Why Do Yo... f This Book?

Here are five reasons why the ninth edition of POWER AND POLITICS IN CALIFORNIA **will help you succeed in your course.**

∞ **The definitive critical approach to California politics.** This new edition expands on the book's tradition of asking you to take a hard and systematic look at what is working and what is not in your state governance. With comprehensive updates on both the historical context and current processes, the ninth edition encourages you to engage in a critical analysis of what changes need to be made for your state to meet the increasingly formidable challenges it faces.

∞ **The most current discussion of California politics.** This new edition provides the most up-to-date political data on all of California's 58 counties, as well as offering in-depth analysis of Governor Schwarzenegger, putting his election and policies in context with the greater history of California politics. This currency throughout the book will better prepare you to meaningfully participate in classroom discussions of contemporary events in California's dynamic political system.

∞ **New comparative analysis of California politics.** Reflecting California's growing role in the national and global community, the authors offer political and demographic comparisons among California, its neighboring states, and the rest of the nation, enhancing your understanding of California politics in a greater context.

∞ **Reorganized discussion on the politics of diversity.** Recognizing the growing influence of diversity on all aspects of California politics, the authors have integrated coverage of the politics of diversity throughout the book. Additionally, a new concluding Part IV will help you analyze how California's response to diversity, its fiscal condition, and its educational system will most crucially shape the state's politics in the future.

∞ **Updated and expanded resources for comprehension and study.** Updated boxes and tables throughout provide illustrative, in-depth examples of key concepts, offer engaging snapshot biographies, and pose critical questions on key issues, helping you to not only better understand what you read, but also to make connections between classroom concepts and current events.

N I N T H   E D I T I O N

Power and Politics in California

Ken DeBow

California State University, Sacramento

John C. Syer

California State University, Sacramento

PEARSON
Longman

New York   San Francisco   Boston
London   Toronto   Sydney   Tokyo   Singapore   Madrid
Mexico City   Munich   Paris   Cape Town   Hong Kong   Montreal

Editor-in-Chief: Eric Stano
Assistant Editor: Donna Garnier
Executive Marketing Manager: Ann Stypuloski
Production Manager: Bob Ginsberg
Project Coordination, Text Design, and Electronic Page Makeup:
    Electronic Publishing Services Inc., NYC
Cover Design Manager/Cover Designer: John Callahan
Cover Photo: Image courtesy of Getty Images
Visual Researcher: Rona Tuccillo
Senior Manufacturing Buyer: Roy L. Pickering, Jr.
Printer and Binder: RR Donnelley & Sons Company/Crawfordsville
Cover Printer: RR Donnelley & Sons Company/Crawfordsville

Library of Congress Cataloging-in-Publication Data
DeBow, Ken.
    Power and politices in California / Ken DeBow.
        p. cm.
    Includes bibliographical references and index.
    ISBN 978-0-205-62219-1
        1. Political participation–California. 2. California–Politics and government. I. Syer,
John C., 1940- II. Title.
    JK8789.D43 2008
    320.9794–dc22

                                                                                    2007051556

Visit us at www.ablongman.com

ISBN-13: 978-0-205-62219-1
ISBN-10:   0-205-62219-4

1 2 3 4 5 6 7 8 9 10—DOC—11 10 09 08

CONTENTS

PART 3
LINKING THE PUBLIC TO THE SYSTEM

Chapter 7
Interest Group Power in California   141

Chapter 8
Political Parties and Media: Linking the Public to the Process   159

Chapter 9
Elections in California   183

PART 4
CALIFORNIA'S POLITICAL FUTURE: FISCAL AND HUMAN CHALLENGES

PREFACE

Barely into the twenty-first century, California was shaken by a series of events that have rearranged its political terrain. Following on the heels of an energy crisis, economic recession, and 9/11, an unprecedented recall of a sitting governor wrenched the state out of any sense of political "normalcy." Out of this turmoil emerged one of the most engaging political figures in California's political history: Arnold Schwarzenegger.

Much of the excitement that surrounded his entrance into state politics still remains; he has in fact established himself as a national, even international, political figure. But now, some five years in office, it is possible to get beyond the personal and evaluate the "Terminator" as a politician and policy maker. This we have attempted to do in several chapters throughout this text. A central point we emphasize, however, is that there are real limits to the power of personality and political leadership at the top; even the most charismatic governor is limited by political, fiscal, and structural realities.

In terms of those structural realities, earlier editions of this book have argued that Californians need to take a harder, more systematic look at the way their political system is put together. What is working, what is not, and what changes need to be made if the state's public sector is to provide us a reasonable chance of meeting the increasingly formidable challenges facing it? The new governor has spoken a great deal about the need to think outside the box, maybe even "blow up" parts of the system. This edition once again asks readers to engage themselves, as well, in this mental effort.

NEW TO THIS EDITION

The ninth edition also offers some important enhancements to the editions that preceded it, both in content and organization. Some of the changes include:

- A revised chapter sequence and organization that better complements the way most California government courses are taught. The chapters on institutions and local government have been moved closer to the front of the text, reflecting instructor feedback that students need to these important fundamentals covered earlier in the course.

- The previous Chapter 4 on "The Politics of Diversity" has been broken up and integrated throughout the book, in recognition of the growing influence of diversity on all aspects of California politics.

- New political and demographic comparisons among California, its neighboring states, and the rest of the nation enhance students' understanding of "where they stand" in relation to the rest of the country.

- An in-depth analysis of Governor Schwarzenegger puts his election and policies in context with the greater history of California politics, allowing students to make meaningful comparisons between current and past administrations.
- Updated information throughout the book related to the partisan leanings of California's 58 counties keeps students abreast of the latest dynamic changes in California politics.
- A new concluding section in Part IV ties together three interrelated factors—California's fiscal condition, its educational system, and its response to diversity—that will be of growing importance and will most crucially shape the state's politics into the future.

ACKNOWLEDGMENTS

As we have admitted before, in a political system as large and complex as California's, even those who have spent much of their life studying it will not know anywhere near as much as they need to. For this reason, we are endlessly indebted to all those "players" in the political process—executive wing, legislative branch, lobbying corps, and political media—who have generously shared their expertise with us. And, of course, we are incalculably indebted to our partners, Linda and Annie, for their support and patience while we were buried, sometimes beyond reaching, in the preparation of this edition.

KEN DEBOW
JOHN SYER

CHAPTER one

CALIFORNIA'S WILD RIDE: A VERY DIFFERENT KIND OF GOVERNOR

W hen, in the unprecedented recall election of 2003, California voters replaced Governor Gray Davis with the politically untried action movie star Arnold Schwarzenegger, they were clearly seeking changes. The exact nature and direction of those desired changes were, however, much less clear. The instant excitement around and the political support for Schwarzenegger were driven more by his star-quality persona than any clear picture of his political ideology, policy positions, or governing style.

The man he replaced, Gray Davis, was, on the other hand, a very well known commodity. And Californians had pretty much decided that they had seen and knew enough about their governor to send him packing. None of this could have been predicted just a few years earlier, however. After winning the governorship in a landslide election in 1998, the moderate, super-cautious Davis, the first Democratic governor in 16 years, enjoyed strong public support over the first 2 years of his tenure. Good times reflect well on the state's governor (whether or not his leadership and policies actually influenced those times) and the last two years of the twentieth century brought mostly good news. Recently enacted education reforms created hope that California's K–12 public school system was moving in the right direction, and the state's crime rate, another major concern of voters, continued to decline. Even Mother Nature seemed to shine on the Golden State. The catastrophic fires, floods, and earthquakes that periodically ravage the state were mostly missing at the century's end. Winters of average to above-average snowfall eased chronic concerns about the state's water supply.

Most crucially, California's economy was soaring. This was the era of the dot-com revolution, and the state's high-tech sector was the world leader of this revolution. By the century's end, California economic output exceeded that of France; in fact only four *nations* had gross national products that were larger than California's! Governors

1

PHOTO 1.1   California's state capitol—architectural grandeur masks a house divided.
(*Department of Government, California State University, Sacramento*)

reap political benefits from good economic times. Generally, as mentioned, good news tends to sweeten voters' appraisal of the state chief executive; more specifically, economic booms generate high tax revenues, making it easier to more generously fund public services while at the same time maintaining or even lowering taxes. Gray Davis was not an exciting, charismatic politician, nor did his aloof and somewhat stiff public style generate a personal bond with average Californians. But in good times, a cautious, even boring, governor may be just fine with most voters.

Thus, at the midpoint of his first four-year term, Gray Davis seemed nearly assured of a successful career as governor. Then, however, things turned very sour very quickly. The "energy crisis" of 2001 was the first setback. The crisis had two components. First, the wholesale cost of energy spiked sharply, leaving the state's public utilities in financial peril because the price they could charge their retail customers, both businesses and homes, was regulated. And if the retail energy prices were allowed to rise as fast as the wholesale prices, the result would be strained household budgets and a competitive disadvantage for California businesses. Second, and even more ominous, it appeared that there might not be enough energy to supply the state's needs. This raised the specter of a summer of rolling blackouts, sweltering homes, and shops and factories shut down for days or weeks at a time. (Imagine, for example, trying to keep a restaurant open without the normal sources of energy for cooking and refrigeration!)

Governor Davis's initial public response, blaming the policies of his predecessor, Republican Pete Wilson, the energy policies of President Bush, and price rigging by energy wholesalers, did little to settle public concerns. Whatever the merits of the governor's attempts to focus the blame on others, many in the public concluded that his own responses were too belated and too indecisive. By the end of 2001 the energy crisis had subsided. But the sheen on the "good-time" governor had been permanently tarnished. And at about the same time, the economic bubble burst.

A GOVERNORSHIP "TERMINATED"

Somewhere between late 2000 and early 2001, the economic boom lost its steam. The subsequent decline, part of a national recession, affected all segments of the economy. But in California, it coincided with the collapse of the dot-com industry. The torrent of capital gains tax revenue generated by the thousands of newly created millionires enriched by the high-tech boom, suddenly vanished. Californians were, by 2002, suddenly facing substantial state budget deficits.

As in the case of the energy fiasco, Davis's responses to the fiscal crisis only reinforced his increasingly negative image among California voters. The 2002–2003 and 2003–2004 budgets were "balanced" only through a combination of borrowing and accounting tricks. Some programs were cut, and some fees (for example, public university student fees and the vehicle license fee) were raised. But the governor was not able to offer a big-picture blueprint of how California might repair its budget problems.

Despite his eroding public support, Davis was able to survive, but only narrowly, the 2002 election. His Republican opponent, William Simon, was a businessperson without California political experience. Simon, whose views on issues such as gun control and abortion were considerably more conservative than those of most voters, ran an ineffectual campaign. Nonetheless, Davis was reelected by only a 5 percent margin.

Very shortly after Gray Davis's second inauguration in January 2003, the reality of the state's massive deficit, now estimated in excess of a staggering $30 billion, became widely known and calls for the governor's ouster took center stage. The initial drive to recall the governor (a full description of the recall process is provided in Chapter 9) was undertaken by an antitax group angered by the governor's plan to sharply raise the vehicle license fee. But most insiders assumed that the recall effort, like many before it, was doomed to failure. Their reasoning was twofold: first, gaining the required number of signatures to force a recall vote is an expensive undertaking, and the recall proponents did not have that kind of cash. Second, the list of known or suspected candidates to replace Governor Davis lacked star quality.

However, as often happens in politics, actual events proved the "experts" wrong. First, the recall campaign received a hefty influx of money from one very wealthy congressperson, Darrell Issa, who hoped he might be the person to replace the Governor. While Issa's own ambitions were a long shot, his nearly two million dollar contribution to the recall campaign gave new life to the ultimately successful signature-gathering effort.

Still, none of the early potential candidates to replace Davis enjoyed widespread name recognition nor had held statewide office. In fact, given this weak field, Democrats initially adopted a strategy of supporting Davis by refusing to put any prominent

:holder on the replacement list. There had been speculation that Republican
, ʌood action movie star Arnold Schwarzenegger might enter the contest, but most
"insiders" were guessing that he would not.

But the insiders were, once again, wrong! As the filing deadline drew near,
Schwarzenegger declared himself a candidate, and the recall election was immediately
transformed from "regular politics" to a worldwide media event. His candidacy quickly
eclipsed that of the other leading Republican challengers; most of them, including Issa,
soon opted out of the contest. The Democrats' early strategy of boycotting the election
gave way when Lieutenant Governor Cruz Bustamante declared his candidacy while at
the same time urging voters to retain Gray Davis.

Initially, the contest seemed to be three-sided: Davis, the sitting governor;
Bustamante, the Democrat next in line; and Schwarzenegger, the exciting, outside
Republican alternative. Bustamante's bid, always complicated by his support for Davis's
retention, was further burdened by allegations—subsequently sustained by the Fair
Political Practices Commission, the state's political watchdog agency—that his campaign violated the spirit, if not the letter, of California's campaign contribution limitation law. At a time when professional politicians and "politics as usual" were blamed
by many voters for the state's problems, these charges were especially lethal to
Bustamante's election prospects. For his part, Gray Davis attempted to "reconnect" with
voters and "humanize" his image by appearing in public dressed down from his standard coat and tie and even, to a degree, admitting he had made errors in the past. But
his image, mostly negative at this point, was not easily changed.

Schwarzenegger, for his part, ran an extremely effective "outsider's" campaign.
Although very short on details, his message consistently stressed the need for a thorough political housecleaning and his ability to deliver the strong leadership obviously
lacking in Sacramento. In addition to his audacious promise to "blow up" Sacramento
politics, his message of fiscal conservatism and social policy moderation was attractive
not only to Republicans, but also to independent and Democratic voters fed up with
Davis. Even last-minute allegations of sexual misbehavior could not derail his run for
the governorship. When, on October 7, 2003, the votes were counted, 55 percent
voted to oust Davis, and with almost 50 percent of the replacement candidate vote,
Schwarzenegger was the runaway replacement winner.

Electing Arnold Schwarzenegger: Did the Voters Get
What They Wanted?

This question assumes, of course, that voters, or least a majority of them, had a clear-cut
picture of how and why state government and politics would be better with Arnold
Schwarzenegger rather than Gray Davis in the governor's office. If by that clear-cut picture we mean specific policy choices or a consistent philosophical or ideological preference for one set of policies over another, then the likely conclusion is that there was no
identifiable purpose that motivated the recall election outcome. Thus, according to this
definition of "rational" voting, the election outcome was based on "irrational" impulses,
such as confusion of the real-life Arnold Schwarzenegger with the invincible action
movie characters he portrayed on the screen, or the assumption that strength of a
world-class bodybuilder could somehow translate into political strength.

But such an analysis misses some underlying sources of the voters' discontent and the "fit" between the voters' sour mood and the allure of the brash political newcomer. Voters were looking for a break from "politics as usual," by which many of them meant government dominated by full-time politicians whose career advancement supersedes the public well-being, and by "special interests" to whom these politicians cater. Politics as usual also includes an image of Sacramento politics that is so mired down in partisan and ideological struggle that the state's broader needs and problems, such as the state budget, education, health care, transportation and the environment, go untended.

Viewed this way, the voters' decision to replace Davis with Schwarzenegger seems consistent with their wishes. The challenger's flamboyant and engaging public persona was the perfect contrast to the aloof, cautious and calculating incumbent. Moreover, Schwarzenegger's public style, brash and unpolished as it sometimes seemed, provided personal reinforcement of his main message: with Arnold as governor, politics in Sacramento would be transformed, and politics as usual would be banished.

So have things worked out as those pro-Schwarzenegger voters hoped and expected? The best quick answer is yes and no. (Please see Chapter 4 for a fuller discussion of the Schwarzenegger governorship.) On the "yes" side, his landslide reelection victory in 2006, a year in which many other Republicans in California and throughout the nation were trounced, indicates that his personal political stock, three years after initially taking office, was still high. He has demonstrated, at times, a feel for public opinion and an ability to change course based on that feel that has kept him ahead of permanent political disaster. For example, he has distanced himself from a fellow Republican, President Bush, whose own standing in California is at rock bottom. He has also embraced popular issues such as global warming and expanded access to health care, issues more usually associated with Democratic politicians. His use of bipartisan rhetoric plays well with many Californians tired of endless partisan bickering in Sacramento. And he still has that Hollywood "buzz" and "sizzle" that guarantees him big audiences for any policy or political ventures he might undertake. In fact, he has attained a political prominence that goes well beyond California borders; he is easily the best-known governor in America, and probably among the half dozen or so most recognizable political figures in the nation.

Those arguing against the claim that Governor Schwarzenegger has lived up to his early billing would cite the missteps and disasters that also characterized his first term in office. At times, he displayed a penchant for making enemies out of political opponents, such as with his contemptuous references to Democratic state legislators, who as the legislative majority, have the power to thwart most of his policy proposals. And his decision to launch full-scale political war against the state's public employee unions was another overstep that he came to regret. (Again, see Chapter 4 for a discussion of these and other episodes.)

Certainly, public support of the governor has been anything but consistently high throughout the first four years in office. In fact, as Table 1.1 indicates, the profile of his standing with the public resembles the undulations of a carnival roller coaster much more than a straight line of consistent public approval.

Moreover, long-term problems and dilemmas facing the state have not vanished. For example, the state government's fiscal resources are still mightily strained to match demands for public spending, the state's transportation system is still rated near the bottom of all the states, and its prison system seems set to implode under the weight of overcrowd-

TABLE 1.1	Peaks and Valleys: Governor Schwarzenegger's Voter Approval Rating					
Percentage of Voters Who Approve of the Job the Governor Is Doing						
Feb 04	**Aug 04**	**Feb 05**	**Sep 05**	**Feb 06**	**Sep 06**	**Mar 07**
56	65	55	36	40	48	60

Source: Field Research Corporation, California Field Poll. *(San Francisco: various release dates).*

ing and mismanagement. These problems did not begin with Schwarzenegger's governor-ship, and he can hardly be blamed because they have not suddenly disappeared. But there are lessons here about the limits of any individual politician's ability to solve deep-seated problems if the state's governmental institutions, political culture, and social and economic realities are not conducive to positive change. Californian voters who believed that a new face and style could transform the nature of state politics and banish forever "politics as usual" were doomed to disappointment.

IS CALIFORNIA STILL GOVERNABLE? SOME BASIC LONG-TERM CONCERNS

To this point, our attention has focused on the factors leading to the political arrival of Arnold Schwarzenegger, and the implications of this for California government and politics. But a central assumption of this entire book is that political personalities are but one factor, and probably not the most important factor, in how the political system performs, and whether that performance enhances or diminishes the lives of California residents. Forces beyond a leader's individual personality, insight, energy, and style, briefly alluded to above, such as the way the political system is structured, the distribu-tion of political power, the expectations of voters, and social and economic patterns, shape and limit what individual politicians can do. One crucial lesson from the Schwarzenegger years seems inescapably clear: big changes in leadership personality and style, such as from Gray Davis to Arnold Schwarzenegger, don't of themselves lead to correspondingly big changes in the overall political system, nor to the disappearance of deeply rooted problems and issues. It is to these broader and less malleable elements of California's political system that we now turn.

The tumult and dislocation of the new century's first years, culminating in the amazing recall election of 2003, may have temporarily obscured, but did not erase, other long-term issues facing the state. One of these problems is the steady decline in the quantity and quality of public services delivered by the state and local governments. Public education is, of course, the most obvious case in point, but it is hardly unique. For example, California's highway and road system ranks at the very bottom of the 50 states, and the quality of its air ranks near the bottom. Peter Schrag, a longtime state political observer and journalist, refers to the state's decline as the "Mississippification" of California's public sector. Associated with this same decline is a seemingly chronic inability of official decision makers, especially the legislature and governor, to formulate and enact major policy and an increasing reliance instead on the initiative process to break the gridlock in Sacramento (Schrag, 1998).

From his extensive study of public opinion in California, Mark Baldassare concluded that the state suffers from a profound lack of unity and consensus. Wide gaps separate state residents along both regional and ethnic/racial lines. Moreover, most Californians feel simultaneously disconnected from and highly distrustful of their state's politicians and political institutions (Baldassare, 2000).

Under the best of circumstances, governing California would be a hugely difficult chore. The state's size, growth, and diversity are, in many ways, unique advantages enjoyed by the Golden State. But these factors also provide challenges to effective governance not found in smaller, less dynamic, and more homogeneous states.

Effective government requires at least a minimum consensus, among both citizens and official decision makers. But as Baldassare points out, more disunity than consensus is found among California residents. And this lack of unity is echoed in Sacramento, where partisan and ideological disagreements often harden into protracted political warfare and policy stalemate.

Effective governance also requires political/governmental structures and processes that facilitate consensus building, deliver effective services, and generate responsive policy answers to problems citizens face. Based on these criteria, most residents, and practically all observers of state politics, agree that California's current political system fails to work well. What is lacking, however, is any general agreement over what changes need to be made.

As discussed above, much of the excitement and optimism surrounding Arnold Schwarzenegger's campaign for and capture of the governorship was based on the hope that a completely new face would bring a whole new spirit and energy to Sacramento politics. And as will be discussed in later chapters, the flamboyant governor clearly changed the atmosphere around the capitol. But most of the old problems and divisions remain: many Californians think our taxes are too high, many others think our level of spending for public education, transportation, the environment, and other purposes are too low; California prisons are overflowing, but are more prisons or more early intervention programs the solution? Six million state residents are without health care insurance. Is it state government's, and hence state employers and taxpayers' responsibility to make this right? These are a sampling of issues over which there is no "California consensus," and thus no easy policy answers. That was true when Gray Davis was governor; it is still true with Arnold Schwarzenegger in the governor's chair.

Concerns over the state's political system's viability and effectiveness do not occur in a vacuum or as part of an "ivory tower" academic debate; governmental failure touches us all in a real, everyday way. Table 1.2 illustrates some of the more glaring "performance gaps" of the state's public sector by comparing California with the other 49 states on a variety of policy and problem areas.

POLITICS BY INITIATIVE

As discussed in much greater detail in Chapter 9, the initiative process allows citizens and private groups to write new laws, amend existing laws, and make changes to the state constitution, all without the participation of the legislature or governor. Over the last

TABLE 1.2	How Well Is California Doing? Some Comparisons with the Other States	California's National Rank
Violent crime rate		6
Percentage of school-aged children fully immunized		39
Number of books in public libraries per capita		44
High school verbal/math SAT scores		43/30
Voter participation rate		34
Overall "Livability Index"		36

Source: Morgan Quitno Corp., State Rankings *(Lawrence, KS: Morgan Quitno Press, 2004).*

25 years, coinciding with citizens' increased distrust of government, the growing policy deadlock in Sacramento, and deepening divisions within the state's population, initiatives have been the primary vehicle for major policy and institutional changes. Some of these initiatives brought changes to the way government itself operates; others dealt with "hot-button" social and cultural issues over which Californians are deeply divided.

As indicated in Table 1.3, the years leading into the twenty-first century witnessed repeated use of the initiative process to deal with these issues. Voters opened the decade of the 1990s by approving term limits for legislators and members of the executive branch. This initiative set in motion a whole series of changes, especially in the legislature, that political scientists, journalists, and other observers of state politics are still trying to sort out. Public dissatisfaction with budget and policy gridlock, revelations of corruption, and a general distaste for "professional politicians" all combined to provide the term limits initiative (Proposition 140) a narrow victory in November 1990. Over the following years, as more and more legislators reached their maximum service (six years in the state assembly, eight years in the state senate) and were thus "termed out," term limits achieved their intended effect. By 2007, there were just three legislators whose legislative experience dated back beyond 1990.

Whether term limits have improved the legislature remains a topic of debate. Those who favored the idea initially tend to believe things are better; those who opposed term limits mostly still think they were a mistake. (See Chapter 3 for a full discussion of the impacts, both positive and negative, of term limits.) But among the general public, term limits are even more popular now than at the time they were passed, and attempts, at least through 2007, to soften or modify their impact have been soundly rejected by the voters.

In the final years of the twentieth century voters also delivered strong majority support of initiative proposals aimed at reducing the power of political parties in the election nomination process, and imposing tighter controls over political campaign donations and expenditures. (These issues are more fully discussed in Chapters 8 and 9.) These new laws were ultimately voided by the federal courts, but their passage underscored most voters' dissatisfaction with the political system's performance and

TABLE 1.3	**An Uneasy Electorate Mandates Fundamental Changes**

Changing the Political Rules of the Game

1990	Proposition 140	Established term limits for the legislature
1996	Proposition 198	Replaced closed primary election with blanket primary system
1996	Proposition 208	Imposed drastic limitations on contributions to political candidates

Responding to the Challenge of Diversity

1994	Proposition 187	Prohibited medical, social, and educational services to illegal immigrants
1996	Proposition 209	Banned affirmative action in state hiring, contracting, and college admissions
1998	Proposition 227	Drastically curtailed use of bilingual education programs
2000	Proposition 22	Limited definition of marriage to heterosexual relationships

their willingness to support fundamental changes to it. Nor has that dissatisfaction disappeared over the succeeding years.

Voters' concerns are not limited to the political system itself either. The state's growing diversity fails to set comfortably with all Californians, especially those who are older, more settled, and, at least until recently, much more likely to vote. Most, though not all, of the diversity-related initiatives over the past decade dealt, in various forms, with racial/ethnic or sexual orientation questions. And the results of these initiatives indicated a certain reluctance on the part of the state's electoral majority to embrace all the assumptions of multiculturalism.

During the same time that voters were approving the political reform measures discussed above, they were also registering their opinions on a variety of social and cultural issues. Adopted by the voters in 1994, Proposition 187 prohibited the provision of public health care, education, and social services to illegal immigrants and their children.

Two years later, by a similar strong majority, voters approved a ban on affirmative action programs that gave preferential treatment to racial/ethnic minorities or women in the areas of college admissions, public employment, and public contracts. Next, returning to an immigration-related issue, voters approved strict limitations, if not outright abolition, of public school bilingual education programs. (Bilingual education allows students not yet proficient in English to attend classes taught in their native language until their English skills develop to the point that they can be taught successfully in English.)

Finally, in the primary election of 2000, voters approved Proposition 22, the Defense of Marriage Act. Proposition 22 legally defines marriage as and restricts it to a relationship between a man and a woman, thus excluding gay relationships from the state's legal definition of marriage. Concern that other states might sanction gay marriages, allowing individuals so married in those states to then come to California and claim married status, sparked this proposition.

Not surprisingly, these propositions' passage led to immediate court challenges based on a variety of state and federal constitutional issues. However, with the exception of Proposition 187, which the courts voided, these successful initiatives survived their legal challenges, and are currently the law in California. But the issues they addressed and the political divisions over them have not gone away. Illegal immigration services, bilingual education, affirmative action, and same-sex marriage, while different issues, generate some shared reactions. And there is a connecting logic behind opposing opinions about them.

"Yes" votes on these propositions were motivated, at least in part, by the sense that, in the pursuit of multiculturalism and diversity, the state was moving too far and too fast at the expense of traditional rules and long-held definitions of shared national loyalties and personal morality. On the other hand, a substantial minority opposed each and every one of these propositions. (Our own studies indicate that a yes or no vote on any of these proposals was a strong predictor for the same vote on all of them.) And with the state's changing demographics, coupled with the replacement of the oldest voters with younger voters, the minority position on these issues may have time on its side. For example, there is some indication that California voters, especially younger voters, may now be less attracted to policies that appear to be anti-gay. But whatever the political balance, it's safe to say that these cultural and racial "hot button" issues will continue to divide Californians for some time to come. (See Chapter 11 for a fuller discussion of these issues.) And it's also a good bet that California voters will also continue to be asked to support ballot propositions that aim, in the name of banishing "politics as usual," to restructure political processes and institutions.

DEMOGRAPHICS

Throughout its history, California has experienced periods of rapid population growth. But unlike the growth of earlier eras, such as the gold rush of the middle nineteenth century and the post–World War II influx of the 1940s, 1950s, and 1960s, current growth is not based on immigration into California from other states. Indeed, over the last twenty years, more California residents left to resettle in other states as came to live in California from the rest of the nation. Instead, current population expansion is based almost solely on two factors: immigration from Asia, the Pacific Islands, Mexico, and Central America and a state birth rate that outpaces the state death rate. In fact, contrary to popular belief, "natural increase"—that is, the high rate of births relative to deaths—accounts for as much of the population growth as does international immigration (California Department of Finance, 2004).

As a result of these trends, in 1998, California officially became a "majority-minority" state when its non-Hispanic white population dipped below 50 percent of total state population. This trend is likely to accelerate because, although the state's overall birth rate is quite high (California ranks third among all fifty states in the percentage of its total population that is 5 to 18 years old), the non-Hispanic white birth rate is low. As a result, the proportion of California children who are white dropped even more dramatically than that of the white population generally. For the past decade, a majority of kindergarten though twelfth grade (K–12) public school students have not been white. Projections indicate that whites will constitute only about 30 percent of the state's public school population in the not too distant future. And as indicated in Table 1.4, the fact that California's immigrant population is young means that the next childbearing

TABLE 1.4	A Fast-Growing, and Even Faster Changing, State	
	1990	**2007**
Total population:	29.7 million	37.7 million
Race/ethnicity:		
White	57%	46.7%
Latino	26	35.2
Asian/Pacific Islander	9	12.2
African American	7	6.7

Note: "Other" and multiple race/ethnicity categories are not included.

Sources: Morgan Quitno Corp., State Rankings (Lawrence, KS: Morgan Quitno Press, 2007); California Department of Finance, Statistical Abstract (Sacramento: 2007).

generation of Californians will number proportionately fewer whites than any preceding generation going back to the gold rush.

Overall, California, already by far the most populous state in the union at about 37.6 million (as of 2007), continues to grow at approximately the same percentage rate, but at a much faster numerical pace, than the nation as a whole. About 12.2 percent, or just under one person in eight, of the nation's population resides in California, and during the initial years of this century, the state population grew by approximately 500,000 each year (an annual growth figure that equals the *total population* of Wyoming) (U.S. Bureau of the Census, 2003; California Department of Finance, 2007). However, population size and population growth are far from uniform throughout the state. The state's nine largest counties (in descending order, Los Angeles, San Diego, Orange, Riverside, San Bernardino, Santa Clara, Alameda, Sacramento, and Contra Costa) all contain at least 1 million residents. Over one in four Californians lives in Los Angeles County, and the total population of these nine largest counties accounts for almost 70% of the state's population. And most of these counties continue to gain population at a steady rate (California Department of Finance, 2007). (See Table 1.5.)

However, very high growth percentages are also found in some of the 49 smaller counties, usually those located at the commuter fringes of the largest metropolitan areas and especially in the San Joaquin Valley. Conversely, most of the very rural counties have the smallest populations, and most are growing very slowly. The combined residency numbers of the 10 least populated counties currently account for less than half of 1 percent of the state's population, and their combined annual numerical growth over the last ten years is less than that of Los Angeles County alone in a single year! (California Department of Finance, 2007).

ECONOMICS

The Macro View

If California were a nation, its gross national product would, as of 2005, rank ninth among all countries in the world. As it is, the Golden State's total annual economic

TABLE 1.5	California's Largest and Smallest Counties (as of January 2007)			
County	Population	Rank	1990–2000 Change	2006–2007 Percentage Change
Los Angeles	10.3 million	1	+0.9 million	+0.7%
San Diego	3.1million	2	+0.4 million	+1.1%
Orange	3.1 million	3	+0.4 million	+0.9%
Riveside	2.0 million	4	+0.3 million	+3.3%
San Bernardino	2.0 million	5	+0.3 million	+1.7%
Santa Clara	1.8million	6	+0.2 million	+1.6%
Alameda	1.5 million	7	+0.1 million	+1.1%
Sacramento	1.4 million	8	+0.2 million	+1.4%
Contra Costa	1.0 million			
Mariposa	18,254	53	+1,400	+0.6%
Trinity	14,171	54	+750	+0.4%
Mono	13,985	55	+50	+1.0%
Modoc	9,721	56	−150	+0.1%
Sierra	3,485	57	−140	−0.2%
Alpine	1,261	58	+70	1.3%

Source: California Department of Finance, Statistical Abstract *(Sacramento, 2000, 2007).*

output, in excess of $1.7 trillion, far outstrips that of any other state (Morgan Quitno Corp., 2007).

Of course, California's total economic output mostly reflects the fact that it is by far the most populous state. But even when the total numbers are divided by state population, thus revealing the per capita economic output, California ranks twelfth highest in the nation. And the Golden State's personal per-capita income is, based on 2005 figures, again twelfth highest in the nation.

But California is not immune to fluctuations of the economic cycle, and downturns are part of that cycle. With the national downturn beginning in 2000–2001, California's economy was bound to suffer some reverses. And the near collapse of the dot-com sector, a main component of the state's recent boom, further complicated the state picture. By 2005 California, along with most of the nation, had climbed out of the recession and was expanding on a solid upward, trajectory though projections indicate that slope is, at least through 2008, likely to level off. The main cause of economic concern is weakness of the housing market, nationally and especially in the Golden State. California led the nation in the explosion of home prices over the last fifteen years or so, and the average price per home far outstrips that in any other state. Thus, the market's decline is especially problematic here, since many Califorians were using the rising worth, and hence equity in their homes, as a source of ready cash to fund major purchases and further fuel the state's economy. (See Chapter 10 for a discussion of these factors in relation to the state budget.)

The Micro View

Up to this point, the discussion of California's economy has focused on the macro level: its overall size and strength. And this focus indicates that, by and large, the state's economic health is solid, relative to most states. But a micro view of the state's economic health, emphasizing how economic wealth and opportunity are distributed within the state, yields a more troublesome picture. Nationally, the gap between rich and poor continues to grow, and this trend has been especially strong in California. Between 1976 and 1994, the actual purchasing power of the nation's poorest 10 percent dropped by 13 percent. In California, that figure was 36 percent (Schrag, 1998). A more recent analysis of income inequality places California sixth among all fifty states in the magnitude of difference in incomes between the state's richest and poorest residents (Center on Budget and Policy Priorities, 2006).

Part of this same trend is a reduction in the size of the middle class and an increase in the ranks of the very poor and very rich. This condition, sometimes referred to as the "two-tier economy," is marked by a reduction of jobs paying middle-class wages (such as those in manufacturing plants) and their replacement with service-sector jobs (waiters, cashiers, non-professional health care workers, food preparers, etc.) that pay at or near the minimum wage level. As a result of this shift, a growing number of persons are employed in jobs whose compensation does not include benefits, most crucially health care. In fact, California is currently fifth among all states in the percentage of its employees who are not covered by any health care plan (Morgan Quitno Corp., 2007).

Thus, even when the state's macro picture is generally positive, the micro reality can be a two-tiered society consisting of an increasing number of working poor, even when "times are good" and unemployment rates are low. In California, this problem is only made worse by a high cost of living, and especially high housing costs. And, of course, when economic trends turn negative, those farthest down the economic ladder are the first and often the hardest hit.

Increasing economic disparities are reflected in both geographic and racial/ethnic patterns. The San Francisco Bay Area, even after the dot-com bust, is the wealth center of the state. The top five counties in terms of per capita or household income (Marin, San Mateo, San Francisco, Santa Clara, and Contra Costa) are all located in this region. This area now ranks as the nation's richest; it also has the highest housing costs, with home purchase costs averaging about $700,000 (and more than $1 million in Marin and San Francisco Counties). Orange County remains Southern California's richest, ranking sixth statewide. Los Angeles County comes in at nineteenth (California Department of Finance, 2007). Conversely, the state's lowest personal income figures are found in rural and/or agricultural counties such as Del Norte, Glenn, Imperial, Kings, and Tehama.

Geographic disparities in wealth are nothing new for California; for many decades, the Bay Area specifically and the state's more urbanized areas generally have enjoyed greater financial wealth per capita than have rural areas relying on agriculture and extractive industries such as mining and lumbering. But this money-geography gap is growing. At the end of the 1980s, the per capita income of the state's lowest five counties equaled 45.5 percent of the same income measure for the five richest counties. By early in this century, this figure had dropped to 38.2 percent (adapted from California Department of Finance, 2007)

Nor is geography the only economic dividing point. Widening gaps also follow ethnic and racial lines. As the middle class gets "squeezed," with relatively more residents now occupying the highest and lowest economic rungs as opposed to the middle rungs, disproportionate percentages of African Americans and Latinos, in addition to rural whites, are clustered on the lower rungs. According to the U.S. Census Bureau, the average household income for California's African Americans is only about 62 percent of the average for white California households; Hispanic households average about 71 percent (U.S. Bureau of the Census, 2005).

Age is yet another economic dividing line. In California, those under 18 are much more likely to live in a household with an income under the poverty level than are those aged 65 or older (U.S. Bureau of the Census, 2003). And, remember, whites are disproportionally represented in the older-than-65 group, while minorities, especially Latinos, are overrepresented in the under-18 category.

A comparison of California with other states puts the emergence of the two-tiered society in sharp profile. As already mentioned, California ranks high, twelfth overall, in terms of personal income. That means that many Californians, compared to those in most states, are doing quite well. But the state also ranks twelfth in the percentage of residents living under the poverty level. Taken together, these numbers paint a picture of California as a place with comparatively high percentages of both the well-off and the very poor.

California enjoys an image as a place of economic opportunity, and for many, that image turns out to be the happy reality. But for a growing number of Californians, the picture is quite different. For example, California's home ownership rate is driven down by the large percentage of under-poverty-level residents coupled with very high real estate costs. In this important measure of economic well-being, only one state (New York) ranks lower than the Golden State. And California leads the nation in its percentage of homeowners spending at least 30percent of their income on housing costs (Morgan Quitno Corp., 2007). This emerging two-tier reality of California's economic life, structured along racial and geographic lines, presents many political and policy problems that will severely test the state's political institutions, regardless of whether new or old faces are running things in Sacramento.

CALIFORNIA POLITICS ON THE NATIONAL AND WORLD STAGE

Certain distinctive characteristics of California's political life set it apart from the other states. On the other hand, political change and political movements often originate in the Golden State and then are imprinted onto the national political landscape. One long-standing element of "California-style" politics is its tradition of weak political parties. (The origins of California's nonpartisan politics go back to the progressives of the early twentieth century and are discussed more fully in Chapters 2 and 8.)

In the absence of strong parties, other forces and organizations moved into the void. Among them was the campaign management industry, which originated in this state because candidates could not rely on their political parties to organize their campaigns, get their messages out, and deliver the voters. The media comprised another force that moved into the vacuum created by weak political parties. And as the state grew larger and larger, the media became the only practical way to reach voters in statewide and often even in legislative election contests.

Hurray for Hollywood!

Hollywood is a California city, and Arnold Schwarzenegger is the most recent, but hardly the first, show business personality to make a major impact on California politics. Several movie and other entertainment figures have gone on to high-level political positions. The most notable, of course, was Ronald Reagan, a two-term governor (1967–1975) and two-term president (1981–1989). Another movie actor, George Murphy, served in the U.S. Senate from 1965 to 1971. Sonny Bono, the male half of the Sonny and Cher singing/comedy team in earlier life, served in the U.S. House of Representatives during the 1990s until he died in a 1998 skiing accident.

Steve Peace, a state legislator in the 1980s and 1990s and Governor Davis's top budget aide, had earlier produced the cult film *Attack of the Killer Tomatoes*. Mike Curb, the state's lieutenant governor from 1979 to 1983, was elected to this office following a career as a record industry executive. Rob Reiner, best known as "Meathead" in the TV sit-com *All in the Family*, is a leading spokesperson and financial backer of liberal and environmental causes, and Woody Harrelson, of films and the TV series *Cheers*, is yet another former actor turned liberal activist. Sheila Kuehl, many years prior to a legislative career that spanned the end of the twentieth century and the beginning of the twenty-first, played the role of Zelda in the television comedy series *The Many Loves of Dobie Gillis*. Hollywood personalities such as Charlton Heston, Clint Eastwood, and Warren Beatty have been touted as potential candidates for major political office.

But the "Hollywood connection" goes beyond its list of political candidates and officeholders. Show business personalities are often featured in political advertising for candidates and ballot propositions. Hollywood is also an important source of political money in the form of campaign contributions for state and national candidates and political movements. Recently, most Hollywood celebrity and money influence has tended to liberal causes and Democratic candidates (movie actor/director Mel Gibson is a major exception). In earlier years, the opposite was true with major show business celebrities and production executives tilting toward the Republican Party and conservative causes.

And, finally, California-produced movies and television shows are often laden with political themes and messages that become part of the nation's political dialogue. For example, Hollywood movie depiction of the Vietnam War ranged from full support (such as *Green Berets*) to condemnation (*Platoon*). Are we about to be offered a series of Iraq War films presenting a similarly diverse picture of that conflict?

In the Limelight and Setting the Trend

California is a place where social and political change often comes first. As indicated earlier, the central role of campaign management companies and the media was a California "invention." California also gave the nation the free speech movement (University of California, Berkeley, 1964) and the tax revolt movement (Proposition 13 in 1978). More recently, the state was in the vanguard of the term limits movement and the national debate over affirmative action.

California has even more recently carved out a leadership role among the states in the area of carbon emissions control and public financial support of stem cell research. The state's receptivity to new ideas and values and the nationwide media attention given to California guarantee that many causes and movements begin here

PHOTO 1.2   Governor goes global—Governor Schwarzenegger at the United Nations. His speech on global warming marked the first time that the UN General Assembly has been addressed by an American governor. *(New York Times)*

and are then transplanted onto the national, and even international, scene. Will Governor Schwarzenegger position California as a world leader in the war against global warming?

Given the media coverage California attracts and the fact that its size gives it by far the biggest single state bloc of electoral college votes (about 20% of the number of electoral votes needed to win the presidential election), one would assume that the state is a pivotal player in presidential politics. Thus it is not surprising that 8 of the last 15 presidential elections, dating back to 1948, featured a Californian as a presidential or vice presidential candidate. It is important to note, however, that all eight were on the Republican ticket, reflecting the fact that, until the 1990s, the state leaned Republican in its presidential voting. For example, in both 1960 (Kennedy vs. Nixon) and 1976 (Carter vs. Ford), California went against the national grain by voting for the losing Republican candidate. In fact, in the ten presidential elections between 1952 and 1988, the Democratic ticket carried California just one time (1964, Johnson vs. Goldwater).

However, this pattern was completely reversed starting with the Bill Clinton's first election. In both 1992 and 1996, Clinton carried California by double-digit margins well in excess of his national vote support. And in 2000, without bothering to campaign in the state, Al Gore routed George W. Bush in California by 12 percentage points. This election marked the first time *in over a century* that California failed to support a Republican presidential candidate who was the national winner. In, 2004, California voters again went against the national Republican tide, providing Democrat John Kerry an easy 10 percent, 1.2 million vote margin in the state. If these trends continue, California may find itself abandoned by the presidential campaigns of both major parties. If the state is assumed to be a "Democratic lock," Republican candidates might well decide to ignore California and concentrate on the "swing" or "battleground" states, especially after George W. Bush's 2000 and 2004 elections demonstrated that it is possible for a Republican candidate to lose California and still win the presidency. And Democratic candidates, confident that California's electoral votes are safely in hand, could also ignore the state and devote their attention and resources to other key states such as Ohio, Florida, and Pennsylvania. On the other hand, California could be the linchpin in a new Democratic "western states strategy" aimed at winning presidential elections in portions of the west, such as Colorado, Arizona, New Mexico, Nevada, and Montana. Victories in these states, added to more traditionally Democratic western states on the Pacific Coast, might be enough to assure national victories even if Democratic presidential candidates lose in Florida and Ohio and are entirely shut out of the deep and border southern states.

Still, the presidential general election is just half of the presidential selection process. The series of primary elections held from February through June every fourth year determines which candidates will compete in the general election. Because California's traditional June primary election date came so late in the game that both parties' nominees were decided before Californians could vote, the legislature moved the primary up to early March, hoping that it would play a pivotal role in selecting the nominees. Such was the case in the 2000 Republican primary, where George W. Bush was being vigorously challenged by John McCain. However, other states have responded by moving their primary election dates up even earlier. In 2004, both the Republican and the Democratic nominations were all but guaranteed before California's voters had the chance to voice their opinions. As a result, the legislature then moved the primary election date back to June. Now, in the latest attempt to be part of the primary election action, lawmakers have yet again changed the date, this time to early February!

Based on the 2000 census, California was allocated 53 seats in the U.S. House of Representatives, an increase of 1 from its 1990 allocation and up from 45 seats in the 1980s. Unfortunately for California, mere size does not necessarily guarantee that a state's congressional delegation will effectively articulate and represent statewide needs and priorities. For that to happen, some basic agreement and sense of shared perspective among the state's members in the House of Representatives are required. Coming from a state as diverse as California, these representatives have been unable to define a "California agenda" around which to unite. Historically and currently, California's congressional delegation has not been particularly cohesive, instead dividing sharply on partisan grounds and thus diluting its numerical strength. Moreover, an ABC (Anywhere But California) syndrome tends to motivate representatives from other states. California has undoubtedly lost research and development, as well as pork barrel projects, because of a lack of delegation cohesion and the ABC syndrome.

POLITICAL DISUNITY

No single political adjective or phrase can capture California's political diversity. In terms of the bulk of state voters, California's crucial geographical division is between the metropolitan counties south of the Tehachapi Mountains and the counties around San Francisco Bay. Between them, these two regions account for about 75 percent of the state's voters and its main partisan and ideological division. The southern counties, with the huge exception of Los Angeles County, are where Republican candidates and conservative ballot measures must run up strong majorities to be successful. Conversely, the San Francisco Bay Area is the numerical heart of Democratic and liberal strength. But the geographical differences don't end there. Generally, in the northern three-quarters of the state, voters become more Republican as you move away from the Pacific Coast toward the state's eastern Sierra Nevada border. In fact, in terms of percentage voting totals, it is the state's rural areas that are most Republican. But because these counties are not heavily populated, their numerical contribution to Republican candidates is, on a statewide scale, only mildly significant.

For example, in 2004, George W. Bush carried 36 of the state's 58 counties, including nearly all of the mountain and Central Valley counties, usually by wide margins. He also carried the highly populated southern counties of Orange, San Diego, Ventura, Riverside, and San Bernardino, which are the key to Republican statewide success. But his margins here were fairly modest, never reaching the 60 percent plateau. For his part, John Kerry easily won the traditionally strong Democratic counties, including Los Angeles County and the counties in the San Francisco Bay Area, with margins well over 60 percent. It all added up to a 1.2 million statewide vote margin for the Democratic candidate.

Beyond this schism, Dan Walters, political columnist for the *Sacramento Bee*, identified no less than 14 distinctive economic/political regions (Walters, 1992). Joel Garreau went so far as to define the northern and southern portions of the state as two distinct "nations" (Garreau, 1981).

Immigration patterns, political history, economic and occupational concentration, political culture, and even weather differences have all been offered as explanations of these regional political differences. Nobody is really sure just how they started and how they endure, but in California, where you live certainly influences where you stand politically. Such political diversity can be positive or negative. On the positive side, the state's politics are infused with a rich mixture of contending ideas and philosophies. Overall, the state remains reasonably well balanced and competitive in terms of partisan, and especially ideological, struggles.

But negative consequences can arise as well. We already discussed the lack of unity within the state's congressional delegation. Part of this disunity is explained by intrastate geographical divisions. Enduring and heartfelt geographical splits, when added to the state's tremendous ethnic and economic diversity, can preclude consensus and stymie effective political and policy decision making. Regional differences of opinion can harden to alienation and a sense of no longer "belonging" to the state, which may have already occurred in the most rural northern counties. Residents of this area, correctly believing that their votes are too few in number to have an impact on statewide elections, voted overwhelmingly in a nonbinding 1992 referendum to split the state between north and south. Subsequently, assembly mem-

B O X 1.1	**State of Jefferson and an Old Idea: Get Us Out of California**

In a state containing many very different regions, it is not surprising that throughout its history California has witnessed many movements to somehow divide the state, usually by separating it along north/south lines. And, as population power has gravitated to the south, it is also not surprising that most "split the state" sentiment has come out of the north. In 1941, something approaching a full rebellion boiled up in a few of the northernmost counties. The idea was to forge a new state out of these counties along with southern Oregon counties also dissatisfied with what they considered neglect and mistreatment by their central state government. The new state was to be called the State of Jefferson. Just as things were coming to a head, Pearl Harbor was attacked and America found itself in World War II; just as quickly, the whole secession idea evaporated.

As a plan for a new state, the State of Jefferson is dead. But it is still a part of the region's vocabulary, cyberspace (there is a State of Jefferson Web site), and landscape (in the form of occasional signs or barn walls referencing "State of Jefferson").

ber Stan Statham, a Republican representing northernmost California, introduced legislation calling for a popular vote on whether to split California into northern, central, and southern parts. His bill actually passed the state assembly, only to die in the upper house. The "split the state" movement is, at this time, moribund. But the restlessness and resentment of those who spearheaded it are alive and well. (Please see Box 1.1 for a brief further discussion of northern California's desire to "secede" from the rest of the state.)

LIMITLESS DEMANDS AND LIMITED RESOURCES

Water Wars

Water is central to California's growth and economic vitality, and an ongoing source of controversy. One physical fact defines California water policy and politics: Most of the rain and snow falls over the state's northern portion, but the bulk of the population and agricultural demand for water is in the south. A variety of dams, aqueducts, and canals bring water from Northern California to Central and Southern California; from the Sierra to the Bay Area and Los Angeles; and from the Colorado River to the Imperial Valley, Los Angeles, and San Diego. Over the years, water battles pitted north against south, farmers against urbanites, environmentalists against developers, California against neighboring states, and the state against the federal government. The financial stakes will continue to be high in the future, given water's scarcity and its vital importance to the environment, the economy, and the growing population's well-being.

FIGURE 1.1   Major aqueducts in California

California's history of moving water from its natural location to where it is "needed" is full of deceit, scandal, and environmental catastrophe. Early in the twentieth century, Los Angeles politicians and developers essentially stole water from Owens Valley in the Sierras to develop the formerly arid San Fernando Valley, whose acreage they owned. As the city grew, so did its water needs, and the streams that fed Mono Lake were next to be tapped. By the 1980s, the lake's water surface had dropped approximately 40 feet, and it was on the verge of becoming a "dead" lake. At this point, the courts interceded, forcing Los Angeles to allow water to once again flow into the lake. No such happy ending attended the story of Hetch Hetchy, a valley just north of Yosemite Valley and once a scenic rival to it. The valley was dammed and flooded to pro-

PHOTO 1.3 Hetch Hetchy project—Yosemite's "Twin Valley" drowned to accommodate San Francisco's water needs. *(California State Library)*

vide a water supply for San Francisco, some 150 miles to the northwest. Unlike Mono Lake, this natural wonder has yet to be reclaimed.

In 1937, the federal government commenced construction of the Central Valley Project (CVP), a long-cherished plan to irrigate the Central Valley with waters from the north. Completed in the 1940s, the CVP moves water originally collected at Shasta Dam in the state's far north through an elaborate interconnection of rivers and canals to the agriculturally rich but dry San Joaquin Valley. Ninety-five percent of the water that flows through this massive system is used for agricultural purposes.

In 1960, California voters narrowly approved the sale of $1.75 billion in water resources bonds. The ensuing State Water Plan (SWP) system begins in the north with the Oroville Dam. Water collected here is released into the river system and moves south to the San Francisco Bay delta, the confluence of the Sacramento River and San Joaquin River (which drains central and southern Sierra streams and flows north). At this point, the second major component of the SWP, the California Aqueduct, picks up delta water and moves it down the western San Joaquin Valley to the valley's base, just south of Bakersfield. Here giant SWP pumps propel the channeled water over the Tehachapi Mountains and down into the Los Angeles Basin. Ultimately, the system terminates in San Diego County. Water agencies, both agricultural and urban, contract for water deliveries from the system all along its route.

In 1981, the legislature authorized construction of a peripheral canal as a part of the SWP. The 42-mile-long canal was to bring water from the Sacramento River to the California Aqueduct, which begins just south of Stockton. However, opponents of the controversial canal gathered enough signatures to force a referendum on the project. The canal raised an array of technical, fiscal, and environmental concerns. But for northern Californians, the peripheral canal became a symbol of the south's robbery of "their" water. An overwhelming "no" vote in the north overcame a much less unified "yes" vote in the south, and the idea of a peripheral canal was killed, at least temporarily.

In the meantime, the state's population continued to grow, putting greater strains on the state's water delivery system. The problem was exacerbated by a series of drought years in the early and middle 1990s. They were followed by heavy winters that created flooding in Northern and Central California and reminded citizens that several urban areas, Sacramento being the most notable, were built on flood plains and subject to incalculable loss in the case of a catastrophic flood. These floods invigorated yet another long-standing controversy about water: Should the state dam rivers and create reservoirs (a proposed dam on the American River some 30 miles east of Sacramento is

---

BOX
1.2   **A Twenty-first Century Water War**

"Build it—damn it!" That was the bumper sticker cry of those who wanted to build a dam on the American River, near the town of Auburn, some 30 miles east of Sacramento in the Sierra foothills. Originally planned back in the 1970s, the Auburn Dam was first delayed by concerns with earthquake potential at the dam site. Subsequently, a congressional coalition of environmentally oriented Democrats and fiscally conservative Republicans succeeded in removing the project from the federal government's water works priority list. Developers and the Republican congressperson from the area continued to fight for restoration of the project and succeeded in blocking federal funding for downriver flood protection not coupled with authorization for the dam. The deadlock was finally broken when dam supporters agreed to drop their opposition to flood control in exchange for federal spending for water supply enhancement that did not include a new dam. Since then, the Democrats gained a majority in the House of Representatives, reducing the power of the local pro-dam congressional supporter, John Doolittle, who announced his decision not to seek reelection in 2008 in the wake of federal Justice Department investigations of his alleged violations of bribery and campaign finance laws.

Whether dead or not, the Auburn Dam controversy epitomizes the political gridlock that surrounds water policy. Opposition to the dam, which would have flooded the largely free-flowing American River, galvanized environmental and recreational interests. Dam supporters stressed the flood protection, water storage, and, most recently, power-generating potential of an Auburn Dam. The worldview and values of the two sides are oceans apart.

Is a beautiful, free-flowing river worth forgoing the economic development and flood protection benefits of a dam? And if not with new dams, how can the state meet increasing water demands, or should it even try? What do you think?

the main focus) in order to provide water storage and flood protection? The fact that new dams might also enhance the state's hydroelectric capacity, and hence contribute to the state's energy supply, adds another element to this complex policy mix. But those who oppose more dams on environmental grounds show no retreat from their opposition. Nor is it clear whether the state and federal governments are willing to provide the necessary funding for these very expensive projects.

Conflicting demands for water allocation among agriculture, urban development, and environmental preservation are nothing new in California's 100-year-old "water wars." Nor are the regional rivalries and distrust between the state's wet and dry regions. But water issues are getting even more complicated and intractable with increasing population and economic development, and future reductions in available water from the Colorado River. Without a massive new water development and deployment system to rival the scope of the Owens Valley, Hetch Hetchy, Central Valley, and State Water projects, Californians are left with little reason to believe that the state can continue to grow and not experience long-term shortages in some water use sectors, or perhaps in all of them. The prospects for a new era of massive water development, given the lack of political consensus, the daunting fiscal and environmental ramifications,

PHOTO 1.4   Southern California's great wildfire of 2007. Drought, global warming, and urbanization of forest land combine to create a natural catastrophe of historic proportions. *(AP Photo/Mike Meadows).*

and other major infrastructure demands (especially in transportation), seem pretty remote.

Californians were reminded by the return of a dry winter pattern in 2006–2007 that the growth in demand for water may be limitless but the supply of water at any point in time is, ultimately, limited. Water supply and water demand in California are on a collision course, and no political solutions on the horizon hold the promise of averting the wreck. Ominously, some long-range forecasts predict a very long dry cycle for the entire West, exacerbated by global warming.

Urban Sprawl

Land-use planning, or the lack of it, is yet another issue that touches on the state's physical well-being. Economics and population increases combine to create strong urbanizing pressures in many of the state's agricultural areas. Housing costs in the metropolitan areas, especially the San Francisco Bay Area, force families working in these places to build and buy homes farther and farther away. A 100-mile commute twice a day becomes a more attractive option as closer-in housing becomes unaffordable.

As a result, housing developments appear on what was once open agricultural land. Farmers, concerned about the availability of water to stay in business anyway (agriculture accounts for about 85 percent of the state's water use), succumb to temptations to sell to developers. A farm acre, worth perhaps $3,000, can fetch $100,000 and upwards if sold for housing development. The result of these pressures is diminishing farmland. One estimate puts the loss at 9 percent statewide over a ten-year period. In Fresno County, one in seven acres was lost to farming over this same period (Kasler, 1998). Over the last 20 years, agricultural land in California has diminished by some 5,000 acres. Some have gone so far as to predict that, in the not too distant future, agriculture will largely disappear from the California landscape (O'Connell, 2003).

Many serious long-term consequences could result if this trend continues. If California ceases to be an agricultural state, it will lose a stable and important part of its economic infrastructure as well as a cultural heritage. Nationally, because California is the most productive farm state, the United States could even move from being an agricultural exporter to an agricultural importer. The environmental and esthetic consequences of paving over farmland with housing developments, gated communities, and big-box shopping malls are no less far-reaching.

In many ways, these issues dealing with the physical integrity of the state are representative of the whole host of major problems (many of them discussed throughout this book) currently facing California. They involve several interests, values, and perspectives, often strongly at odds. Solving them requires political institutions that can foster consensus around viable and broadly accepted compromises. In a state like California, where diversity and division are more prevalent than uniformity and agreement, this is no small task for even ideal institutions.

Limits to water supply and adequate land are physical factors that shape water and land use policies. But there is a whole host of other issues for which another shortage, that of money, poses major constraints. Education and health care are the state's two biggest examples. California public student test scores for reading and math languish near the bottom of the fifty states, this in a state where education is the key to individual economic advancement and the overall health of the state's economy. State *spending totals* in California dwarf those of any other state, yet our *per student* spending is in the lower half of all the states, and our class size and student/teacher ratios are among the nation's largest.

Health care is the second largest item in the state's general budget (K–12 education is the biggest expense), but California's overall health picture is at best mixed. In its percentage of citizens covered by a health insurance plan, or the amount of money spent *per capita* for public health, the Golden State is far from golden, ranking in the bottom fifth of all the states.

Education and health care, like a host of California political dilemmas, have not been allowed to languish on purpose, or through inattention. There is little political disagreement that these systems require revitalization; but there is no agreement as to how this should be accomplished. The divisive issue here is money. How much more can the state afford to spend on education? Or could the need for higher expenditures be moderated by adoption of educational reform along the lines of a voucher system, greater school accountability, or other measures?

Similar complexities complicate the search for health care solutions. Should all or most employers be forced to pay some share of their employees' health care coverage costs, or should the state itself guarantee universal health care, thus transferring coverage costs to the taxpayers? Or would expanded opportunities for individuals to buy private health coverage be a better, more efficient answer?

Of course, in a perfect world there would be plenty of money to go around, and even to experiment with competing policy proposals. In the real world, however, money, or the lack of it, constrains options. Bigger public expenditures to lower class size or provide more individual training for at-risk students must be financed by higher taxes or squeezing other public programs. A universal state health care coverage plan would likely involve the same choices. Mandating employer provided health insurance would impose costs of doing business in California, perhaps jeopardizing the state's economic competitive position, and thus its tax revenue base.

Note again that the issue is not overall spending; California's total yearly spending on education and health care, like other policy areas, dwarfs that of practically every other state. But the sheer size of the state, and more crucially annual state growth, present major fiscal challenges. Just keeping per-capital sending at current levels would require hefty annual increases to accommodate increases in the demand for public education and public health. To increase spending beyond simply keeping up with growth to deliver better health care and more effective education would require increased spending of a substantial magnitude. Over this prospect there is no current consensus. Would a lot more public spending create substantial improvement? What should be the relative roles of the public and private sectors in improving education and health care? If more taxes are necessary, who should bear the brunt of the new tax load?

Fiscal constraints, like the physical limitations discussed earlier, cannot be wished away. They present policy dilemmas whose solutions will require innovation, imagination, sacrifice, and compromise that would challenge even the best constructed and most effective political institutions and processes. When those institutions and processes are substandard, prospects for successful issue resolution become even bleaker.

INSTITUTIONAL CHANGE

This introductory chapter has attempted to provide a current snapshot of the state's political landscape with some discussion of background factors that help define California politics and examples of long-range issues facing the state. Following Chapter 2's outline of the state's political history, the next several chapters will examine individual components of the state's political institutions and processes. This format was adopted for organizational clarity, but ought not be taken to imply that these institutions and processes exist in their own vacuum, or that changes in our political system should be approached piecemeal.

In fact, we urge you to read this book with an eye toward possibilities of comprehensive, broad-based changes, even though most of these chapters limit their discussion of possible reform to those chapters' specific subjects. A recurring argument, and in fact the underlying theme of this book is that many of the arrangements and practices that make up what we call "California politics" are relics of much different times and not well suited, and in fact are counterproductive, to what Californians need and deserve out of their political system.

To the contrary, some might argue that nothing is inherently wrong with California's political institutions that the selection of a few capable leaders could not cure. The voters' imposition of term limits on the state's legislature and executive branch reflects the hope that new faces in Sacramento can succeed where career politicians have failed. And at the heart of Arnold Schwarzenegger's political appeal, and the public's positive response to it, is an assumption, or at least a hope, that smarter, more energetic, and better focused leadership is the key to overcoming political problems.

Unfortunately, California's 15-year experience with legislative term limits undercuts the credibility of the theory that new faces are sufficient. Few would argue that public policy, the end result of the legislative process, is improved over what it was in the "bad old days" of professional, lifetime legislators. Nor have the state's basic problems disappeared under the leadership of a new, charismatic "non-politician" governor. This point is made to argue not that leadership is unimportant but rather that it is not enough. California needs both excellent leaders and sound institutions—institutions that grant leaders the latitude and the power to solve public problems while maintaining their accessibility to the public.

Political Structures—How Can They Be Changed?

Several methods are available to California to rearrange its political structures. Depending on how sweeping the proposed changes are, one of the following forms of alteration may be undertaken.

1. *Legislative Constitutional Amendment.* After an assembly or senate constitutional amendment passes both houses of the legislature by a two-thirds vote, the proposed amendment is placed before the California electorate. A legislative constitutional amendment is adopted in California when a majority of those voting on that precise item approve it.

2. *Initiative Constitutional Amendment.* When signatures amounting to 8 percent of the total number of votes cast in the last gubernatorial contest are collected on petitions, an initiative constitutional amendment is placed before the voters at the next statewide election. An initiative constitutional amendment is adopted when a majority of those voting on that precise item approve it. Initiative amendments are limited to specific constitutional provisions and may not be used for wholesale changes to the constitution, although "wholesale" is not specifically defined, and is instead subject to judicial interpretation on a case-by-case basis.

3. *Constitutional Convention.* The state legislature is empowered to call a constitutional convention on a two-thirds vote of both houses. A majority popular vote on the question of holding such a convention must be obtained from the electorate. After the convention drafts a new constitution, the proposed document must be approved by a majority of those voting on the issue. In other words, popular votes are required both before and after a constitutional convention, but the convention's finished product is not subject to legislative approval.

4. *Constitutional Revision Commission.* The state legislature may create a commission to review the basic law of California and to recommend changes to be made to the constitution. Changes proposed by the revision commission must be adopted by two-thirds votes of both houses of the legislature and by majority vote of those members of the electorate voting on the changes statewide. Thus, unlike the case of a constitutional convention, the legislature has the power to squash any ideas coming out of a revision commission simply by failing to pass them. For example, the revision commission authorized by the legislature in the early 1990s proposed numerous constitutional revisions in 1996. None of them was approved by the legislature.

5. *Split the State.* This radical departure would not only change state government but also obliterate its current form. It is clearly a "last resort" proposal, which might be considered if the failure of less sweeping reforms indicates that the state has become too big, too complex, and too fragmented to ever be made right. It would require the new states arising out of what was the single entity we call California to create new state governments based on their specific needs and circumstances and on their understanding of what worked and what failed in the "old California."

Piecemeal Constitutional Change

Compared with the U.S. Constitution, California's document is easily amended. The national constitution has no provisions for initiative constitutional change, and amendments proposed by the Congress must be approved by three-quarters of the states. In California, constitutional change can originate with an initiative or in the legislature, and ratification requires only a simple majority of "yes" votes at the next statewide election. As a result, the California Constitution has been amended more than 500 times since its adoption in 1879, which contrasts with just 17 formal changes in the U.S. Constitution since the adoption of the Bill of Rights 220 years ago. Ease of amendment has resulted in a state constitution that is very long, quite specific and detailed, and often the reflection of the priorities of interest groups rather than broader constitutional concerns. As more specific organizational and policy details are grafted onto the constitution, rather than relevant statutory code sections, future changes require still further rounds of constitutional amendments.

Moreover, interest groups with the resources to mount a signature-gathering and ballot-measure campaign increasingly see advantages to pursuing the initiative route over more conventional legislative lobbying tactics. In the first place, a provision inserted into the constitution is more difficult to change than a normal law. Second, the details of interest groups' pet projects may be subject to close review and analysis as they pass through the legislative process. Such inspection may be avoided by circumventing the legislature and putting the question before an electorate unlikely to read or understand a ballot initiative's fine print.

Thought might be given to making it more difficult to amend California's basic law. Several alterations could be made. First, the percentage of signatures required to qualify an initiative constitutional amendment could be raised from 8 to 10 or 15 percent, as is now the law in several states. Second, about a dozen states now require that legislative constitutional amendments be passed during two consecutive sessions of the legislature before the item is put out for ratification by the voters. Third, voter approval of constitutional amendments could be made more difficult by requiring a two-thirds popular vote for ratification, as is now the law in New Hampshire. Alternatively, the voter requirement could be a majority of those voting in the election as a whole as opposed to a majority of those voting on the amendment itself. If the vote is much heavier for president or governor at the top of the ballot than it is for a constitutional amendment at the bottom, this proviso would block amendments from slipping into the constitution with only a majority of a diminished electorate. Along these same lines, the constitutional revision commission in 1996 proposed that constitutional amendment initiatives be placed only on general election ballots, where more citizens vote, rather than on either general or primary election ballots, as allowed under the current law.

Ironically, California's constitutional health is threatened by two seemingly contradictory problems. On the one hand, the initiative process allows for frequent, piecemeal amendment, often in the service of narrow interests. On the other hand, the state's basic constitutional framework has not been seriously addressed since the early years of the twentieth century. For observers of California politics who believe fundamental constitutional reform is required, this latter problem is especially troublesome. It is one reason why the deliberations and suggestions of the most recent constitutional revision commission attracted a great deal of attention and why their quick rejection by the legislature was so disappointing. Throughout this book, we ask the following question: Should California retain its current political institutions and processes, change them marginally, or subject them to a fundamental overhaul?

A Political Response

Given the nature, severity, and diversity of problems besetting California, it is possible that even the best-conceived constitutional changes, necessary as they might be, would not be sufficient. At the most pessimistic end of the scale, many argue that the state as we know it might be beyond saving and that we need to divide it up into smaller, more manageable segments. But most would probably agree that less drastic approaches should be tried before giving up on the state altogether.

It is easy to place this burden on the elected politicians, whose perspectives need to be wider and longer than what voters normally see. But responsibility for a better political system does not begin and end with the political professionals; Californians generally must demand better and do better. Voters can hardly expect elected officials to rise above personal, career, and partisan perspectives if they themselves are unwilling to think beyond their own immediate and personal needs in order to consider what is good for California and their fellow Californians.

California in National and Western State* Perspective

Population
California: #1
Smallest: Wyoming

National Rankings of Other Western States
Washington #14
Arizona #16
Oregon #27
Utah #34
Nevada #35
New Mexico #36
Idaho #39
Montana #44
Wyoming #50

Size
California: #3
Largest: Alaska
Smallest: Rhode Island

African-American Population Percent
California: #27
Highest: Mississippi

National Rankings of Other Western States
Montana #4
New Mexico #5
Arizona #6
Nevada #7
Colorado #8
Oregon #9
Wyoming #10
Utah #13
Idaho #14
Washington #18

Household Income
California: #12
Richest: Connecticut
Poorest: Louisiana

National Rankings of Other Western States
Colorado #8
Wyoming #10
Nevada #14
Washington #16
Oregon #28
Arizona #38
Montana #41
Idaho #42
New Mexico #45

Hispanic Population Percent
California: #2
Highest: New Mexico
Lowest: West Virginia

National Rankings of Other Western States
Arizona #4
Nevada #5
Colorado #6
Utah #11
Oregon #14
Idaho #15
Washington #16
Wyoming #22
Montana #40

Lowest: Montana

National Rankings of Other Western States

Nevada #23

Colorado #33

Arizona #35

Washington #36

New Mexico #38

Oregon #41

Utah #42

Wyoming #44

Idaho #48

Asian-American Population Percent

California: #2

Highest: Hawaii

Lowest: Montana

National Rankings of Other Western States

Washington #5

Nevada #6

Oregon #12

Colorado #19

Arizona #20

Utah #26

New Mexico #34

Idaho #39

Wyoming #48

*"Livability"***

California: #30

Most Livable: New Hampshire

Least Livable: Mississippi

National Rankings of Other Western States

Wyoming #6

Utah #11

Idaho #18

Colorado #20

Montana #21

Nevada #24

Washington #25

Arizona #29

Oregon #33

New Mexico #41

*"Western states" refers to California and the ten contiguous states of the western United States.

**"Livability" rankings are based on an index adding positive elements such as good weather, wealth, and education levels, then subtracting negative elements such as high crime rates, teenage birth rates, and high taxes.

Source: Morton Quitno Corp., State Rankings *(Lawrence, KS: Morgan Quitno, 2007).*

CHAPTER *two*

CALIFORNIA'S POLITICAL
HISTORY

T hough few Californians took much notice of it, California celebrated a sesquicentennial, or 150-year anniversary, over the last two years of the twentieth century. The
sesquicentennial commemorated the discovery of gold and subsequent 1849 gold rush,
which changed California forever. In January of 1848, James Marshall, repairing a sluice
box on the American River just north and east of what is now Sacramento, spotted a gold
nugget. News of the discovery quickly spread and, by the next year, the race to California
in search of the precious metal was on. For better or worse, California would never be
the same. Its population—at that time overwhelmingly Native American, Spanish, and
Mexican—swelled from fewer than 15,000 non–Native Americans in 1848 to 250,000
just four years later. The gold rush brought, in addition to the near annihilation of
California's native population, Anglo numerical and political dominance to California at
the same time that the United States was establishing its military supremacy and political
dominion over most of that vast area that we now call the American West. However, even
though these events constituted the pivotal turning point in the state's modern political
history, they were hardly the beginning of California's human history.

CALIFORNIA BEFORE THE GOLD RUSH

The Portuguese navigator Cabrillo explored the California coastline for Spain in 1542,
but permanent settlement by Europeans did not occur for another two centuries. At
the time of Spanish exploration, some 300,000 Native Californians lived throughout
California in numerous tribes. Indians inhabited California for thousands of years prior
to the arrival of the Spanish, who found anything but an empty landscape. Not until

1769, however, did Captain Portola and Father Serra lead an expedition from the Spanish colony of Mexico to found a European settlement and Franciscan mission at San Diego. The chain of 21 missions ultimately founded by Father Serra was confined to a narrow band of land bordering the Pacific shoreline. Native Californians in this area were either made the object of missionary efforts by the Franciscan padres or displaced into the interior region of California.

Spanish rule in its colony to the north of Mexico was characterized by insufficient investment and uncertainty as to leadership and direction. Due to warfare on the European continent with France and England, as well as the remoteness of the colony itself, Spain was not able to provide ample support for the colonization effort. With the often involuntary assistance of Native Californian labor, the missions grew economically powerful on the strength of cultivated crops and livestock herds. The military presidios and civilian pueblos did not thrive to such an extent, and discord between the military and religious authorities in California was common.

With Spain increasingly unable to administer its far-flung colonial empire, Mexico obtained its independence from Spain in 1821 and thereafter assumed control of California. Actually, Mexican control of its northern province was never complete. Years of inattentive administration by Spain had produced independent attitudes among the European residents of California. Governors sent from Mexico City found their authority was not accepted by local leaders. Although relatively bloodless in nature, military engagements between factions from Northern and Southern California did occur.

Two developments were of more long-term significance than the feuding among Mexican provincial officials. First, the Mexican government in 1834 decided to secularize the missions in California and to distribute the mission properties to those settlers desiring land grants. The Spaniards had dispensed only a limited number of land grants, but the pace of granting large parcels of land accelerated dramatically in the late 1830s and early 1840s. Grants of up to 48,000 acres were made to individuals. Because each member of a family could obtain a grant, vast ranchos—some reaching one-quarter of a million acres in size—were accumulated by related persons. Second, citizens of the United States began to appear in California in greater numbers. Preceded by intrepid mountaineers and maritime traders, the first U.S. settlers to cross the Sierra Nevada into California were the members of the Bidwell party, which arrived in 1841. Lieutenant John C. Fremont brought U.S. military expeditions into California in 1844 and 1846, thereby defying the authority and provincial rule of the Mexican government.

U.S. Military Occupation

As a result of a dispute concerning the location of the southern boundary of Texas, the United States declared war on Mexico in May of 1846. During this war, Commodore John D. Sloat occupied the Pacific port of Monterey for the United States, and General Stephen W. Kearny made his way across the Southwest to take control of the southern portion of California. Los Angeles was initially entered without resistance because ranking Mexican officials had fled to Mexico. However, Captain José Flores led those Mexicans who chose to stay and fight in a five-month campaign against the U.S. forces. But by January 1847, the United States was in full possession of California.

It was during the interim period in which U.S. military rule and the remnants of Mexican law prevailed that James Marshall discovered gold. Later in 1848, the United

States signed, and Congress ratified, the Treaty of Guadalupe Hidalgo. The treaty formally concluded the war with Mexico, which ceded California to the United States. The treaty also provided that Mexican Californians wishing to become U.S. citizens could do so and that titles to land established by earlier grants from Mexico and Spain would be honored. With legal responsibility for the area now transferred and the population rapidly growing due to the frenzied search for gold, it became imperative to organize a civilian government in California.

CALIFORNIA'S FIRST CONSTITUTION

A constitutional convention, consisting of 48 delegates representing various regions of California, was held in the fall of 1849. It was a relatively youthful assemblage—the average age of the delegates was just under 38 years—with wide variation in length of residence in California. Seven delegates had spent all their lives in California, whereas 13 members of the convention had been in California for one year or less (Mason, 1973, p. 87). From the standpoint of the document ultimately crafted, it was significant that the nonnative Californians at the convention had been born in 13 different states (as well as 5 foreign countries) and that they collectively had resided in 21 of the then 30 states. California borrowed heavily from other states in writing its first constitution. Largely due to the presence of a delegate who earlier had participated in Iowa's constitutional convention, 66 of the 137 sections of the California document were taken from basic Iowa law. Probably as a result of the fact that 12 former New Yorkers were convention delegates, 19 sections of the California Constitution originated in the Empire State.

The convention document, which was approved overwhelmingly by the voters in November 1849, established a government very much like today's. However, unlike its national counterpart, in which the provisions concerning a citizen's rights were attached at the end, the California Constitution of 1849 began with a Bill of Rights. A plural executive branch of six separate officials chosen by statewide election was formed. A legislature with two houses—the senate and the assembly—was created. Whereas other articles were based on U.S. precedents, the section establishing the elected judicial branch with four levels of courts reflected California's experience with such an arrangement during the quarter century of Mexican rule. Only white men over 21 years of age were given the right to vote; Native Americans were denied this right pending a two-thirds vote of the legislature granting them the franchise. Official pronouncements and documents of state government were to be printed in English and Spanish. Of interest some 14 years later, when efforts were under way to build a rail line across the Sierra Nevada, was the provision that the legislature could not incur a debt in excess of $300,000 without a vote of approval from the electorate. Interested in solidifying its hold on the region, and perhaps dazzled by the mineral wealth being unearthed there, the U.S. Congress accepted the constitution of 1849 and on September 9, 1850, admitted California as the thirty-first state.

THE BIG FOUR

As the 1860s began, no one could have foreseen the chain of events about to be set in motion by four Sacramento merchants, but it would have a profound and lasting impact on political life in California. The extraordinarily powerful transportation monopoly created at this time was to dominate state politics for more than four decades, and reaction to it ultimately led to major modifications in California's political processes.

Leland Stanford, Collis Huntington, Charles Crocker, and Mark Hopkins formed the Central Pacific Railroad in 1861 for the purpose of building a rail line across the Sierra Nevada north of Lake Tahoe. Realizing the importance to the state and to the nation of a rail line between the East and West Coasts, the group sought government support for its expensive undertaking. The U.S. Congress in 1862 (and later in 1864) made massive land grants and long-term loans available and named the Central Pacific as the corporation responsible for the western portion of the proposed line. Having run successfully for governor of California, Stanford used his office during 1862 and 1863 to secure outright monetary subsidies and additional loans from the state legislature for the railroad. Given the previously mentioned limitation on indebtedness in the state constitution, these financial arrangements were of questionable constitutionality. Fortified with public funds, together with private capital, the Central Pacific commenced construction up the western slope of the Sierra in early 1863.

The leaders of the Central Pacific had a rare, complementary mixture of diverse abilities. Stanford enjoyed public office (he was later to be a U.S. senator) and served as corporate president of the Central Pacific. Huntington was the group's East Coast representative and lobbyist in Washington, D.C. Tireless, yet shunning public attention, Huntington also planned the railroad's political operation throughout the length of California and held the position of corporate vice president. Although named only a director of the corporation, Crocker was the driving force behind the work crews laying track up and over difficult mountain terrain. At first due to a labor shortage, but later due to their proficiency as workers and their lower wage demands, Crocker employed some 12,000 Chinese in the construction effort (Howard, 1962, pp. 235, 303). Less assertive than his three companions, Hopkins was treasurer of the Central Pacific and responsible for assembling the many supplies and materials needed to continue building the rail line to the east.

Given the size of California and the limited number of entry points into the state, transportation within and into the state was bound to be of crucial importance to the development of the region. Sensing this critical element, the leaders of the Central Pacific—soon dubbed the "Big Four"—acquired railroad companies capable of linking regions within the state as well as providing connections to Oregon and Arizona. One of these acquisitions, the Southern Pacific Railroad Company, later became the corporate identity by which the entire system was known.

Although people in California originally supported the growth of rail transportation, the mood changed by May 1869 when the Central Pacific linked with the Union Pacific at Promontory Point (north of the Great Salt Lake) to form the first rail line across the United States. Controlling 85 percent of the track in California gave the Big Four powerful economic leverage, particularly with their ability to vary freight rates. If the railroad supported a particular business, it would provide secret discounts for shipments. It could also raise freight charges to the point where a shipper would be unable to move goods by rail. The railroad expected subsidies from county and city governments for the privilege of rail service. Should such monies not be forthcoming, it would bypass the local government in question entirely or establish a rival community nearby to serve as a rail center. For example, San Bernardino would not subsidize the Southern Pacific, so the company established the town of Colton for use as a depot (McAfee, 1973, p. 123). Under these circumstances, localities wishing to prosper would generally subsidize the laying of track in their area. Note that the Southern Pacific received financial assistance from national, state, and finally local governments.

Efforts by disgruntled Californians to develop less expensive means of shipping were met head on by the Big Four. When shippers between San Francisco and Los Angeles shifted their freight to coastal steamships to avoid high rail rates, the Southern Pacific acquired the steamship line to eliminate the competition. Transportation companies traveling the inland waterways between San Francisco and Sacramento or Stockton met the same fate. If a rail line offering fair rates was established somewhere in the state, the railroad giant would temporarily cut its freight charges on that route to next to nothing. While the large corporation recovered its losses on that route by elevating its rates elsewhere, the upstart competitor was forced out of business.

Apart from these types of economic power, the Southern Pacific was by far the largest landholder in the state. Having received up to 12,800 acres from the public domain for every mile of track laid under provisions of federal laws passed in 1862 and 1864, the railroad came to control 11.5 million of California's 100 million acres (Robinson, 1948, p. 157). Although the railroad could not select acreage covered by a validated land grant made prior to statehood, the acquisition of so much land by the railroad was a genuine source of economic strength.

To forestall the implementation of governmental policies that might hamper their widespread interests, the Big Four and the Political Bureau of the Southern Pacific became thoroughly involved in politics at all levels of government. While Huntington sought favorable treatment for the corporation from the federal government, political agents of the railroad were active at the state capitol in Sacramento and in county courthouses throughout the state. State party conventions were attended by locally chosen delegates, so the railroad's operatives made every effort to see that representatives friendly to the Southern Pacific were selected. These delegates, in turn, nominated candidates to run for state offices. In addition, generous contributions to prorailroad candidates ensured that many individuals sympathetic to the Big Four took office.

Ample financial resources permitted the Southern Pacific to provide free train passes for officeholders and their families, to pay the expenses of visits to San Francisco (the corporate headquarters) by political supporters, and to extend "legal fees" to lawyer-politicians. To obtain favorable press, the corporation subsidized those newspapers with the "correct" attitude about the railroad. Should a particular periodical be especially troublesome, not only would the Southern Pacific withdraw any subsidy then in effect, but also it would initiate efforts to have major shippers remove their advertising. In an unusually flagrant example of the use of money in politics, Leland Stanford's brother, Philip, openly paid voters on the streets of San Francisco to cast ballots in favor of a municipal stock subscription that would provide construction capital for the Central Pacific (Lewis, 1938, p. 358). Finally, the political style of the Big Four is aptly illustrated by Governor Stanford's naming of Charles Crocker's brother, Edwin, to the state supreme court. Edwin Crocker was head of the railroad's legal department at the time of his appointment, and he did not relinquish this post when he joined the state's highest court.

CALIFORNIA'S SECOND CONSTITUTION

During the mid-1870s, the state's economy weakened. Numerous businesses failed and the ranks of the unemployed grew. As often the case in California during periods of economic downturn, many citizens vented their frustrations against foreigners. In this case, the targets were Chinese returning to California from Utah and Nevada after completion of the transcontinental railroad. Corporations were criticized for controlling too much land, charging unfair rates, and encouraging the importation of Chinese laborers. The Workingmen's Party was formed in San Francisco in September 1877 in response to these issues. Dennis Kearney, who supported himself by transporting goods around the city in a cart, became a vocal leader of this group. Kearney's statements included the following: "The rich have ruled us until they have ruined us. We will now take our affairs into our own hands," and "To an American, death is preferable to life on a par with the Chinese" (Swisher, 1969, p. 11). Kearney served a brief jail term for threatening a member of the Big Four with physical violence and for participating in a riot near the mansions of Stanford and Crocker on San Francisco's Nob Hill.

Because of the lack of detail in the constitution of 1849 and the numerous changes in the state in the intervening decades, the state legislature called for the election of delegates to a constitutional convention to be held in June 1878. Individuals with corporate interests turned their attention to the election of as many delegates opposed to Kearney's views as possible. However, even though the Workingmen's Party (or Kearneyites) was able to elect only one-third of the 152 delegates to the constitutional convention, their presence, and occasional alliance with small farmer delegates, led to the adoption of a number of provisions dealing with corporations.

Some of the language approved for the new constitution dealt with corporations in general and some with railroads in particular. Stockholders were made responsible for their share of the debts of a corporation; members of a corporation's board of directors were made liable for all monies embezzled or misappropriated by corporate officers; and no corporation could hold real estate unnecessary to its business for more than five years. The provisions regarding railroads forbade giving free passes to officeholders; prohibited raising rates that had been reduced to compete with a rival line; required that short-haul fares be less than long-haul fares traveling over the same track in the same direction; and, most important, established a Railroad Commission of three persons to be elected every four years to set transportation rates and to correct abuses by the carriers. The delegates wrote this regulatory commission into the constitution so that the legislature could not disband it.

The delegates also approved an article prohibiting the employment of Chinese on public works projects or by corporations chartered in California. This so-called Chinese exclusion provision remained in the state constitution until it was repealed in 1952. Although the all-male convention debated extending the right to vote to women, a motion to that effect was defeated. The California Constitution of 1879 remains in effect to this day, although it underwent major revision in the 1910s, 1960s, and 1970s. In addition, approximately 500 individual amendments, originating in legislative action or the initiative process, have been added to the document since its 1879 passage.

The railroad unsuccessfully tried to block the constitutional convention of 1879, argued against placing language on corporations and railroads in the constitution, and urged voters to deny ratification of the finished document. Faced with strong sentiment in favor of regulating the railroad, the Big Four then "managed to 'influence' two of the three members of the state railroad commission (one by open bribery), and the entire machinery of regulation collapsed" (Lewis, 1938, p. 404). Referring to the ultimate impact of the Railroad Commission, an authority on this era concluded, "Indeed, the railroads seemed to profit by the scheme, in that they appeared to submit to a political agency, which in fact they were themselves able to control" (Swisher, 1969, p. 113). Celebrations over the supposed demise of the Southern Pacific were premature; in fact, its period of dominance was less than half completed.

THE CALIFORNIA PROGRESSIVES

By 1900, all the members of the Big Four had died, and the ownership of the Southern Pacific had passed to E. H. Harriman. With its control of the state legislature still intact, the transportation corporation saw to it that the legislators appropriated no funds to carry out the Railroad Commission's regulatory activities. Determined to liberate their party and the legislature from the influence of the Southern Pacific, a group of reformers set about encouraging antirailroad delegates to attend the next Republican state convention. This partial success at the 1908 convention led to the election of a significant number of state legislators who were not indebted to the rail company. During the legislative session of 1909, these progressive reformers enacted a direct primary law that removed from party conventions the responsibility of selecting nominees to run for public office. Whereas a small number of convention delegates, usually controlled by the railroad, had chosen candidates for various races prior to 1909, henceforth all registered voters in a particular party could participate in primary elections to determine the nominees of their party.

Having instituted the primary system, the progressives moved quickly to take advantage of the opportunity it afforded. Despite opposition from the Southern Pacific in both the Republican primary and the general election, progressive Republican Hiram Johnson swept to victory in the 1910 gubernatorial election. He had promised voters that he would "kick the Southern Pacific out of politics." Declining to ride on trains and refusing to be identified in any manner with the railroad, Johnson had campaigned throughout the state in an automobile driven by his son. With Johnson's election and with both houses of the state legislature also solidly progressive, the stage was set for the introduction of the most important political changes ever made in California.

Although a consensus is lacking concerning the meaning of the term *progressivism*, scholars generally concede the progressives believed in (1) taming unrestrained corporate influence in the political process, (2) regulating concentrated economic power, (3) expanding citizen participation in politics, (4) protecting the environment, and (5) improving adverse working and living conditions stemming from industrialization and urbanization (Gould, 1974, pp. 2–5). Progressives hoped to rid government of corruption and to establish efficient, expert management in the public sector. The progressive point of view was not found exclusively among Republicans, nor were all Republicans necessarily progressive in their orientation. Democrat Theodore Bell, Johnson's opponent in the general election of 1910, was considered a progressive as well.

PHOTO 2.1   Hiram Johnson—leader of California progressivism, state governor (1911–1917), and U.S. senator (1917–1945). (*California State Library*)

Under Hiram Johnson's administration, the following changes in political institutions were either placed in the state constitution or enacted as statutory law in 1911 and 1913.

1911

- The Railroad Commission was expanded from three to five members; made appointive by the governor instead of elected; given jurisdiction over utilities (i.e., gas, electricity, and telephones) as well as railroads; and provided with the means to enforce its rate decisions.

- The direct democracy devices of initiative, referendum, and recall were made available to the people of California. (Refer to Chapter 9 for extended discussion of these items.)

- Local government, judicial, and school board elections were made nonpartisan, which meant that party labels could not appear next to candidates' names on the ballot.

- Women were extended the right to vote. (The U.S. Constitution was not amended to incorporate women's suffrage until 1920.)

- The party column ballot, which facilitated straight-ticket voting (i.e., selecting all the candidates of one party), was eliminated in favor of the office bloc ballot.

1913

- City, county, and special district elections were made nonpartisan.

- The leadership and operation of the official political parties in California were prescribed in detail, thereby weakening these organizations. (Refer to Chapter 8 for extended discussion of this point.)

- Candidates were permitted to "cross-file" into more than one primary election contest, which meant that a prospective officeholder might appear simultaneously on the ballots (and possibly win the nomination) of two or more parties (Olin, 1968; Mowry, 1951).

As is evident from this list, several reforms dealt with political parties. The progressives thought that parties were the vehicle by which the Southern Pacific exercised its domination over the state. Therefore, the reformers undertook to weaken them. Making elections nonpartisan reduced the number of offices for which someone bearing a party label could run. Altering the ballot and introducing cross-filing made it more difficult for parties to be sure that their rank-and-file members were voting for party candidates. Governor Johnson and the legislature approved a bill in 1915 to do away with party labels for all state offices, legislative and executive, just as partisan elections were eliminated at the local level. Essentially, this action would have been a death blow to political parties in California because only elections for national offices would have remained partisan. Ironically, the voters used a device made available by the progressives themselves—the referendum—to defeat this measure sponsored by the progressive leadership in the state.

Apart from changes in political institutions, the progressives attempted to curb industrial accidents, to improve conditions for immigrants and migrant agricultural workers, and to preserve the state's natural resources. Much less admirably, the progressives also responded to racist sentiment among some whites in California by enacting an Alien Land Law, which prohibited Asians (but not Europeans) who were ineligible for citizenship from owning land. This law was finally declared unconstitutional in 1952.

In 1914, Hiram Johnson became the first governor in the state's history to win election to a second term in office. However, he completed only two years of this term before moving to the U.S. Senate, where he served until his death in 1945 ended the longest U.S. Senate tenure in the history of California.

Johnson's exit from California to Washington marked the end of Progressivism's high tide in California, though it continued to be a force, particularly within the Republican Party, the state's dominant party until the 1930s. Leadership of the party, particularly in the person of the Governor, swung back and forth between Republican progressives and conservatives, with policy cycles that reflected the changing political fortunes of the two Republican factions.

DEPRESSION ERA POLITICS

Beginning with the stock market crash in late 1929, the Great Depression shook the nation's economic system to its roots and ended a three-decade era of almost complete Republican Party dominance over national and California politics. At the national level, the Democratic Party established itself as the majority party, and maintained this status over the next 30 to 40 years. Republican control over California politics was similarly

---

B O X
2.1

The Meaning and Legacy of California's Progressives

Though California's progressives controlled state politics for only a brief period, it is hard to overestimate their lasting impact. It is also difficult to neatly label their philosophy or ideology. The state's weak political parties, its heavy reliance on the initiative process, and the nonpartisan nature of its local governments are just three of the more obvious enduring legacies of the progressives. The way most Californians think about politics—for example, taking pride in "voting for the best candidate, not the party label"—is also crucially shaped by the progressives' vision.

Yet these men and women defy easy categorization. In certain ways—for example, in their support of women's right to vote, environmental protection, and improved workplace conditions—they were forward-looking and "liberal" in their politics. But progressives also looked to the past, or at least their conception of the past, for their political guidance. They were alienated by the growth of large organizations, whether corporations or labor unions, that characterize a modern economic system. Like some contemporary conservatives, they saw government as an instrument to buttress basic moral standards. And, not unlike some Californians today, they were fearful of the immigrant "flood," which, in their eyes, threatened to tear the social fabric. Least appealing, progressivism (though certainly not all progressives) was tainted by racism, focused most directly on Asians.

Their leader, Hiram Johnson, is equally difficult to characterize. His career in public service was long; after serving as governor 1911 through 1916, he went to the U.S. Senate, where he served for 38 years, a California record. Johnson not only influenced politics in California, but also was an important national political actor. He was Teddy Roosevelt's Bull Moose Party vice presidential running mate in the 1912 election and harbored strong presidential ambitions.

The Republican nomination always eluded him, however, and he was an early supporter of Democratic President Franklin Roosevelt. That relationship quickly turned sour when Johnson, an irreconcilable isolationist, bitterly opposed the interventionist policies of Roosevelt. Increasingly, he was alienated from both Republicans and Democrats, casting the only Senate vote against ratification of the United Nations charter. He died on August 6, 1945 (the day the atomic bomb was dropped on Hiroshima), an isolated and alienated political figure.

Johnson's influence on the development of California politics was singular. He was his own person, never really at home in his Republican Party and not comfortable with the newer-style liberalism of the New Deal Democrats. One Johnson biography is fittingly titled *A Bloc of One* (Lower, 1993).

---

challenged as California voters supported the presidential election and reelections of Democrat Franklin Roosevelt. But the California State Republican Party was able to largely insulate itself from the anti-Republican national tide, winning most of the gubernatorial and legislative elections until the late 1950s.

The 1934 campaign for governor was the first major challenge successfully turned back by the Republicans. This election offered voters a stark choice between Republican Frank Merriam, the Lieutenant Governor, and Democrat Upton Sinclair. Sinclair advocated a radical program of economic redistribution titled End Poverty in California (EPIC) that featured government operated farms and factories to employ the out of work, and increased taxation of individual and business wealth. Merriam countered by deriding the "empty promises in California" of his opponent.

This very bitter election, dubbed "the campaign of the century," was a prototype of the negative campaigns waged today (Mitchell, 1992). Because of his plan to tax their industry, owners of Hollywood studios unleashed newsreels distorted against Sinclair. (Newsreels were the television news and blogger space of that day and age.) Sinclair backers were depicted as hobos and bums migrating to California, while Merriam's supporters were shown as responsible citizens. Though Merriam succeeded in defeating Sinclair in 1934, the continuing depression and the national tide against Republican officeholders kept up the pressure on California Republicans. Merriam would be a one term governor.

These tides led to the victory of Democrat Culbert Olson over Merriam in 1938. Olson was the first Democrat to be elected governor in California in the twentieth century. But help was on the way for tottering Republican state control. This same election provided a glimpse of the future as the district attorney from Alameda County, Republican Earl Warren, became state attorney general by successfully using cross-filing to win the Republican and Democratic primary elections.

EARL WARREN AND THE POLITICS OF NONPARTISANSHIP

Governor Olson intended to preside over a rebirth of progressive programs—chief among them being public hydroelectric power, stronger government regulation of the oil industry, and compulsory health insurance—but conflict with the legislature precluded passage of his reforms. Olson lost the governorship to Republican Earl Warren in 1942. Appointing Republicans and Democrats alike to state administrative positions, Warren typified the progressives' nonpartisan orientation to state government. His support of better pensions, unemployment insurance, and health insurance was also reminiscent of progressive policies. For the first and only time in the state's history, Warren carried the nonpartisan spirit to its zenith by winning the Republican and the Democratic nominations for governor in 1946 through a successful cross-filing effort. It could also be argued that Warren's nonpartisan approach, appealing to Democrats, Independents, as well as his Republican base, maintained Republican power in the state for another decade. (See Chapter 4 for a discussion of parallels between the Warren and Schwarzenegger governorship.) In 1950, Warren became the only governor of California ever elected to a third term, but he did not complete that term due to his appointment as chief justice of the U.S. Supreme Court in 1953, where he served until 1969. The Warren Supreme Court's most famous decisions declared racial segregation unconstitutional.

Leaving Sacramento, Warren was probably the most popular governor in the state's history; indeed he may still own that title. Despite his long and distinguished career (he was also the Republican vice-presidential candidate in 1948), there is a major blemish on Warren's record. That was his support and approval of the relocation of West Coast Japanese-Americans to "relocation" camps in 1942. This policy was hatched up in the hysteria immediately following the Pearl Harbor attack and justified by the argument, subsequently proved baseless, that these Americans were somehow a threat to national security. Of his role in this tragedy, he later wrote, "I have since deeply regretted the removal order and my own testimony advocating it, because it was not in keeping with our American concept of freedom and the rights of citizens" (Warren, 1977).

Republican Goodwin Knight, the incumbent lieutenant governor, became governor upon Warren's departure for Washington, D.C. Business interests thought Knight would be sympathetic to their point of view, but this assumption proved to be only partially correct. Governor Knight did not support health insurance or create numerous new state programs, but he did permit increased appropriations for existing government activities, such as workers' compensation and disability insurance, as well as embracing the aims of organized labor. The Democrats had climbed ahead of the Republicans in terms of registered voters in 1934. Migration to California to jobs in military construction plants during World War II and the Korean Conflict further augmented the size of the state's Democratic Party. Following Warren's example, Knight understood that to be retained as the state's chief executive, he would need the votes of both Democrats and Republicans. Pursuing a relatively nonpartisan campaign, and with labor's backing, Knight was elected governor in his own right in 1954. The Warren and Knight strategy was a successful response to the new reality of a Democratic majority among the state's voters. But other forces within the Republican Party favored a different, more confrontational approach.

PHOTO 2.2 Earl Warren—master of the politics of nonpartisanship and California governor (1943–1953) and U.S. Supreme Court Chief Justice (1953–1969).
(California State Library)

THE END OF REPUBLICAN DOMINANCE

The 1958 election proved to be pivotal in California politics. Having just completed eight years as state attorney general during the Republican administrations of Warren and Knight, Edmund G. (Pat) Brown was nominated as Democratic candidate for governor. Although Knight was planning to campaign for reelection, California's U.S. Senator William Knowland announced his intention to run in the Republican gubernatorial primary in his home state. To avoid a bitter split in the Republican Party, and at the urging of Vice President Richard Nixon and the *Los Angeles Times*, Knight decided to attempt an exchange of offices with Knowland by campaigning for the U.S. Senate instead of the governorship. The big switch failed as both Republican candidates lost. Unlike Warren and Knight before him, Knowland's reputation as a strongly partisan, antilabor Republican hindered his appeal across party lines. This image was only sharpened when he endorsed a Right to Work ballot initiative aimed at weakening California labor unions. Both Knowland and the initiative went down to landslide defeat.

Along with Pat Brown's victory in the gubernatorial race, the Democrats won control of both houses of the state legislature for the first time in the twentieth century. Once in power, the party that fared poorly under cross-filing quickly eliminated this aspect of primary elections from future use in California. Saying that he hoped to lead California to accomplishments as significant as those made during the bipartisan administrations of Hiram Johnson and Earl Warren, Brown expanded aid to local educational districts, the highway system, and the state's university campuses. He inaugurated a consumer protection program to control unscrupulous business practices. Governor Brown also successfully advocated for State Water Project reservoirs on the Feather River north of Sacramento to capture water that would then be transported through an aqueduct system to the dry central and southern portions of the state.

Following former Vice President Richard Nixon's unsuccessful attempt to unseat him in the election of 1962, a number of problems plagued Governor Brown's second term. Brown's conflict with the Democratic speaker of the state assembly, Jesse Unruh, hindered good relations with the legislature and weakened party cohesiveness in the state. Student protests, dubbed the free speech movement, on the Berkeley campus of the University of California in 1964 and riots in the south-central Los Angeles ghetto of Watts in 1965 provided opponents with issues to use against Brown as he tried to duplicate Warren's feat of being elected to a third term. Campaigning on a platform to limit taxation and the growth of state government, as well as advocating firm measures to deal with student unrest, Ronald Reagan defeated incumbent Pat Brown by 1 million votes.

CALIFORNIA GOVERNORSHIP: NO EXPERIENCE NEEDED

After decades of experienced leadership by the likes of Earl Warren and Pat Brown, 1966 marked the beginning of a 16-year period during which California's chief executives learned the job while occupying the governorship. Having never held public office, former actor Ronald Reagan endeavored to deliver on his campaign promise to cut government spending. He did reduce state appropriations for higher education and for mental health, but with inflation and population growth, Reagan was not able to stop the absolute growth of state expenditures. However, he claimed to have reduced the *rate of increase* in government spending. Having received strong campaign assistance from the business community, Reagan appointed numerous persons from industry to state posts formerly occupied by individuals supportive of labor, consumerism, or environmentalism.

Like many California governors, Ronald Reagan quickly captured a great deal of national interest. Having been in office less than two years, he was emboldened to seek the 1968 Republican presidential nomination. By coming close to edging out the front-runner, Richard Nixon, he established his credentials as a national politician to be reckoned with.

Like other Republican governors who followed him, Ronald Reagan had to contend with a legislature controlled by Democrats. Although Reagan was elected to a second term as governor by defeating Democrat Jesse Unruh by 500,000 votes, both houses of the legislature returned to Democratic majorities by narrow margins. In all, Reagan's party controlled the legislature for less than two of his eight years as governor, demonstrating the proclivity of California voters to forsake partisan loyalty and vote for a person, not a party. By splitting their tickets, voters returned a Republican to the governor's office while handing leadership of the state legislature to the Democrats. This voting pattern occurred regularly over the next four decades. As is often the case when legislative and executive branches are controlled by rival parties, Governor Reagan's second term was characterized by partisan gridlock. Beyond his policies, however, Reagan deeply affected state politics, especially Republican politics, for years after his departure from Sacramento to the White House. The Earl Warren style of Republicanism—nonpartisan, non-ideological, and moderate—gave way to a much more conservative, ideological, and some would say contentious, partisanship. And of course his subsequent two-term American presidency has left indelible marks on national politics.

In 1974, sensing the public's support for political reform during the year of Watergate and Richard Nixon's resignation from the presidency, Secretary of State Jerry Brown, son of former governor Pat Brown, entered the Democratic gubernatorial primary. Brown and his staff had helped to draft the Political Reform Act, which appeared on the primary ballot in 1974 as Proposition 9. In brief, the ballot measure sought to curtail public officials' conflicts of interest, require fuller campaign finance disclosure, and regulate lobbyists. During the campaign for the Democratic nomination for governor, Brown vigorously supported the reform initiative while his opponents were reluctant to do so. Both Brown and Proposition 9 swept to victory in the June 1974 primary. In the wake of Ronald Reagan's decision not to seek a third term, State Controller Houston Flournoy captured the Republican nomination for governor. With a large lead over Flournoy in the early polls, Brown ran a cautious campaign for the governorship. Given the handicap of being a Republican candidate when the Watergate scandal had forced a Republican president out of office, Houston Flournoy lost the general election to Brown by a surprisingly narrow margin of 180,000 votes.

Pat Brown, Jerry's father, had in his earlier stint as governor presided over a dramatic expansion of state government programs. But Jerry Brown, early in his administration, declared an "era of limits" and, in keeping with this theme, proposed few new government programs. He did play a major role in 1975 in the passage of an agricultural labor relations statute that established procedures for the conduct of union elections on

PHOTO 2.3   Ronald Reagan—only California governor (1967–1975) to also serve as U.S. president (1981–1989).
(California State Library)

California farms. Although Brown's legislative accomplishments were not numerous, his record in the area of appointments was indeed noteworthy. Jerry Brown appointed the first woman, the first and second African Americans, and the first Latino to the California Supreme Court. His cabinet featured a number of female members. Brown named minorities and women to boards, commissions, and departments throughout state government. Environmentalists liked Brown's support of alternative energy programs (e.g., solar and wind) and his opposition to the licensing of Pacific Gas and Electric's (PG&E's) Diablo Canyon nuclear facility. Interested in energy conservation, he discouraged the use of single-occupant motor vehicles and encouraged the use of mass transit and car pools. His spartan lifestyle (no limousine or mansion) and his penchant for asking tough questions of civil servants intrigued the public and contributed to his high standing in the polls during his first term.

Things did not go so well during his second term. Although reelected in 1978 by a huge majority over his Republican challenger, Attorney General Evelle Younger, Brown's popularity began sliding quickly. He had opposed Proposition 13, the property tax reduction initiative that overwhelmingly passed at the June 1978 primary election. Upon its passage, however, he embraced the content and spirit of Proposition 13 by imposing a hiring and spending freeze on the state bureaucracy. Although this move put him on the side of the state's voting majority, it alienated many Democratic politicians, especially in the legislature, who were strongly opposed to Proposition 13 and the antitax, antigovernment agenda that animated it.

As well, Brown, like so many California governors, caught a very bad case of "Potomac fever," the itch to run for President. He mounted a brief, unsuccessful bid to derail Jimmy Carter's nomination in 1976; in 1980, he tried for the big prize again. His campaign was no more successful this time, and Californians were tired of their traveling governor. Finally, his reluctance to use aerial pesticide spraying against a medfly epidemic further eroded his standing, especially in the agricultural community. By the end of his second term, the legislature, still firmly in the hands of a Democratic majority, was overriding his vetoes, and in the minds of many citizens, Jerry Brown had become a caricature of himself rather than a politician to be taken seriously.

Jerry Brown left the governorship at the end of his second term in 1982 and ran for the U.S. Senate against an up-and-coming Republican, Pete Wilson. Wilson won handily, and Brown disappeared, for a while, from the political stage. He was fond of saying, "The first rule of politics is to be different." And that he was.

CALIFORNIA GOVERNORSHIP: RETURN OF THE PROFESSIONALS

After 16 years (1967–1983) of governors possessing little governmental experience at the time they took office, 1982 featured a gubernatorial race between two veteran political leaders. With 9 years as mayor of Los Angeles to his credit plus service on the city council, Tom Bradley easily captured the Democratic gubernatorial primary, becoming the state's first, and still only African-American major party nominee for governor. In his come-from-behind win against Lieutenant Governor Mike Curb in the Republican gubernatorial primary, Attorney General George Deukmejian highlighted his 20 years of experience in the legislative and executive branches. Once again overtaking an opponent in the closing days of a campaign, Deukmejian defeated Bradley by just 93,345 votes out of some 7.8 million votes cast for governor. Despite losing the governorship and a U.S. Senate seat in 1982, Democrats retained control of both houses of the California legislature and also captured all other statewide offices in the executive branch.

Unlike his flashy predecessors, Governor Deukmejian ordinarily was characterized as unspectacular, bland, and predictable. His lack of charisma was so evident that Deukmejian himself joked about it. Despite his low-key style, Deukmejian used his budgetary and appointment powers to bring about new priorities in state government. Governor Deukmejian's budgets contained major increases for prisons and highways. Programs that suffered reductions included the state public defender office, family planning, Medi-Cal, the Coastal Commission, the Agricultural Labor Relations Board, the Air Resources Board, and Cal-OSHA. By paying overtime to civil servants and by contracting out some tasks to the private sector, Deukmejian slightly decreased the number of employees working in state government during his first term. The governor especially appreciated the opportunity to appoint what he called "commonsense" judges to the bench. He showed a preference for appointing former prosecutors and those with judicial experience to court vacancies. But as was true for Republican governors who preceded and followed him, much of Governor Deukmejian's first term was consumed with partisan wrangling with the Democratic-controlled legislature.

The 1986 election, a rematch between Bradley and Deukmejian, was as much about Rose Bird and the state supreme court as it was about the candidates for regular elective office. Governor Deukmejian made his opposition to the retention of Bird and her allies the centerpiece of his reelection campaign. (The Bird episode is examined in Chapter 5.) The combination of the "Duke's" high job ratings, his well-run campaign, and the Bird issue resulted in a landslide Deukmejian victory in 1986. But once again, a Republican victory at the top of the ticket was accompanied by continued Democratic control of the legislature, and Democrats retained all the remaining statewide offices.

Not only did the supreme court issue contribute to Deukmejian's victory, but also it gave him a chance to remake the state's high court. When the voters refused to retain Bird, Joseph Grodin, and Cruz Reynoso, they created three vacancies for the governor to fill. In doing so, he was able to usher in an era, one that would last into the twenty-first century, of high court decisions more amenable to Republican policy and philosophies.

But Deukmejian was unable to match his success in changing the direction of the high court with corresponding success in getting the legislature to see things his way. Following the death of Treasurer Jesse Unruh in 1987, Governor Deukmejian nominated U.S. Representative Dan Lungren to the vacant post. And although the assembly consented, the senate rejected Lungren in February 1988. The opposition to Representative Lungren stemmed from his record as a strongly partisan Republican. Also, ethnic groups, particularly Asian Americans, fought his confirmation because he had voted in Congress against reparations (payments) for individuals who spent World War II inside internment camps. Viewed as a strong fund-raiser and an energetic campaigner, Lungren was opposed by Democratic legislators who wanted to deny him a stepping-stone to higher office.

Early in 1989, George Deukmejian announced that he would not seek a third term as governor in the elections of 1990. His announcement, signaling an end to a 28-year public service career, contributed to a more cooperative relationship with the legislative branch. During 1989, the governor and the legislature approved a ban on certain semi-automatic assault weapons, reforms in workers' compensation law, and a new regulatory commission to deal with solid waste materials. The greatest achievement of 1989 was a grand compromise between Governor Deukmejian and legislative leaders to seek popular approval for gas tax increases and modifications in the state appropriations limit (the so-called Gann limit, discussed in Chapter 10). This compromise was approved by the California electorate as Proposition 111 in June 1990.

Governor Deukmejian's final year as chief executive saw a return to bruising combat with the California legislature. The state's economy entered recession in 1990 and actual revenues collected failed to meet projections. To cope with declining revenues, Governor Deukmejian proposed that the school funding guarantees contained in Proposition 98 be suspended. Legislators from both political parties refused to go along with the governor's request. Protracted negotiations finally produced a state budget one month into the new fiscal year. The continuing decline of the state's economy, and hence tax revenues, made it clear that this compromise budget would be badly out of balance. Under darkening fiscal skies, the governorship changed hands in January of 1991.

A New Governor Reaches for the Political Center

Aside from their obvious gender difference, the two major party nominees for governor in 1990 had much in common. Both Pete Wilson (R) and Dianne Feinstein (D) were centrists who shared the same positions on a number of issues. Both opposed offshore drilling, supported capital punishment, and claimed to be pro-choice on the abortion issue. Wilson had no major opposition in the Republican gubernatorial primary, whereas Feinstein needed to expend a great deal of money and effort in defeating Attorney General John Van de Kamp in the Democratic primary. Wilson ultimately prevailed in a tightly contested general election on the strength of more seasoned campaign managers and superior funding. Feinstein's margin of defeat was less than pollsters expected, and she would be heard from again.

Democrats maintained their hold on all but one of the statewide offices. One of those Democratic winners was state controller candidate Gray Davis, Jerry Brown's former chief of staff, who traded in his seat in the state assembly to begin a long climb up the executive branch ladder.

Pete Wilson began his governorship amidst high hopes and, relatively speaking, bipartisan support. The former U.S. senator and San Diego mayor was seen as a "moderate" and "pragmatist" who might be able to deal effectively with the Democratic majority in the legislature. However, partisan wrangling with the legislators, both Democrat and Republican, continued economic decline, and, perhaps, the governor's combative personal style, stymied Wilson's attempt to govern through a broader consensus. State Republicans had prevailed upon him to give up his U.S. Senate seat to run for the governorship. With little chance of capturing a legislative majority and a new round of redistricting due in the early 1990s, the Republicans feared a repeat of the 1980s redistricting, in which a legislature controlled by Democrats had created a set of district maps that Republicans felt cheated them out of several congressional and legislative seats. A Republican governor, with the power to veto redistricting bills, could save Republicans from the same fate. But although nearly all Republicans agreed that Wilson was the strongest possible candidate, a view that was substantiated by his successful candidacy, the new governor was not at all popular with the conservative wing of his own party, especially the more conservative assembly Republicans.

This intra-Republican feud had deep roots. Wilson had not been an early supporter of Ronald Reagan's early presidential ambitions, and his support for environmental policies and, crucially, his pro-choice position on abortion only widened the gap between the new governor and many Republican legislators. Finally, Wilson's willingness to "meet the Democrats halfway" in closing the budget gap through tax increases as well as spending cuts further alienated many of his Republican colleagues in the legislature.

As if this intra-party animosity were not enough, Governor Wilson increasingly found little ground for agreement and cooperation with the legislature's Democratic majority. The early 1990s saw a series of fiscal disasters. Even in good years, the increased monetary demands on Sacramento caused by population growth and rapidly expanding education, welfare, and prison-inmate caseloads would have stretched, if not broken, the state budget. California also suffered a seemingly unbroken string of natural and human-induced disasters—fires, flooding, earthquakes, and civil rebellion. During this period of almost unprecedented fiscal needs, the state's economy continued to fail, thus creating a state government revenue shortfall. Wilson's early rhetoric about the need for "preventative policy" was buried under an avalanche of fiscal woes. His attempts to balance the annual budgets by cutting expenditures for health, welfare, and education created annual impasses with legislative Democrats opposed to reductions in these areas. The public was treated to a series of budget deadlocks, often extending weeks beyond the state constitution's July 1 deadline. The final products, officially "balanced" based on unrealistic projections of federal revenues, raids on special funds and local property taxes, short- and long-term loans, and various accounting tricks, did not please Republicans, Democrats, or the public.

Election year 1992 was a great one for California Democrats. Bill Clinton easily carried the state, becoming the first Democrat since 1964 to garner California's electoral college votes. Both Democratic U.S. senatorial candidates, Dianne Feinstein and Barbara Boxer, were triumphant. (Democrats had not controlled both seats since the 1976 election.) Moreover, Democrats maintained seemingly solid majorities in both houses of the state legislature, despite the fact that the new district lines, first in effect in 1992, were thought to favor the Republican Party. No wonder, then, that as Governor Wilson approached the end of his first term, many pundits concluded he had virtually no chance to be reelected. Californians' confidence in their state government, including the governor, was at a low ebb. The state was still mired in economic depression, and Governor Wilson had few friends, either Republican or Democrat, in Sacramento.

Polling results in late 1993 and early 1994 gave his most likely opponent, Treasurer Kathleen Brown, a double-digit lead. Brown, the daughter of Governor Pat and sister of Governor Jerry, seemed poised to continue the family dynasty. Her election hopes were further buoyed by the 1992 success of the two women candidates for the U.S. Senate. But what followed instead was a masterful Wilson campaign that emphasized two hot-button issues, illegal immigration and crime. Two ballot issues, one mandating the elimination of educational and social services to illegal immigrants and the other imposing enhanced or lifetime prison sentences for repeat felony offenders, helped to keep the election focused on Wilson's issues. As the campaign wore on, Wilson passed his challenger in the polls, and she could not regain her early momentum. Pete Wilson, whose political career most experts had prematurely written off, easily captured a second term in the governor's office.

Overall, the 1994 election reversed the partisan tides of 1992. In addition to maintaining their hold on the governorship, Republicans captured three other statewide positions previously held by Democrats. Democrats could take only slight solace from the facts that Gray Davis successfully exchanged his position as state controller for that of lieutenant governor, thus continuing his slow succession toward the governorship, and Democrat Dianne Feinstein successfully, but only by a razor-thin margin, held off the challenge to her U.S. Senate seat mounted by U.S. Representative Michael Huffington.

Even these substantial statewide Republican gains were overshadowed by the completely unexpected loss of the Democrats' majority in the state assembly. When all the votes were counted, Republicans emerged with a 41–39 margin in the lower house, their first assembly majority in 25 years. As discussed in Chapter 3, the new Republican majority was thwarted in its attempts to immediately seize the speakership and organizational control of the assembly. And Democrats maintained a narrow majority in the state senate. But, clearly, in 1994, state Republicans successfully rode the national Republican tidal wave that gave them control over both houses of the U.S. Congress for the first time in 40 years.

The political landscape of 1995 was much different from that of the preceding year. State Republicans, ascendant in both the legislative and the executive branches, looked to gain the initiative in policy-making denied them during the decades-long Democratic domination of the legislature. Governor Wilson, having achieved a reelection triumph thought impossible a year earlier, seemed well positioned to lead the Republican revolution in California. The 1994 elections registered broad public support for the governor's positions on crime and illegal immigration. It seemed quite possible that, for the first time since 1958, the Republican Party was poised to become the state's majority party, enjoying regular control over both the executive and the legislative branches, as it had over the first half of the twentieth century. Over the next four years, however, the Republican tide would be stopped and then reversed. By 1998, California Republicans' high hopes would be replaced by pessimism and despair.

A broken promise started the Republican decline. During his reelection campaign, Wilson promised that, if reelected, he would not seek the Republican presidential nomination. But during the summer of 1995, rumors and predictions about his imminent entry into the race began to percolate. Late that summer Governor Wilson made official what was already assumed: He would seek the Republican presidential nomination.

At its beginning, the governor's presidential bid seemed realistic enough. He had proved himself a tough, effective, and well-focused candidate in four statewide elections. He was generally considered a pro-choice moderate in a Republican field dominated by conservative, generally pro-life candidates, but he could appeal to his party's conservative primary voters with his strong stands against illegal immigration and affirmative action. But nothing went right in his ill-fated campaign. Throat surgery delayed the campaign's beginning and limited his public speaking engagements. His immigration issue failed to generate much excitement outside of California. Out of money to finance his campaign and trailing far behind in the polls even in his home state, Governor Wilson canceled his campaign even before the start of the official election year.

In 1996, President Clinton carried California as easily as in 1992, despite national Republican claims that they would make the state a key battleground. More surprising, Democrats recaptured control of the state assembly, moving up from 39 to 43 seats. Republican control of the lower house had been short-lived indeed. Still, Republicans could look forward to 1998, a nonpresidential election in which, traditionally, turnout is lower and the Republican party usually does better.

In the meantime, the stalemate between Governor Wilson and the legislature continued. In the 1996 elections, Wilson strongly backed Proposition 209, a measure that banned the use of racial or gender preferences in public hiring, public contracting, and public higher education admissions. The measure won easily, but the division between the governor, who came to office with the label of "moderate," and Democrats in the legislature deepened. Wilson's long-standing feud with organized labor reached new heights when he backed an unsuccessful ballot initiative that required permission of individual union members before any of their dues money could be used by their union for political purposes.

Even good economic news did not ease the increasing tensions between the governor and the legislature. The governor insisted that the surplus available for the 1998–1999 budget be dedicated to tax cuts and, in particular, to reductions in the state's automobile registration fees. Legislative Democrats were already incensed by Wilson's support of the 1996 anti-affirmative action initiative (Proposition 209) and the anti-union political activity initiative (Proposition 226). Now, with extra budget money finally available, they bridled under the governor's insistence that the additional funds be devoted to tax cuts rather than to the expansion of social programs.

Entrance and Departure of Gray Davis

By 1998, Wilson was termed-out as governor, but Republicans had his replacement in line: Dan Lungren, who after shaking off the legislature's refusal to confirm him as state treasurer, had been elected and then reelected as attorney general. Republican clarity on their choice contrasted with confusion on the Democratic side. Everyone agreed that U.S. Senator Dianne Feinstein was their strongest potential candidate, but she ultimately declined to enter the race. When Feinstein finally decided not to make the run, many pundits were ready to concede Dan Lungren the governorship. As attorney general, Lungren held the position that historically offered the best stepping stone to the governorship. He was also considered a tough debater and an effective television campaigner.

Gray Davis, the Lieutenant Governor, won the Democratic nomination by defeating a wealthy businessman and a congresswoman. While his opponents had plenty of campaign money, they lacked statewide recognition. But his primary election victory, based on his long track record in California politics, did not, at the beginning, seem to offer much hope that Democrats could end 16 years of Republican control of the governorship.

Republicans also had every reason to believe that they were on the verge of recapturing one of the state's U.S. Senate seats, as Barbara Boxer, a winner in the 1992 Democratic landslide year, was considered vulnerable. On the primary election night, Davis emerged as a surprisingly easy winner in the three-way Democratic contest, while Lungren cruised to victory in a Republican field without serious challengers. Matt Fong, elected to the treasurer's position in the 1994 Republican landslide, won the Republican nod to square off against Barbara Boxer.

What was supposed to be a Republican election year in California turned out to be a Republican disaster. Davis's early lead over Lungren in the polls did not, as was the case with Kathleen Brown in 1994, diminish. Instead, as the campaign moved forward, that early lead reached double digits and, on election night, turned into a landslide victory of nearly 20 percent. Barbara Boxer won by half that margin, still a comfortable 10 percent edge. Democratic majorities in the legislature also increased. When the dust settled, the assembly stood at 48 Democrats to just 32 Republicans, with a 25-to-15 Democratic majority in the senate. The Democrats also reclaimed two other statewide positions from the Republicans and held onto the positions they already owned. At century's end, just two Republicans held statewide office: Charles Quackenbush as insurance commissioner and Bill Jones as secretary of state. And in June 2000, Quackenbush was forced to resign his position under the cloud of scandal.

The 2000 and 2002 elections continued more bad news for state Republicans. In 2000, Californians supported Al Gore as strongly as they had Bill Clinton; Dianne Feinstein was a landslide winner in her U.S. Senate reelection bid; and strong Democratic margins in the legislature became even more lopsided. The state legislature began the twenty-first century with Democrats enjoying lopsided majorities in both houses. Republican ranks in the state's delegation to the U.S. House of Representatives shrank from 24 to 20. In 2002, Republicans did pick up two additional seats in the assembly and one in the senate. But Democrats reclaimed ownership of the secretary of state post and swept the remaining state executive positions, leaving the Republicans, prior to the 2003 recall election, without a single statewide elected official.

Davis's gubernatorial career was outlined in the preceding chapter. Suffice it to repeat that his cautious, bland style stood him well when things were going well. But when troubles mounted, especially the energy crisis and state budget collapse, his support levels fell through the floor. California voters, seemingly content just two years earlier, were, by 2003, hopping mad, and itching for change. Never personally popular with most voters, Gray Davis and his long and varied political career fell victim to the sense of change and excitement swirling around a brand new face.

The Arnold Era: Republican Comeback, or the Politics of Personality?

Arnold Schwarzenegger's smashing 2003 recall victory fostered new conjecture about California's future partisan balance. Did his victory mark the end of the Republican Party's decline and the beginning of its electoral resurgence? Or was the Republican capture of the state's highest office a fluke, one-time event explainable by the special dynamics of a recall election and the star appeal of the candidate? Will Schwarzenegger's blend of fiscal conservatism, social policy moderation, and bipartisan rhetoric become the new Republican party themes, perhaps echoing and duplicating Republican successes in the Earl Warren era? Or will long-term Republican hopes prove as illusory and short-lived as those following the 1994 election?

Predicting what will happen next in California politics is a very risky proposition. But results of the 2004 and 2006 election tended to dampen Republican hopes that their state party would soon enjoy a big political comeback. Besides George W. Bush's weak showing here, Republican U.S. Senate candidate Bill Jones was thoroughly trounced by incumbent Barbara Boxer, a Democratic officeholder Republicans had long considered vulnerable. In addition, big Democratic majorities in the state assembly, state senate, and in California's House of Representatives delegation were returned completely intact.

In 2006, Schwarzenegger was an overwhelming election winner; yet most other state Republicans had a tough election night. When all the votes were counted, Democrats had increased their majority of the state's House of Representatives delegation by one, held Diane Feinstein's U.S. Senate seat by a margin of victory even bigger than Schwarzenegger's, and captured all but one of the statewide offices below that of governor. Democrats also maintained their lopsided majorities in the state assembly and senate. At this point, Republican Schwarzenegger's popularity and electoral attractiveness do not seem to have spread beyond the man himself. (The past, present, and future strengths of California parties is more thoroughly analyzed in Chapter 8.)

SUMMARY

California's modern political history, compared to the preceding thousands of years of Native American habitation, covers a relatively short span of time. But over the last 160 years or so, the state's political contours have been shaped and reshaped by events, movements, and individuals. The discovery of gold and subsequent gold rush very quickly ushered in an era of Anglo political domination that only now may be receding.

The "Big Four" railroad dominion of the late nineteenth century ultimately gave way to the progressive movement, led by Hiram Johnson, fostering institutional changes and a political outlook that continue to flavor the state's politics almost 100 years later. The first half of the twentieth century witnessed almost unbroken Republican control of state political power, in its later stages under the "bipartisan" banner of Republican politicians such as Earl Warren. The second half of that century, until the 1990s, witnessed strong two-party competition, often marked by Republican control of the governor's office along with Democratic legislative majorities. The last decade of that century saw a decline in Republican electoral fortunes and Democratic domination in Sacramento and over the state's presidential voting. The intriguing question now is whether the "age of Arnold" has ushered in yet a new era of California politics.

REFERENCES

Gould, Lewis L., ed. *The Progressive Era.* Syracuse, NY: Syracuse University Press, 1974.

Howard, Robert W. *The Great Iron Trail: The Story of the Transcontinental Railroad.* New York: G. P. Putnam's Sons, 1962.

Lewis, Oscar. *The Big Four.* New York: Alfred A. Knopf, 1938.

Lower, Richard. *A Bloc of One.* Stanford, CA: Stanford University Press, 1993.

Mason, Paul. "Constitutional History of California." *Constitution of the State of California (1879) and Related Documents.* Sacramento: California State Senate, 1973, pp. 75–105.

McAfee, Ward. *California's Railroad Era: 1850–1911.* San Marino, CA: Golden West Books, 1973.

Mitchell, Greg. *Election of the Century.* New York: Random House, 1992.

Mowry, George E. *The California Progressives.* Berkeley: University of California Press, 1951.

Olin, Spencer C., Jr. *California's Prodigal Sons: Hiram Johnson and the Progressives* Berkeley: University of California Press, 1968.

Robinson, William W. *Land in California.* Berkeley: University of California Press, 1948.

Swisher, Carl B. *Motivation and Political Technique in the California Constitutional Convention: 1878–79.* New York: Da Capo, 1969.

Warren, Earl E. *The Memoirs of Earl Warren.* Garden City, NY: Doubleday, 1977.

CHAPTER three

THE CALIFORNIA LEGISLATURE

Long time capitol observers with very good memories fondly remember the 1960s and 1970s, when the California legislature was rated the best in the land. Having embarked on a program of professionalization in 1967—with full-time sessions and full-time legislators, generous legislative salaries and perks, and ample expert staff—California's legislature was rated as the nation's "most professional" by the early 1970s. It was also a period of energetic public-sector expansion and policy innovation. During this time, the state created the most extensive freeway network in the nation and the most prestigious system of public higher education; it also undertook a massive engineering program to provide water reservoirs, pumping stations, and canals to move that precious liquid from where it fell as rain or snow to where it was demanded by the state's burgeoning population. In addition, California established itself as a leader in environmental and civil rights policy during this period. California, which had become the most populous state in the union in 1962, was clearly on the move, and California's professional legislature seemed to be at the center of the action.

By 1990, all the luster had worn off the California Senate and California Assembly. Voters' disenchantment was punctuated in 1990 by the narrow victory of Proposition 140, an initiative establishing term limits for the state's elected officials and substantially cutting the legislature's own operating budget. Professional politicians, and especially the professional legislature, were now seen as part of the problem rather than a positive source of solutions. Since 1990, public approval of the legislature's performance has never reached the 50% mark, and only infrequently has risen to 40% (Field Research Corp., 2007).

What were, and are, the main criticisms leveled against the state's professional legislature? Should California return to an "amateur legislature," or would that only make things worse? What other changes might improve legislative performance that Californians should be considering? We return to these questions after describing the state's legislative structure and process.

LEGISLATIVE DISTRICTS

California state government has functioned with a bicameral or two-house legislature throughout its statehood. The 80 members of the state assembly (lower house) are elected to two-year terms. The 40 members of the state senate (upper house) serve four-year terms, with half of the senate districts conducting elections every two years. It should be noted here that California, the state with by far the largest population, has a relatively small legislature. For example, tiny New Hampshire elects more than 300 members to its lower house, compared with the mere 80 elected to the California Assembly. As a result of the discrepancy between California's huge population and its small legislature, districts are by far the biggest in the nation. A state senator represents approximately 900,000 residents, more than reside in congressional districts, and the average size of an assembly district is about 450,000. (See Box 3.1 for a fuller discussion of the small legislature–large district issue.)

After the U.S. Census Bureau completes its work each decade, the California legislature redraws the district lines of the state assembly and state senate (as well as congressional districts). Until the 1960s, California's legislative district lines adhered to the "little federal plan," meaning that its lower house districts were based on population but its upper house districts reflected county lines and not population. The intent was to mimic the U.S. Congress, where the Senate representation is equally apportioned among all the states regardless of their populations. This system was discarded following a 1964 U.S. Supreme Court ruling that state legislative districts must contain equal populations. Since that time, both state legislative houses' representational base is population, with upper house districts containing twice the population of the lower house districts.

The legislative majority party has the power to draw district lines in such a way as to maximize its own strength and minimize that of the minority party, a process known as gerrymandering. It involves "packing" as many of the minority party voters into as few districts as possible. Even though this process does produce a few safe seats for the minority party, the remainder of the districts now favor the majority party because so many of the other side's voters were used up in creating the few safe districts. In this way, the majority party enhances its prospects for maintaining its majority in the legislature and in the California congressional delegation over the next ten years. The drawing of district lines, then, involves politics at the highest stakes.

When the governor is of a different party than the legislative majority, that majority's power to gerrymander is severely constrained because the remapping plans, like other legislation, require the governor's signature. The remapping that took place in the 1970s and 1990s followed this scenario: Democratic legislative majorities were checked by Republican governors (Ronald Reagan in the 1970s, Pete Wilson in the 1990s). In both instances, the stalemate was broken only when lines were drawn under the direction of the judicial branch.

BOX
3.1
Political Math: Small Legislature + Huge State = Super-Sized Districts

With a population approaching 40 million, California is far and away the biggest state in the nation. Yet its legislature, with just 40 senate and 80 assembly seats, is comparatively small; only 16 other state legislatures are smaller than the Golden State's. What that means is that our legislative districts contain many more residents than is true for the other 49 states. At the other end of the spectrum, New Hampshire's lower house contains 400 members, whose district sizes average about 3,000 residents.

There are some real drawbacks to such large districts, including the fact that there is little chance that most voters will have any personal knowledge of "their" representatives in Sacramento. Minority factions might have a harder time getting their needs and ideas heard if they are lost in the midst of a huge districts. Campaign costs, driven by the number of voters that need to be reached, rise with the size of a district, meaning that interest groups who donate the necessary campaign funds to candidates may gain even more power.

As appealing as smaller districts might appear, however, there is no chance that giant California could ever shrink to the size of its districts to those of New Hampshire. To replicate the size of New Hampshire lower house districts, we would need an assembly with about 13,000 members, meeting either in a football stadium or electronically through interactive technology. Even doubling the size of the legislature would still leave California with much larger than average legislative districts.

So can anything be done? One modest approach would be to allow the legislature to grow along with the state's population, increasing it by the percentage population growth every ten years. This would prevent the continued spiraling of district sizes. More radically, the assembly could be increased several fold, perhaps to 500, the approximate size of legislative bodies such as the U.S. House of Representatives or the British House of Commons.

Under this plan, the senate could be kept at or near its current size, leaving one very large, and one very small legislative chamber. The lower house would represent smaller, more localized viewpoints (with a district size of 70,000–80,000 based on current population), while the senate would represent broader, more regional and diverse perspectives.

The 1980s were a far different story. Democrats controlled both the legislature and the governor's office and produced maps with a decidedly Democratic tilt. Republicans fought back with all the tools at their command, including a referendum setting aside the first set of Democrat-drawn maps and an initiative to replace the district lines with new ones drawn up by Republicans. In the end, however, these strategies failed, and Democrats ruled the remapping process. Republicans spent the rest of the decade rowing upstream against the districting plan imposed by the Democrats. It was this experience that energized them to recruit U.S. Senator Pete Wilson to run for governor in 1990 so as to prevent another redistricting disaster.

As the 2000 census approached, Republicans faced the nightmare of 1980 all over again. The legislature was still controlled by Democrats, and the governor was Democrat

Gray Davis rather than Republican Pete Wilson. But as things turned out, the 1980s Democratic gerrymander was not repeated this time around. Instead, the new maps generally maintained the status quo by protecting practically all incumbents, both Republicans and Democrats, rather than more radically reconfiguring the districts in order to threaten Republican-held seats. One reason was that the number of Republicans in the legislature was already so small, just 16 in the senate and 30 in the assembly, leaving relatively few "targets of opportunity" for the Democrats. Second, the fastest-growing areas, hence those requiring more legislative seats, are not in regions where Democrats have an easy time winning. Redistricting will again be a background issue for the 2010 gubernatorial election, when Arnold Schwarzenegger will be termed out. Assuming that Democrats still control the legislature, Republicans will be especially concerned with holding onto the governorship and preventing a new round of redistricting controlled by the Democrats.

Given the high political and partisan stakes in this process, many reformers continue to argue that allowing politicians to draw lines that vitally impact their own careers creates a hopeless conflict of interest and that redistricting should take place in a nonpartisan arena, under the direction of judges, or a nonpartisan or bipartisan commission. Such an idea has been presented to voters on a number of occasions, including as part of Governor Schwarzenegger's four part reform plan rejected by the voters in a 2005 special election. It is an issue that few voters really grasp, and the majority party in the legislature has successfully played to this confusion by spending large sums of money on ads against initiative attempts to change the redistricting process.

But even if an "impartial" group could be created, the definition of what is a "fair" set of district maps is not as clear-cut as it might appear. In truth, many of the criteria for a "good set of maps" are, in fact, contradictory. Some of those criteria are mandated by the federal government, starting with the basic federal constitutional principle that all districts must contain equal populations at the time of their creation. Beyond this mandate, the federal government, through the federal Voting Rights Act, requires that district lines be drawn so as not to dilute ethnic and racial minority voting power. The California Constitution requires that all districts be contiguous. In addition, "good government" reformers argue that district boundaries should be compact, should not divide local jurisdictions (such as cities and counties) between different districts, and should not divide geographic/economic areas or other "communities of interest." But others would argue that, in the name of political competition, more emphasis should be placed on creating districts in which either party has a chance to win rather than districts that are "safe Democratic" or "safe Republican."

The problem is that when we examine all these criteria, it is clear that even a "neutral" board or commission's mapping plan would not satisfy everyone because the criteria conflict. For example, in order to include a "community of interest" in a single district, it may be necessary to ignore city and county lines and to draw districts whose shapes are not "compact." Nor are districts drawn in such a way as to maximize compactness, communities of interest, or minority voting power likely to serve the goal of political competitiveness, since such districts will likely be dominated by Republican or Democratic sympathies. Clearly, even the most nonpartisan approach to redistricting involves "politics" because the process requires choices between competing goals and values.

BOX
3.2

Redistricting and "Safe Districts"

When the legislature got down to the business of redrawing district lines in 2001, the stakes of the game went far beyond the usual distribution of seats between Democrats and Republicans. With the partisan division in the U.S. House of Representatives so close and with California having 53 congressional districts to divide up, the two national parties and their congressional caucuses were attentive audiences. But to national Democrats' dismay and Republicans' relief, what emerged instead was a status quo set of congressional districts that seemed to leave the existing division of seats pretty much intact. This was accomplished by adding Democratic voters to those districts already represented by Democrats, and Republican voters to those districts already electing Republicans. In another words, districts were made "safe" for incumbents of both parties. This tactic not only protects those already in office; it also assures that most districts will remain under the same party control even after the current U.S. representatives, state senators, and state assembly members have left their office.

The "success" of this strategy has been borne out over the last several legislative elections since the new lines went into effect in 2002. The numerical party balance between the 53 U.S. representative seats, 40 state senate seats, and 80 assembly district seats has remained almost exactly the same as it was in 2002.

Is this a good thing? Most reformers would argue it is not. First, our notions of democracy generally include the possibility of competitive elections, but safe legislative seats are built to be noncompetitive. Second, in safe districts, the winner of the dominant party's nomination is just about assured that he or she will easily win the general election, and hence the office. Such officeholders need not attempt to appeal to independents nor the other party's concerns and issues. Instead, they are free to take hard-line, no-compromise Republican or Democratic positions rather than seek out compromise policy solutions. The end result is legislative bodies that are mired in ideological and partisan stalemate, and are thus unable to formulate broad policy capable of generating general consensus approval.

LEGISLATIVE FUNCTIONS

Legislators fulfill several responsibilities besides enacting laws. Deliberating on the several thousand bills introduced in each two-year session is work enough, but assembly and senate members must attend to other business as well. These additional duties are not altogether separate from making laws because ideas obtained in the course of non-legislative work can often be incorporated into legislation. Reviewing the various responsibilities of legislators provides a fuller picture of their activities and clarifies why lawmakers are not able to devote more time to considering legislative proposals.

Lawmaking

Each member of the assembly and of the senate may introduce bills, resolutions, and constitutional amendments. By introducing a measure, a legislator becomes known as its "author." Unfortunately, this terminology gives quite a misleading impression of the actual work done by elected members. Legislators themselves seldom undertake serious writing. What they do, in fact, is discuss with their staffs the desirability of introducing legislation on certain topics. After consultation with legislators' offices, the Office of Legislative Counsel—literally the legislature's own law firm—completes the detailed drafting of legislative measures. Legislators themselves are far from the only source of ideas for new legislation. Numerous lobbyists, state executives, private citizens, and legislative staffers contact legislators with ideas for new laws. Although putting a legislator's name on a bill allows it to be introduced as a piece of legislative business, a member's signature does not indicate how much (if at all) he or she will actually work for the measure's passage. Legislators sometimes introduce a measure as a courtesy, though they have no intention of expending effort on its behalf. In short, "authoring" really means "introducing."

Some legislators agree to introduce scores of bills during a two-year session, whereas other members may "author" only ten or so. The volume of measures introduced by a member is not a valid indicator of legislative productivity for several reasons. First, bills differ greatly in terms of the degree of difficulty associated with their passage. A comprehensive, path-breaking piece of legislation entails far more work than several technical bills to correct minor flaws in existing statutes. Second, if the objective is to record a high number of introductions, it is a simple matter for a legislator's office to send numerous bill requests to the Office of Legislative Counsel. This office dutifully drafts whatever members' request, so high introduction levels do not necessarily reflect a great deal of effort on the part of a member. Third, the real test of an effective lawmaker is whether he or she is capable of "working" or "carrying" a measure through all phases of the legislative process, not whether he or she authored a large number of bills. Some legislators inflate their bill introduction totals to appear competent to casual observers of state politics. However, serious students of the California legislature, such as lobbyists and members of the press corps, know which officeholders are capable of pushing major legislation through and which are not.

Once the decision to introduce a proposal has been made by a legislator, the proper vehicle must be selected. If changes in the state's body of statutory law (known as the California Code) are desired, assembly bills (ABs) or senate bills (SBs) may be introduced. Constitutional amendments originating in the legislature, not to be confused with initiative constitutional amendments, may be introduced in the assembly (ACAs) or in the senate (SCAs). Resolutions may be introduced in either chamber to make the views of the California legislature known to the U.S. government, to establish rules and committees within the state legislature, and to express the sentiments of legislators (as in condolences and congratulations).

Budget Passage

The annual budget is taken up as a bill and could have been discussed in the foregoing section on lawmaking. However, passage of the budget is such an important and distinctive legislative responsibility that it deserves separate treatment. The budget is a massive document written in the executive branch. The governor transmits a revenue and spending plan to the legislature each year on or before January 10. The governor's proposed budget must be "balanced," at least on paper.

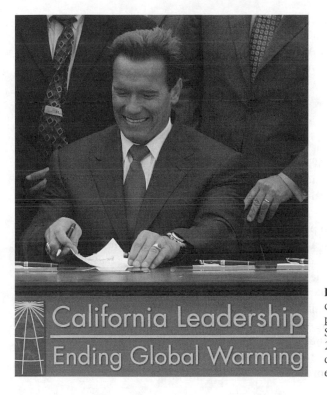

PHOTO 3.1 "Successful conclusion of the legislative process: Governor Schwarzenegger signs sweeping 2006 legislation aimed at curtailing global warming emissions." *(Associated Press)*

Like the extraordinary majorities needed for constitutional amendments, for urgency measures, and for overrides of gubernatorial vetoes, passage of the state budget and other appropriations bills requires a two-thirds vote in both chambers of the state legislature. The budget must, theoretically, be sent back to the governor by June 15, so the legislature has slightly more than five months to review billions of dollars of state expenditures. However, this June 15 deadline is frequently missed. (For an expanded discussion of budgetary process and politics, see Chapter 10.)

Confirmations

Members of the California Senate have the responsibility of approving or rejecting, by simple majority vote, hundreds of gubernatorial appointments. Persons named to head the cabinet agencies, as well as the department directors beneath them, must be confirmed by the senate. In addition, gubernatorial appointments to such bodies as the University of California Regents, Public Utilities Commission, the Water Resources Control Board, the Air Resources Board, and the Agricultural Labor Relations Board are subject to senatorial confirmation. First, the five-member Senate Rules Committee studies the nominee's background, hears testimony on the fitness of the nominee, and recommends approval or disapproval to the full membership of the upper house. Second, at least 21 votes on the senate floor are needed to confirm an appointment.

Important exceptions do not require senate confirmation. For instance, the governor's personal staff (i.e., chief of staff, press secretary, legislative liaison, appointments secretary, scheduling personnel, and legal affairs secretary) need not be confirmed by the senate. Likewise, the California Senate does not approve or block judicial appointments by the governor. Appellate court appointments are confirmed by the Commission on Judicial Appointments, and trial court nominations are reviewed only by the electorate.

Constituent Relations

Legislators and their staffers allot a substantial portion of their time to cultivating positive impressions among voters. When a district resident notifies his or her legislator of a problem with the state bureaucracy, the member's office endeavors to resolve the dilemma by contacting the relevant executive agency and then communicating with the citizen. This process is known as constituent casework. Beyond providing this service, legislators go to great lengths to project a competent image in their districts. They conduct polls of their constituents' attitudes, respond to letters requesting their positions on pending legislation, and write congratulatory notes to district residents who won awards or celebrated anniversaries. They prepare press releases (perhaps on bills they introduced) and write letters to editors of local newspapers in hopes of obtaining free media coverage. Legislators usually spend Fridays and weekends in their districts meeting with specific groups, holding town hall meetings open to the public, and receiving constituents in their district offices. These activities, a part of legislators' representative functions, can compensate for any unpopular votes members may have cast in Sacramento, and hence also improve their reelection prospects.

Oversight

Members of the legislature oversee or monitor the manner in which the executive branch carries out statutes passed during earlier sessions. If the legislative intent behind a certain program is not being met due to faulty implementation, lawmakers can investigate the situation and urge corrective action. If simple publicity is insufficient to bring about the desired change in the executive branch, more drastic steps may be taken. The legislature may delete from the budget the salaries of recalcitrant department directors. Budget control language requiring that specified actions be taken may be attached to an agency's appropriation.

The constitution grants the assembly the power to vote articles of impeachment on statewide executives as well as on members of the state judiciary. Impeached officials are tried in the state senate, where a two-thirds vote is needed for conviction and removal. Legislative hearings on alleged statewide executive malfeasance in office can also lead to those executives resigning prior to the commencement of formal impeachment hearings. This was the case in 2000 with then Insurance Commissioner Charles Quackenbush. The same scenario led to the resignation of Secretary of State Kevin Shelley in 2005.

Generally, however, careful monitoring of the executive wing can consume a great deal of legislative time, and it is not always clear that such an effort would yield a legislator political credit commensurate with the effort involved. In short, greater political incentives are present to concentrate on bill introduction and constituent service rather than careful oversight of executive wing activity.

THE LEGISLATIVE PROCESS

After a measure is introduced by its author in either the assembly or the senate, it is numbered and referred to a policy committee. For example, a bill proposing that fuel-efficient cars be allowed to use the "diamond lanes" on the state's freeways was referred to the Transportation Committee; a bill calling for the abolition of sex education in public schools would be sent to the Education Committee. To allow members of the public and the press to become informed about a specific proposal, no committee action may take place until a bill has been in print for 30 days. Committee hearings permit interested individuals, lobbyists for organizations in the private sector, and legislative liaisons from state executive departments and local governments to give their views concerning a particular bill. The members of the committee may recommend approval of a bill and send it to the chamber floor without alteration, recommend modifications to a bill and recommend approval on the floor as amended, or allow a bill to die in committee. The great majority of items that fail to be enacted into law are killed in committee.

Not all bills that pass their initial policy committee go directly to the floor, however. Any bill that would result in more than a trivial money expenditure by the state or by local governments must also, after policy committee passage in the senate or assembly, be referred to that house's Appropriations Committee. In addition, bills dealing with subject matters that fall under the jurisdiction of two policy committees may be assigned to both those committees before they can be sent to the floor or to the Appropriations Committee.

A measure sent to the floor is debated by the membership of the chamber. Amendments to a bill may be made by the legislators prior to the vote on the issue. Approval of legislative business ordinarily requires a simple majority of the full membership of each chamber (41 in the assembly and 21 in the senate). However, legislative amendments to the state constitution, appropriations bills and the annual budget, urgency measures to take effect immediately upon passage, and votes to override a gubernatorial veto all require a two-thirds majority (54 in the assembly and 27 in the senate).

Given the bicameral structure of the legislature, bills must pass both chambers in identical form before being sent to the governor for signature or veto. As soon as a bill passes one chamber, it is immediately sent to the other house for its committee review and floor action. Because bills may be amended both in committee and on the floor, a bill passing the second chamber is likely to contain different language than the bill that passed the chamber of origin. To resolve differences in wording, the originating chamber may simply concur in the changes made by the other house, in which case both chambers pass identical bills. Failing concurrence, a conference committee consisting of three senators and three members of the assembly is established to recommend common wording for the bill. The report of the conference committee is sent to the floor of each chamber, where it must be accepted in its entirety to be adopted. If either chamber refuses to accept the conference committee report, a new conference committee is selected and another report with compromise language is prepared. Three conference committees—meeting one at a time, not simultaneously—may be attempted on a single bill. If the report of the third conference committee is not accepted by both chambers, the bill dies.

The preceding account of the legislative process suggests an orderliness that often is not evident in actuality. Political compromises may not have been achieved prior to the measure's introduction. To reserve a number and to have a bill begin meeting the deadlines contained in the legislative calendar, members sometimes introduce legislation that they know is not likely to be passed as initially drafted. In fact, the bill amendment process is the primary policy-making device. Amendments are made to improve the technical quality of bills. Most important, this process is also a way to "soften" bills and remove partisan or interest group opposition. Typically, bills as introduced are stronger in their policy implications than are bills that survive the process and are sent to the governor. In the California legislature, most amendments are the work of the bill's author, though bills can be amended by committees or on the floor. Legislative amendments are at the heart of the legislative process, where the original goals of a bill's author and sponsors face compromise with the political and partisan realities that spell ultimate success or failure for any piece of legislation.

Also, the legislative process in reality does not always follow the tidy "how a bill becomes a law" scenario described in most civics books. Whereas a noncontroversial item might follow the formal steps in the legislative process to the letter, ideas that generate considerable debate may be negotiated behind closed doors, outside the public scrutiny of a committee hearing or a floor session. In legislative parlance, this informal approach is known as negotiating a moving target. After an agreement is struck in private, the resulting compromise is amended into a measure that emerges at an advanced stage in the legislative process.

This method of cutting deals in private and then manipulating the formal legislative process to enact the informal agreement presents several drawbacks. If the contents of a bill are completely replaced during floor consideration or if a bill containing a deal is rushed through three committees in one day, committee review essentially is circumvented. Given the staff analysis prepared on all bills heard in committee and given the opportunity for public input at committee hearings, bypassing committees should not be taken lightly. Private negotiating sessions do not involve coverage by the press corps and may not involve all persons with an interest in an issue. On the other hand, defenders of informal negotiations contend that following formal legislative procedures closely may produce weak legislation or none at all. If every lobbyist has the chance in committee to water a bill down with amendments, the resulting legislation may be little improvement over existing law. Likewise, why follow the formal legislative process carefully only to have the governor veto the enactment? If representatives of the governor have not been active on a given bill during committee review, it may be necessary to meet privately with individuals in the executive branch to find out what the chief executive must have in the measure to guarantee she or he will sign it. No doubt informal negotiations have produced accomplishments, but at what price? When a major legislative package is hastily adopted in the waning hours of a session—the energy deregulation bill of 1996 being one example—a close reading of such a compromise after the legislature adjourns may reveal surprises for legislators and lobbyists not invited to the private negotiations.

POWERS OF LEADERSHIP

Given the thousands of bills, two annual budgets, and assorted confirmations to be dealt with in a typical two-year session, decisions must be made concerning which members will have primary responsibility for what measures and how business will be routed through the legislative labyrinth. Organizational decisions by those in power in the assembly and in the senate can greatly influence the outcome of legislation. In discussing legislative leadership, it is important to distinguish between positions with real power and those offices that are more ceremonial than influential. Traditionally, real power in the assembly was wielded by a single individual, the assembly speaker, while in the senate that power had been exercised in a more collegial manner by the Rules Committee. Changes in both houses, however, have recently blurred, and in certain ways reversed, that distinction between leadership and power styles in the two chambers.

Assembly Speaker

Beginning in the early 1960s, assembly speakers enjoyed such extraordinary powers, impinging on every point in the legislative process, that they were routinely referred to as the second most powerful California politician and the most powerful state legislator in the land. However, term limits probably preclude the kind of omnipresent power that characterized assembly speakerships from the 1960s through the middle 1990s. Traditionally, the speaker's arsenal of parliamentary powers includes the following:

- The speaker determines the number and the titles of standing committees, special committees, and subcommittees.
- The speaker establishes the schedule for committee meetings.
- The speaker appoints members of the assembly to (and removes them from) standing committees, special committees, and subcommittees, excluding the Assembly Rules Committee.
- The speaker appoints (and removes) chairs and vice chairs of all assembly committees, including the Assembly Rules Committee.
- The speaker provides guidelines to the Assembly Rules Committee regarding the referral of bills to particular committees.
- The speaker is an ex officio nonvoting member of all assembly committees.
- The speaker is presiding officer of the assembly and, as such, recognizes members during debate, renders opinions on points of order, names members to temporarily perform the duties of speaker, and clears the gallery when necessary.
- The speaker assigns members their office space in the capitol.
- The speaker appoints the majority floor leader, who expedites floor proceedings by making appropriate motions and points of order.
- The speaker appoints three members of the assembly to serve on conference committees after the senate has rejected assembly language on certain bills.

This combination of leadership powers may be deployed to promote or to hinder the passage of bills as well as to help or to hurt the careers of individual members. Mindful of the vast powers available to the presiding officer, members of the lower house, especially those in the Speaker's party, ordinarily cooperate with the speaker. Should members of the assembly defy the speaker, they run the risk of losing their committee assignments, their office space, and their staff—not to mention their pending bills. Only on rare occasions did Speaker Willie Brown find it necessary to utilize his punitive powers against legislators who challenged his authority. But when he did he the impact was twofold: the immediate threat was quashed and future potential challengers were effectively deterred from risking the Speaker's ire.

As crucial as these formal roles are, they do not encompass the sum total of the speaker's powers. In fact, these formal powers may be most crucial because they provide access to an even more potent source of clout: the ability to attract huge sums of electoral campaign money. Because of the centrality of the speakership to the legislative process, that office is a magnet for interest group campaign donations. Recent changes in the law limit the amount of money that one politician can "transfer" to another. But legislative leaders can certainly "steer" potential donors to partisan incumbent colleagues facing a tough electoral challenge or, in the case of an open seat, to their favored candidate for use in the primary and then the general election. Within the majority caucus, then, the speaker should be able to count on the support of partisan colleagues who may owe their own legislative careers to him or her or who may desperately need help in the future. Formal legislative power thus merges with and reinforces campaign funding power in a way that enhances the job security of both the speaker and the members of the majority caucus.

But the power wielded by contemporary speakers pales next to the examples of Jesse Unruh, Bob Moretti, Leo McCarthy, and Willie Brown. Term limits mean that no one today can hold the job long enough to establish that sort of power. Unless a first-term member is selected, an incoming speaker's tenure is, at most, four years, the last two as a lame-duck speaker. In 2004, Democrats entered new territory by selecting a first-term member, Fabian Nuñez, as the speaker. But how much power can a first termer, with less than two years of total legislative experience, really wield? And by the time he settles into the position, his time in office is sharply limited by his own upcoming term limit. For better or worse, the days of the all-powerful speaker— Willie Brown referred to himself as the "Ayatollah of the Assembly"—are probably gone forever.

Between 1962 and 1995, some 33 years, just four assembly members served as speaker. In just the first 12 years following Willie Brown's departure, the assembly witnessed a parade of eight assembly speakers. It was, admittedly, a period of unusual turmoil, with a revolving-door speakership during 1996, when the parties deadlocked and partisan majority control changed twice. But until the Nunez speakership, no one had held the post for more than 2 years, and, again, the term-limit clock is clicking on his tenure. The speakership is now a temporary job.

Assembly Rules Committee

This committee operates as the executive committee of the lower house. It is responsible for formally hiring and firing legislative staff, recommending amendments to assembly rules and procedures, renovating assembly facilities in the capitol, and referring bills and resolutions to committees. Prior to December 1980, the speaker had the power of bill referral, but one of the concessions Willie Brown made to the Republicans who helped elect him speaker was to shift this responsibility to the Assembly Rules Committee. In the Brown era, this formal transfer of power was probably not very significant; everybody knew who was in charge. But in an era of weak speakers, this, as well as other powers of the Rules Committee, is likely more crucial.

President of the Senate (Lieutenant Governor)

The lieutenant governor of California serves as president of the senate on the basis of a provision in the state constitution. This post is largely ceremonial. The lieutenant governor may cast a vote in the senate only when it would be decisive—that is, in cases of a 20–20 tie. (Because it takes 21 votes to pass measures in the senate, the lieutenant governor's vote is not decisive in cases of ties at lower numbers.) Because the upper house is saddled with a president that is not of its own choosing, senators long ago revised their rules to strip the post of its once formidable powers. Prior to World War II, the senate president assigned members to committees and referred bills to committees as well. In 1939 and 1940, these duties shifted to the Senate Rules Committee.

President Pro Tempore of the Senate

In the absence of the president of the senate, the president pro tempore (abbreviated to "pro tem" around the capitol) becomes the presiding officer of the upper house. The president pro tem may name any senator to preside over meetings of the senate, provided the lieutenant governor is not present. Serving as presiding officer is not the president pro tem's most significant responsibility; chairing the five-member Senate Rules Committee is. Traditionally, the Senate Rules Committee exercised much the same power as the assembly speaker, but it did so in a much more collegial, nonpartisan manner. The 1980s witnessed a transformation in upper house leadership style with the ascendancy of David Roberti, a Democrat from Hollywood, to the position of pro tem. In 1980, Roberti was able to win the support of the Democratic caucus in his bid to capture the position by promising to raise money for senate Democratic election purposes; in effect, he sought to emphasize the fund-raising aspects of the position in the manner of assembly speakers. Roberti was largely successful in doing so, protecting Democratic upper house majorities throughout his 14-year tenure. It was also a period where the older nonpartisan ethos of the senate gave way, at least in part, to a greater emphasis on partisanship, though not to the same degree as in the assembly.

In 1994, Roberti, who had also established himself as a powerful policy leader, was forced to leave the senate by term limits. In a smooth succession of power, the pro tem position was filled by Bill Lockyer, a Democrat from Alameda County. Given continued instability in the assembly, Lockyer assumed the role of the capital's leading legislator and continued the Roberti tradition of hefty fund-raising, successfully protecting Democratic senate majorities in the 1996 elections. Termed-out in 1998 and gearing for a run for state attorney general that year, Lockyer stepped down at the end of 1997, and in a relatively quick and easy transfer, John Burton of San Francisco assumed the mantle of president pro tem. Like his immediate predecessors, Burton used the office to establish himself as a key policy player and as the guardian of Democratic senate electoral fortunes. Coming out of the 2000 elections with an enhanced 26–14 majority, Burton was clearly California's most powerful legislator until his term limit date of 2004.

The leadership tenure of Bill Lockyer and John Burton was indicative of a power shift between assembly and senate leadership. In the lower house, term limits mean that speakers assume that office with relatively little legislative experience. In the senate, neither Lockyer nor Burton achieved their leadership posts with a great deal of senate experience. But both previously served in the assembly and were seasoned legislators. In 2004, senate Democrats chose Don Perata to replace the termed-out John Burton as the new president pro tem. He is the first senate leader to have begun his legislative career after term limits, and hence he does not have the experience of his predecessors. Nevertheless, he did bring a total of eight years of legislative service (two in the assembly) to the job. In sum, given the combination of a somewhat less restrictive senate term-limit rule (eight years versus six years) and the prior assembly experience possessed by most senators, the senate leaders can probably be expected to possess a considerable experience advantage over their assembly counterparts.

Senate Rules Committee

This five-member executive committee of the upper house is composed of two senators nominated by the minority party caucus, two senators nominated by the majority party caucus, and the president pro tem, who serves as chair. After nomination by the party caucus, all five members must receive 21 votes on the floor of the senate to be placed on the Rules Committee. (If a nominee fails to secure the necessary votes, the appropriate party caucus submits another name.) Because of the composition and the responsibilities of the Senate Rules Committee, leadership in the senate traditionally was more collective and less partisan than that found in the assembly. Recent changes in the senate, however, make this generalization less applicable than it once was. As a review of the committee's duties demonstrates, the Senate Rules Committee undertakes, at least formally, what amounts to the work of both the assembly speaker and the Assembly Rules Committee.

- The Senate Rules Committee appoints senators to (and removes them from) standing committees, subcommittees, select committees, and conference committees.
- The Senate Rules Committee designates (and removes) the chair and vice chair of each committee.
- The Senate Rules Committee refers bills to committee.
- The Senate Rules Committee proposes amendments to the senate rules to help expedite legislative business.
- The Senate Rules Committee grants requests to waive the rules (or withholds approval of the same).
- The Senate Rules Committee employs and discharges all senate staffers.
- The Senate Rules Committee approves payment for studies prepared at the request of the senate and its committees.
- The Senate Rules Committee assigns senators their offices and committees their hearing rooms.

- The Senate Rules Committee supervises renovation of senate facilities.
- The Senate Rules Committee reviews gubernatorial appointments before they are sent for confirmation votes on the senate floor.

With the consolidation of power in the pro tem position over the last quarter century, the individual power of that position increased. The pro tem is now far more than one-fifth of the executive committee of the upper house. In addition to his or her campaign finance role, the pro tem is the central leader in reviewing gubernatorial appointments and a key player in the policy compromises fashioned in the state capitol.

LEADERSHIP SELECTION

In contests for the posts of speaker and president pro tem, the majority party caucus in each house is the key battleground. If this caucus is able to unify behind one candidate for speaker or pro tem, the choice of chamber leadership will be the majority party's alone. If the majority caucus splits into opposing camps during leadership selection, then a bipartisan coalition involving the minority party will be needed to elect a presiding officer. Historically, the legislature has moved back and forth between these two methods in the election of speakers and presidents pro tem.

Assembly

At the end of each two-year session, the speakership is automatically vacated, to be filled again when the new legislative session convenes. It takes 41 votes to elect or reelect a speaker. Installation as speaker, however, provides no guarantee of tenure. A speaker can be removed at any time during the legislative year if 41 members support a motion to vacate the speakership. Assembly history is full of speakership fights. Because the 41 votes can come from anywhere, two methods can be used to elect a new speaker. The speakership candidate, if a member of the majority party, can capture a majority of that party's caucus. Then, if that caucus unifies around its own plurality choice and votes as a unit, the candidate will be installed. In 1974, Leo McCarthy, a Democrat from San Francisco, defeated fellow San Francisco Democrat Willie Brown 26–22 in a Democratic caucus vote. Brown released his supporters, the caucus then united around McCarthy, and he became speaker.

A majority caucus plurality is not always a sure ticket to the speakership, however. Five years later Speaker McCarthy was challenged by West Los Angeles Democrat Howard Berman, who captured a 26–24 plurality in the Democratic caucus. McCarthy refused to release his own caucus supporters, however, and Berman found himself far short of the 41 votes he needed. In this case, the Republican members held the balance of power, but they refused to commit to Berman. The issue remained stalemated, with McCarthy remaining the nominal speaker but lacking control of his own caucus until after the 1980 elections when the new legislature reconvened. Ultimately, Willie Brown put together a bipartisan coalition of 28 Republicans and 23 Democrats to gain the speakership that was vacated at the ending of the last session. This was the first, but hardly the last, time Willie Brown's career was given a major boost by assembly Republicans.

At the time, most observers predicted a short, weak speakership for Mr. Brown. After all, he had been elected by a shaky bipartisan coalition rather than a unified majority caucus vote. Moreover, Brown promised, in order to get the necessary Republican votes, to give up certain traditional speaker's powers over appointment of Republicans to committees and assignment of bills to committees. These concessions were part of a two-year pact between Brown and the Republican caucus.

As it turned out, of course, Brown's 15-year reign set a tenure record that, with term limits, can never be broken. Even though opinions vary as to his vision and success as a policy leader, Brown's persona unquestionably dominated the legislature and perhaps the entire capitol over the next decade and a half. Brown moved quickly to mend fences in his own caucus and, after his first two years as speaker, took back some (though not all) of the power he initially gave over to assembly Republicans. Brown also put together a campaign machine that kept the Democrats in the majority during a period when Republicans were winning many statewide offices. For assembly Democrats, Brown was the key to electoral success and advancement within the legislature. To the general public, Brown was the symbol of Sacramento politics, and to part of that public, he was a symbol of what is wrong with Sacramento politics. Brown was also the Democrat Republicans loved to hate.

PHOTO 3.2   Willie Brown—assembly speaker (1980–1995) and self-proclaimed "Ayatollah of the Assembly." *(California State Library)*

Yet, curiously, Brown's career as speaker, launched with Republican support, was saved during two periods of crisis by Republican support. In 1987–1988, five dissident Democrats, dubbed the "Gang of Five," challenged Brown's speakership. Their votes, along with the 36 assembly Republicans, totaled the magic 41 number necessary to remove Brown. But Republicans refused to go along, and the revolt evaporated.

Six years later, the elections of 1994 brought a sweeping Republican victory, nation-wide and in California. When the smoke cleared, Republicans claimed 41 assembly seats, their first numerical majority in a quarter century, presumably meaning that Brown would be replaced as speaker by a Republican. But Brown wasn't quite finished yet. When the new assembly met for its organizational meeting, Paul Horcher, a Republican earlier befriended by Brown, broke party ranks and voted to keep Brown in the speakership, thus creating a 40–40 deadlock.

For the next year, the assembly was consumed by partisan guerrilla warfare over control of the lower house. In response to Horcher's "independence" or "treachery," depending on one's individual viewpoint, Republicans mounted a successful recall movement against the Los Angeles County assembly member, the first such successful state-level recall in memory. Another Republican renegade, Doris Allen, who accepted the speakership with the votes of only herself and the entire Democratic caucus, was later also removed from office by recall. But before leaving, Allen passed off the speakership to yet another Republican, Brian Setencich, who like his predecessor was the choice of Democrats but not of the Republican caucus.

Ultimately, by the end of the year, Willie Brown left the assembly to become mayor of San Francisco, and new Republican loyalists took the seats of the recalled Republican rebels. Finally, a full year later, assembly Republicans actually had the votes to take advantage of their numerical control. In January 1996, they ousted the "pretend" Republican speaker Brian Setencich and replaced him with the Republican of their choice, Curt Pringle.

After losing a precious year, the legislation Republicans were able to get through the assembly in the waning months of the 1995–1996 session tended to die in the Democrat-controlled senate. In the November 1996 elections, Democrats reclaimed a solid assembly majority, and the brief window of opportunity for Republican assembly leadership and a Republican legislative agenda was suddenly closed.

Senate

In contrast to the more partisan lower house, the senate traditionally was known for its bipartisanship. The representation of both major parties on the powerful Senate Rules Committee contributed to this style. Also, the senate was regarded as a club where a live-and-let-live norm prevailed. Senators observed the bipartisan character of the upper house by not helping challengers try to unseat incumbent senators of the opposition party. The 1970s service of state senator James Mills (D, San Diego) as president pro tem well reflected the senate style of muted partisanship.

The 1980 general election results toppled Mills and produced a far more partisan president pro tem. Destroying what was once the senate norm, then state senator H. L. (Bill) Richardson provided financial support to Republican John Doolittle in his upset victory over long time Democratic incumbent state senator Al Rodda. If the widely

BOX
3.3

Willie Brown, Last of the Powerful Speakers

Whether you loved him or hated him, Willie Brown was never boring. Highly articulate, Brown combined intelligence, volatility, and mischievousness in a way that made him, hands-down, the most engaging politician in the capital. When he left Sacramento to become mayor of San Francisco, where he served for eight years, he also left a huge personality and charisma void.

Whether his speakership, and powerful speakerships generally, is something we should miss is an open question. If power corrupts, then the old system was ripe for political corruption. Much of the power of the speakership rested on the office's role as a magnet for interest group money, and we will never know how many times policy needs took a backseat to fund-raising needs (Clucas, 1995). Also, one could argue that a single assembly member, elected like all 80 in the house by voters from a single district, should not wield such disproportionate power.

On the other hand, little would indicate that the assembly works all that well without powerful speakers. It might be that a legislative body of more than just a few members actually needs strong leadership if it is to get anything done. It could also be argued that strong speakers, able to hold the majority party together on crucial policy issues, provide the best chance to pass meaningful legislation and to crystallize accountability so that voters know whom to credit or blame for those policy choices.

respected Rodda could be voted out of office, senate Democrats realized that they, too, were vulnerable to electoral defeat by well-funded Republicans. Concerned Democrats quickly replaced Mills with Roberti, whose long reign was only occasionally threatened by revolt. Roberti's successors have also successfully utilized their fund-raising advantages to guarantee their job security.

LEGISLATIVE STAFF

Under the leadership of Jesse Unruh, speaker of the assembly from 1961 to 1968, the California legislature entered the modern era. Sessions were lengthened to conduct more business. Legislative salaries were improved to decrease the need for additional gainful employment by legislators. Committee rooms and personal offices for members were constructed to provide ample locations for meetings to take place. Most important, legislative staffing was expanded in the hope of reducing reliance on the executive bureaucracy and interest groups for information needed during the lawmaking process. The intent behind these changes was to make the California legislature as self-sufficient and as independent as possible and to increase its capacity to respond to public issues.

Since the late 1960s, widespread use of support staff for a variety of tasks has been one of the most noteworthy attributes of the California legislature. Personal staff (both in the capitol and in the district) help members with constituent relations and with legislative proposals. Committee consultants analyze bills prior to public hearings. Party caucus staffs do research on the opposition party, write speeches, and study voting trends. A floor staff in each chamber records roll-call votes, prepares legislative publications, and gives parliamentary advice. Party leaders hire specialists in various policy areas to help them with the legislative agenda. When not responding to some immediate crisis, the Senate Office of Research conducts long-range studies of California's future.

Most of these staff work for a portion, but not all, of the members of the legislature. Only three offices serve the entire membership of the legislative branch. First, as discussed earlier, the legislative counsel drafts actual bills and amendments for all 120 members of both chambers. This office also prepares opinions on the constitutionality of various proposals. Should the legislature become involved in a court case, the legislative counsel (or outside attorneys retained by this office) handles the legal work in the judicial proceeding. The legislative counsel also helps in drafting language for initiatives if so requested, but few backers of propositions take advantage of this service. Attorneys working in the office of legislative counsel are expected to be absolutely impartial and never to become involved in supporting or opposing pending legislation.

Second, the legislative analyst prepares a critique of the annual budget submitted to the legislature by the governor. This office is also expected to be impartial and to conduct a thorough examination of the budget regardless of the party affiliation of the governor or the partisan complexion of the legislature. In addition to working on the budget, the legislative analyst determines the fiscal impact of other legislative proposals and ballot measures.

Third, the auditor general conducts both fiscal and management audits on behalf of the legislature. This office determines whether state funds are being spent as authorized and whether state agencies are being efficiently and effectively managed. All audits are public information after their submission to the legislature.

Until 1990, legislative staffing was a "growth industry," with many jobs paying $75,000 or more per year. Proposition 140, passed in November of that year, imposed limitations on how much the legislature could spend on its own operations. The immediate effect of the new cap was to require a cut in legislative spending of about 40 percent. The great bulk of this reduction had to come through staff cuts. In 1991, a massive exodus of staff from the legislature resulted from a "golden handshake offer" made to those staffers who voluntarily left their jobs. Many who left were among the most experienced, senior people in the legislature. Since that time, the lack of continuity caused by term limits has spread to the legislative staff itself and has caused a steady movement of old staffers out of and new people into these positions.

In addition to the loss of staff experience and expertise related to term limits, there has been some concern with the politicization of legislative staff. As mentioned above, most staffers work for an individual member, not the entire chamber. In effect, their own careers and job security are tied to the electoral and political fortunes of their boss. This was always the case for personal staff, those who serve in individual legislative offices. But many observes have noted that, over the last three decades, policy and fiscal committee staff are increasingly used as adjuncts to the committee chair's individual operations; in effect, the once strong demarcation between personal staff and committee staff has been blurred. When this happens and the tenure of committee consultants is tied to the chair's reelection and maintenance of the chairpersonship, these consultants' policy objectivity and the quality of their expert advice about policy questions may be compromised. To the extent that this has occurred, the original justification for generous committee staffing comes into question.

Add to this the number of legislative staffers now housed in explicitly political and partisan offices such as the Republican and Democratic Caucuses in both the assembly and the senate and the majority and minority party leadership offices. The picture that emerges is a very large legislative staff, the largest of all the 50 states despite the relatively small number of legislators, that often seems more a part of the political and partisan warfare that characterizes the legislature than a source of independent, expert policy advice.

TERM LIMITS

More than a decade after the voters approved legislative term limits, no consensus indicates whether it was a good idea or not. On one level, limits certainly have worked: legislators now move in and out of the lower and upper houses at a greatly accelerated pace. As Table 3.1 indicates, the average experience of assembly and senate members in their chamber is only about one-fourth of what it was in 1990, the last legislative year before implementation of Proposition 140.

TABLE 3.1	Impact of Term Limits on Legislative Experience and Seniority in the State Senate and Assembly			
	State Senate		*State Assembly*	
	1990	**2007**	**1990**	**2007**
Average years of service in chamber	10.3	3.5	8.4	2.8
Average years of total legislative experience	14.4	8.4	8.4	3.1
Experience in current chamber:				
0–2 years	3	22	8	55
3–4 years	4	7	9	23
5–6 years	2	10	3	0
7–9 years	11	1	20	1*
10 or more years	20	0	40	1*
Members with prior experience in the other chamber	26	38	0	4

Two current members of the assembly served in that body prior to the imposition of term limits and have since returned. Their earlier years of service are not counted against their six-year limit.

But is this "greening" of the legislature a good thing? Term-limit advocates argue that ending entrenched incumbency has increased diversity among legislators. More Latinos and considerably more women hold seats in the assembly and senate now than before 1990, and the forced retirement of veteran legislators, mostly Anglo males, certainly played a role in this increase.

In addition, a fear raised by term-limit opponents that lobbyists and/or legislative staff would, by dint of their greater experience, come to dominate the inexperienced legislators does not seem to have been realized. Lobbyists doubtless do have greater experience and knowledge vis-à-vis legislators than was once true, but that advantage has probably been canceled out by the fact that "insider lobbying," based on an advocate's long-term personal networking with established key power players, has been disrupted by the accelerated rate of legislators' movement into and out of the assembly and senate. At the beginning of each new session under term limits, lobbyists face a legislature consisting of many total strangers. Nor has legislative staff taken over the building. As already discussed, many of the most seasoned legislative employees took a "golden handshake" after 1990 and left the building. Since then, legislative staff turnover accelerated over what it was before 1990; many or most staff are now just as inexperienced as the members whom they serve.

On the other hand, some predicted that governors would gain the upper hand over the legislature in the natural struggle between the executive and legislative wings. Relative power between governors and legislators is not easily calculated. One factor is whether the same party controls both wings or whether they work under divided partisan control. The latter case held while Pete Wilson was governor, whereas partisan unity of control accompanied Gray Davis as governor. Given the vast experience gap between these two governors and legislative leadership, especially on the assembly side, it's hard not to believe that the governorship has gained relative strength. This power shift is probably most true for complex issues, such as those surrounding the annual budget negotiations.

With the recall election of Arnold Schwarzenegger to the governorship, divided control was reestablished, though this time with a much less experienced governor. But the governor does possess certain advantages, personal and political, that may be all the more potent due to the lack of legislative leadership experience in the legislative wing. He has already proved himself adept at appealing above and around the legislature to the public in order to gain support for his policy initiatives.

The effects of a lack of experience are not limited to legislative leadership. The assembly side, in particular, seems to be subject to a loss of "institutional memory," a shared knowledge and experience relating to recurring policy questions. Essentially, when perennial questions, such as water allocation, transportation priorities, or educational reform, resurface as current issues, term-limited legislators must learn the basics surrounding these problems; experienced legislators already know the basics from having worked on the issues before. For example, education policy issues such as classroom size reduction, vouchers, and funding formulas are nothing new; they have a long legislative record. The absence of lawmakers who experienced earlier attempts to deal with these issues means that most current legislators confront these policy issues without historical context or knowledge.

The main criticisms of term limits, beyond the fact that they have robbed the legislature of a great deal of experience and expertise, revolve around what term limits promised but failed to deliver. A purported advantage of limiting terms was the elimi-nation of "professional politicians." In the eyes of term-limit advocates, it meant getting rid of lawmakers who were overly ideological and partisan—and overly concerned with their own careers. In their place would come citizens without personal and political agendas who would apply common sense in dealing with the state's issues. In this way, the support for term limits was based on some of same assumptions that underlaid support for Arnold Schwarzenegger's candidacy.

But, at least in terms of the legislature, it now seems clear that none of these bene-fits happened. Had term limits spawned a new-style "citizen legislator" less prone to careerism and partisan rigidity, the 1995 speakership fight that paralyzed the assembly would not have occurred, since a large majority of that year's assembly members were elected under the new rules (DeBow, 1996). The term-limited legislature has demon-strated the same old susceptibility to gridlock that characterized the "bad old days" before passage of the term-limit initiative. For example, there were only four years between 1968 and 1998 when the budget was not signed until August, although the con-stitutional deadline is July 1. All four of those protracted delays occurred since the imposition of term limits. During the revenue-rich budget deliberations of 1999 and 2000, the budget was passed on time. But beginning in 2001, the previous pattern of very late budgets again became the norm. Budget passage in 2004 was four weeks late, and seven weeks late in 2007.

Term limits also failed to produce legislators willing to spend a few years in Sacramento as "temporary help." What they have produced is legislators in an even big-ger hurry to move up the ladder in order to stay ahead of their impending term limits. Legislators are no less "professional politicians" now than they were before 1990, but their career paths have been accelerated by limited terms, especially in the assembly. Prior to term limits, many assembly members were willing to spend decades there. Now, with the six-year limit, assembly members attempt to move up—to the state senate, U.S. Congress, or a statewide office—as quickly as possible.

In turn, this change affects the balance between the state assembly and state senate. As Table 3.1 indicates, the senate's advantage over the assembly in terms of its member-ship's total legislative experience is much more pronounced now than prior to term limits. In fact, as Table 3.1 again indicates, the senate formerly contained many mem-bers from a local government or private-sector background. Now, practically all senators come to the upper house directly out of the assembly. In this sense, even though term limits created a more "amateur" state assembly, they produced an even more "profes-sional" state senate.

An amendment to the current term limit provisions, scheduled for the 2008 bal-lot, might alleviate the "experience gap" suffered by the assembly. Under this pro-posal, the current limits, six years in the assembly, eight in the senate, would be replaced by a single twelve-year overall legislative service limit. Under this system, assembly members would not have an incentive to jump from the lowest house as a way of extending their legislative careers, since the entire twelve years could be served in the lower house, and moving to the senate would not push back their term limit date. The ballot measure, proposed by the legislature itself, is hardly a sure bet to win voter approval. An earlier attempt to modify and soften legislative term limits went down to resounding electoral defeat.

IS AN AMATEUR LEGISLATURE
THE SOLUTION?

Whatever its lofty rankings in the 1970s, the California legislature has garnered few high marks for its performance since the 1980s. What went wrong? What most people saw when they looked at the senate and assembly was partisan and ideological gridlock, an obsession with political fund-raising, rhetorical grandstanding, more interest in insider power "caucus games" than public service, and a scarcity of major policy accomplishments. They also saw documented corruption and a legislature seemingly out of touch with the needs and realities of everyday Californians. Many of these problems were laid at the doorstep of legislative professionalism.

According to critics of the professional legislature, the high pay and other perks available to elected legislators create an obsession with reelection and career advancement rather than with finding solutions to the state's problems. Legislative professionalism also breeds a level of partisanship that gets in the way of good policy making. As well, it creates an atmosphere where the needs of well-heeled interest groups take precedence over the needs of average citizens. The full-time legislator, increasingly isolated in the capital, loses touch with the folks back in the district.

Is a return to a nonprofessional legislature really the answer to these issues? It is not impossible that voters will, perhaps in the near future, be asked to decide this question. Part of the puzzle concerns just how amateur the new legislature would be. Would the now unlimited session time be reduced to six months, four months, or what? Would legislative salaries and compensation, now exceeding $150,000 per year, be reduced to the scale of the most amateur legislatures, well less than $50,000, or would the cut be much less drastic? Would legislative staff be decimated or merely pared down? Clearly, the form and extent of any "deprofessionalization" of the legislature are central questions.

But the whole question of a professional versus an amateur legislature perhaps requires some serious thinking about two interrelated issues. The first of these is whether it is feasible and wise to entrust the legislative branch to part-time lawmakers, who will be on the job only a portion of the year and who, unless they are independently wealthy or retired, may have to moonlight on their "real" jobs in order to make ends meet. The annual state budget approaches $150 billion, far exceeding that of any private corporation, let alone most nations of the world. Can "common sense" and a desire to do right, qualities that some believe would characterize amateur lawmakers, be enough to overcome the lack of experience and contact with the issues raised by the passage of a yearly budget? Are policy questions, such as those surrounding education, water, transportation, and health care, answerable by these same part-timers, once we get politics and partisanship out of the equation? (Remember, too, that under a pure amateur model, there will be much less staff on whom legislators can rely for technical information.)

Part of the allure of an amateur legislature is that, presumably, it would be less partisan and ideological; members, no longer burdened by political careerism, would bring a problem-solving mentality to Sacramento. Policy innovation and progress would replace the current stalemate and deadlock. But this theory assumes that the legislature's failure to lead results from its professionalism, when perhaps other factors are to blame. One thing that limits policy innovation is budgetary constraints, and as discussed in Chapter 10, such constraints have been the rule rather than exception over the last 20 years.

Another limiting factor is the political divisions between the executive and the legislative wings, a constant reality between 1982 and 1998. With the governorship of Gray Davis, that partisan division disappeared, but it has now been reinstalled by the voters. Policy innovation requires a shared commitment and vision between a legislative majority, and often a two-thirds majority, and the governor. But California's Republican and Democratic Parties represent contrasting viewpoints and constituencies. Compromise is good, but so is defense of the policies and principles that elected officials pledged to support when they won election from their respective constituencies. So whose fault is it when legislative Democrats and Republicans can't agree or when a Democrat-controlled legislature is stalemated with a Republican governor? In fact, it can be argued that California as a state—not merely politicians in Sacramento—is badly divided over the critical issues facing the state. Without a general consensus among the state's residents, it is difficult to see how any state legislature, be it professional or amateur, can agree on broad policies and take specific and major policy actions.

Critics of the current legislature rightly cite the obsession with reelection or moving up the ladder that gets in the way of productive policy making. And there's little doubt that, as discussed in Chapter 7, the role of campaign donations also can work against

---

BOX 3.4	**Who Needs Two Legislative Houses Anyhow?**

Prior to the U.S. Supreme Court's "one-person–one-vote" decisions, a two-house state legislature made a lot of sense. Like the federal system, where Senate representation is based on state lines and House representation is based on population, the state senate represented county lines while the assembly districts were drawn according to population. But California's system was invalidated by those court decisions in the 1960s. Now both state legislative houses must consist of districts containing equal populations.

Thus, the two-house legislature is "redundant" in terms of its representational base. It is also duplicative, since legislation must pass through two separate committee and floor vote processes. Wouldn't a one-house legislature make it easier for the public to follow the process and to pinpoint responsibility for legislative deeds, good or bad? Wouldn't one large chamber result in smaller districts and better representation?

Maybe, but so far only one state (Nebraska) has adopted a single-house, or unicameral, legislature, and that happened 70 years ago. Some would argue that a two-house legislature allows each of them to "check" hasty or careless legislation passed by the other and that this safeguard is more valuable than any increased "efficiency" and minor cost savings that could be realized through the adoption of a unicameral body.

public-interest–oriented policy making. Amateur legislators might not have career goals that get in the way of public-interest–oriented policy making, but there is no guarantee. Few Californians remember much about the California Assembly and California Senate before they professionalized, but the California legislature of the 1940s and 1950s was hardly free of lobbyist influence or of outright corruption. Remember, too, that term limits were supposed to reduce the power of campaign contributions, though few would argue that they did. Moreover, perhaps the problem here is not that legislators are always looking ahead to the next election—after all, their election concerns are our best source of control over them—but rather that legislative elections in California are too expensive. And there are no guarantees that election to an amateur election would necessarily be less extensive.

ARE THERE OTHER FEASIBLE REFORMS OUT THERE?

Some critics of the California legislature propose changes other than those to end legislative professionalism. Robert Monagan, a former Republican assembly speaker (1969–1970), argues that legislative careers should still be full-time but that legislative sessions should be much shorter so that members could spend more time in their districts and get a feel for the communities they represent (Monagan, 1990). This same approach was advocated by the Commission for Constitutional Reform (California Constitutional Revision Commission, 1996). Monagan and others also argue for a larger legislature, which would thus permit smaller districts. Such districts might allow more sharply focused representation and would also be less expensive to campaign in. Concern with the legislative "experience gap" has engendered calls to ease term limits, but a 2002 attempt to do just that was decisively rejected by the voters. The latest proposed uniform 12-year limit, discussed earlier, will also have to win approval of a skeptical electorate.

Another avenue of reform concerns the way California elects legislators. Perhaps it is time to change the way legislative lines are drawn in order to create more-competitive districts that would send more moderate, as opposed to hard-core Republican and Democratic, legislators to Sacramento. Another approach would be to institute multi-member, as opposed to single-member, legislative districts. Under this system, several legislators would be elected from a large geographical district. This might allow, again, the election of more centrist candidates as well as candidates of parties other than the Republican and Democratic Parties.

These and other proposals deserve public analysis and discussion. The current legislative system was adopted in a much earlier age and may be in need of a radical updating. For example, when the current 40-member senate was adopted, the state's entire population was about the same as the current population of a single senate district. One major hurdle, of course, is the legislature itself. Absent a constitutional convention, a major overhaul such as creation of a unicameral legislature would have to go through the legislature itself before the voters could decide. (Constitutional initiatives can be used to propose amendments but not basic revisions to the state constitution.) Absent a huge public outcry, legislators are unlikely to forward an idea that would radically

California Legislature in National and Western State Perspective

Membership Size

California: 120 (Rank: #35)

Largest: New Hampshire, 424

Smallest: Nebraska, 49

Residents per Legislator

California: 308,000 (Rank: #1)

Smallest: New Hampshire, 3,000

National Average: 41,000

Other Western States

Arizona: 55,000	Utah: 23,000
Colorado: 46,000	Idaho: 13,000
Washington: 41,000	New Mexico: 18,000
Oregon: 39,000	Montana: 9,000
Nevada: 33,000	Wyoming: 6,000

Legislative Staff per Legislator

California: 19.6 (Rank: #1)

Least Staff per Legislator: New Hampshire, 0.39

National Average: 4.7

Annual Legislative Salary*

California: $113,098 Rank: #1

Lowest Salary: New Hampshire, $100

Other Western States

Washington: $36,311	Oregon: $18,408
Colorado: $30,000	Idaho: $16,116
Arizona: $24,000	

Level of Legislative Professionalism**

(1 = most professional; 5 = most amateur)

Level 1: California (along with Michigan, New York, and Pennsylvania)

Level 2: None

Level 3: Arizona, Colorado, Oregon, Washington

Level 4: Idaho, Nevada, New Mexico

Level 5: Montana, Utah, Wyoming

*Figures based on annual salary only and do not include per-diem pay. Some states pay only per-diem and were not included in these listings.

**Professionalism scale based on legislators' salary, session length, and number of staff.

Source: National Conference on State Legislatures (Denver, CO: 2007).

change their own political environment.

SUMMARY

Criticism of the California legislature abounds. The way district lines are drawn, the fights over internal power, and the nature of legislative professionalism have all come under fire, especially recently, and the debate over the desirability of term limits goes on. Perhaps the most serious criticism is that the legislature no longer is the source of practical and workable policy aimed at the state's most important problems. Practical and workable solutions to current legislative shortcomings, however, are hard to come by. For example, even though practically everybody wants "fair" and "equitable" redistricting, those words include different criteria that might not be compatible. Although it is easy to criticize the current highly professionalized legislature and its obsession with fund-raising, internal caucus games, and partisanship, it is much less than certain that going back to an amateur legislature would be any kind of improvement. California's experience with term limits indicates that changing the rules of the legislative game doesn't necessarily guarantee a better legislative product.

REFERENCES

California Constitutional Revision Commission. *Final Report and Recommendations to the Governor and the Legislature.* Sacramento: 1996.

Clucas, Richard A. *The Speaker's Electoral Connection: Willie Brown and the California Assembly.* Berkeley, CA: Institute of Governmental Studies, 1995.

DeBow, Ken. "Decline of the California Legislature: Why New Faces Won't Help." Paper delivered at the Western Political Science Association. San Francisco, March 17–20, 1996.

Field Research Corporation. *California Field Poll,* San Francisco: March, 2007.

Monagan, Robert. *The Disappearance of Representative Government: A California Solution.* Grass Valley, CA: Comstock Bonanza Press, 1990.

National Conference on State Legislatures. Denver, CO: 2007.

CHAPTER four

THE EXECUTIVE BRANCH

Given California's national media prominence, the performance of the state's chief executive is of interest to a much wider audience than simply the residents of the Golden State. Any governor of California is a figure of national importance. Early in his administration, Gray Davis was often mentioned as a member of the "short list" of potential Democratic candidates for the 2004 presidential election, and even before his first gubernatorial inauguration, Arnold Schwarzenegger's potential as a future Republican presidential nominee was a hot topic for political pundits. (See Box 4.1 for a discussion of Schwarzenegger's presidential prospects.) Immediately prior to these last two governors, Pete Wilson was one of a long line of governors who, in 1996, succumbed to presidential ambitions, or "Potomac Fever." After unsuccessful attempts in 1968 and 1976, Ronald Reagan won the presidency in 1980, six years after he left the governorship. Jerry Brown's two terms as governor were also marked by unsuccessful presidential bids in 1976 and 1980. Like Reagan, Brown made yet a third attempt long after departing the governor's position, but unlike Reagan, his third attempt (in 1992) was also futile. Two other California governors, perhaps the state's two most popular ever, Hiram Johnson and Earl Warren, were vice-presidential candidates on unsuccessful national tickets: Johnson with Teddy Roosevelt on the Bull Moose ticket in 1912 and Earl Warren with Thomas Dewey in the losing Republican effort in 1948. Both Johnson and Warren nursed strong presidential ambitions of their own. Even losers of gubernatorial elections in California can become president. After losing his race for governor in 1962, Richard Nixon was victorious on the national level six years later.

Important though governors may be in national politics, however, the executive branch in California involves much more than the operation of a single office. The governor, the most powerful and visible person, shares executive power with seven other elected individuals as well as the five members of the Board of Equalization, who are also picked by the voters. This chapter begins with a description of the various components of the executive branch. The second part deals with the official and unofficial powers of the governor. The final part focuses on the last six governors. Contrasting these chief executives illustrates the political styles of contemporary governors, compares their use of power as the leader of the most populous state, and shows how the dynamics of California politics can result in the election of widely different types of governors, whose prospects for success are shaped by institutional factors, their own personal skills, political tides, and just plain good or bad luck.

BOX
4.1

Arnold Schwarzenegger for President: A Long-Odds Bet?

As Arnold Schwarzenegger's recall election campaign gathered momentum, some observers started looking into the future and projecting this new face as a potential Republican presidential nominee. Over his first term, marked by political ups and downs, some of this excitement has subsided. But his landslide 2006 reelection victory demonstrated a breadth of political support that might bode well, with some luck in his second term as governor, for a future presidential run. He is, obviously, a very skilled campaigner who projects a persona that appeals to a broad array of voters—Republicans, independents, and even some Democrats. If Democrats capture the presidency in 2008, Schwarzenegger might be primed for a 2012 run, when he would still, by presidential candidate standards, be a young man. (Incidentally, he will be termed out of the governorship in 2010.)

There are, however, a couple of huge questions concerning his viability as a candidate for the White House. The first is constitutional. Eligibility to become president requires not just citizenship but also "natural-born" citizenship. Austrian-born Schwarzenegger has long been a naturalized citizen, but only a change in the U.S. Constitution would allow him to run for the presidency. Such an amendment, requiring two-thirds approval in both houses of Congress plus the assent of 38 of the 50 state legislatures, is hardly a sure thing. In fact, given the current bitter controversy over the issue of immigration, particularly within the Republican Party, passage of such an amendment seems to be a very long shot.

The second hurdle is political. Schwarzenegger is considered a moderate to conservative on economic issues such as taxation and business regulation, but moderate to liberal on social issues, especially abortion. And his position on global warming was seen as a direct repudiation of Republican president George Bush. That's a winning combination in California, and perhaps for a national general election electorate. But could a pro-choice, "green" candidate, especially one whose wife (Maria Shriver) has strong Democratic connections, win the hearts of those Republican presidential primary voters who determine that party's nominee? That seems a tall order, even for the Terminator.

At this stage, a better bet on Schwarzenegger's future political moves might be a 2010 election bid to unseat three-term Democratic U.S. Senator Barbara Boxer.

PHOTO 4.1   More than just a state leader: Governor Schwarzenegger confers with British Prime Minister Tony Blair. *(Associated Press)*

STATEWIDE ELECTED EXECUTIVES

Prior service in elective office is ordinarily a prerequisite for those desiring to move to the governor's job, but when voters are fed up with "professional politicians" and "politics as usual," a lack of state political experience can be a campaign plus. This was the case for Ronald Reagan, Jerry Brown, and Arnold Schwarzenegger, all of whom emerged during periods of public antipathy toward politicians and successfully portrayed themselves as above and beyond normal politics and hence especially equipped to turn the state around. In fact, two of these, Reagan and Schwarzenegger, had never held public elective office prior to becoming California governor.

In addition to the governor, seven persons are elected to serve in individual offices within what is known as the plural executive. Like the governor, these officials are limited to two four-year terms. The *lieutenant governor* is selected independently of the governor. Unlike the election of the president and vice president as a team from the same party, in California the governor and lieutenant governor are elected in separate elections, and hence may be from different parties. In fact, it happened exactly that way for five straight elections, beginning in 1978 and extending through the election of 1994. Only in 1998 did voters create partisan unity between the two positions by electing Democrats Gray Davis governor and Cruz Bustamante lieutenant governor. Under the Schwarzenegger governorship partisan division between the two offices has returned: Democrat Cruz Bustamante served as Lieutenant Governor in Schwarzenegger's shortened post-recall election, term, and in 2006 voters elected Democrat John Garamendi to the number two post.

But even partisan unity does not guarantee a sense of partnership or teamwork between the governor and lieutenant governor. In the case of presidential elections, the parties' nominees for president handpick their vice presidential running mates. In California, however, governor and lieutenant governor nominees are chosen through separate primary elections, meaning that a party may field two candidates who are not close personally or politically. For example, the "partnership" between Gray Davis and Bustamante was decidedly not collegial.

Under the state constitution, the lieutenant governor becomes acting governor, with all the powers of the governorship, anytime the governor leaves the State of California. This provision was obviously crafted in an era prior to jet plane travel and instantaneous communication and under the assumption that it might be days or weeks before an absent governor could be reached or get back to the state. Today, it is a recipe for mischief, especially when the lieutenant governor is a political rival to the governor. Instant response to a true emergency in the temporary absence of the governor is a legitimate use of the acting governor provisions, as it was used in 1989 when Lieutenant Governor Leo McCarthy set the state's emergency operations in motion after the Loma Prieta earthquake, which occurred while Governor George Deukmejian was visiting a trade office in Germany. However, when the lieutenant governor takes advantage of the governor's absence to make judicial or administrative appointments or to veto legislation—in other words, to "play governor"—he or she clearly oversteps the reasonable bounds of the position. This became an issue during Jerry Brown's second term as governor (1979–1983) when Brown sometimes found himself racing home to undo the work of Republican Lieutenant Governor Mike Curb.

Relations between the next lieutenant governor, Leo McCarthy, and the two Republican governors with whom he served, George Deukmejian and Pete Wilson, were less confrontational. The "partnership" voters created in 1994 by reelecting Republican Pete Wilson governor while also selecting Gray Davis to fill the lieutenant governor's position was a bit chilly, however. At one point, Wilson proposed that the lieutenant governor's office be physically removed from the capitol and relocated downtown. Arnold Schwarzenegger and Lieutenant Governor Bustamante were, of course, the leading rivals on the replacement ballot of the 2003 recall election; the likelihood of them forming a cohesive "team" was no greater than the prospects for an amicable, productive partnership between, say, George Bush and John Kerry.

In addition to the "acting governor" designation, the other seemingly important constitutional power granted to the lieutenant governor is his designation as "president of the state senate." This somewhat empty title offers real power only in its ability to cast a tie-breaking vote, should the senate be deadlocked at 20–20. Because legislators reflexively oppose any imposition of executive authority over their own house, senators go out of their way to avoid such a split. Since 1975, only two votes have been cast in the senate by the lieutenant governor.

Although the day-to-day powers of lieutenant governors are minimal, they do serve as ex officio members on boards and commissions of some relevance. Probably most important of these are the State Lands Commission and the University of California Board of Regents. (Lieutenant governors also serve as trustees of the California State University System.) The State Lands Commission supervises the leasing of offshore mineral rights and oversees the use of some 4 million acres of state land and waterways. The membership on the Board of Regents, a high-profile, often controversial body, can provide the lieutenant governor with real news-generating potential. For example, in his ex officio role, Lieutenant Governor Gray Davis took a public pro–affirmative action stance on the Board of Regents, in direct confrontation with Governor Pete Wilson, who prevailed on the regents to end the University of California's affirmative action program.

The position in the executive branch often considered next most powerful to that of the governor is *attorney general.* This individual is the chief law officer for the state and head of the state Department of Justice. As such, the attorney general handles the legal work for civil cases involving agencies of state government. (Under certain statutory exceptions, some executive departments, such as the Department of Transportation, are allowed to hire their own lawyers to undertake legal cases.) The attorney general also is responsible for arguing all appeals that arise from criminal proceedings in the trial courts. To make sure that the laws of California are enforced in a uniform manner, the attorney general has supervisory power over all county district attorneys and sheriffs. The state attorney general may take over criminal cases in the event a county district attorney refuses to prosecute or the case raises issues of conflict of interest for the local prosecutor. For example, in the fall of 2001, the attorney general's office took over the investigation of an alleged assault and battery in San Francisco. The reason? The district attorney for San Francisco County also happened to be the father of the suspect.

The attorney general is allowed some discretion in terms of the legal areas, such as organized crime, environmental law, domestic violence, or gambling operations, to which he or she can devote special attention and Department of Justice resources. All attorneys general tout the "top cop" element of their job, even though the position is much more that of an attorney than of a cop. Attorneys general are quick to claim credit when the crime rate drops and to sound the call to alarm when it goes up. Their association in the public's mind with crime fighting is a political plus; it is the main reason why the attorney general position has been the best stepping-stone to the governorship. Earl Warren (1942), Pat Brown (1958), and George Deukmejian (1982) all used the attorney general spot as their immediate stepping-stone to the governorship. Evelle Younger (1978), and Dan Lungren (1998) also parlayed the position into their party's nomination for the governorship, although they lost in their general election bids. All things being normal, Republicans, associated with a tough law-and-order stance, usually had the inside track for the attorney general position. But over the last three elections, it was the Democratic nominee who prevailed. The current occupant of the position, Jerry Brown, was of course governor a quarter century ago, and has reemerged as a statewide office holder. Will this be his final office, or might he be, in 2010, a candidate for the governor's office he left three decades ago?

The *controller* issues checks to pay state employees, lottery winners, and other bills against the State of California. It is the responsibility of the controller to audit the books of state government (and each of the localities therein) and to determine the legality of any financial claims against the state. By virtue of being controller, the occupant of this office serves on a myriad of boards and commissions in fiscally related areas. The controller chairs the Franchise Tax Board, which collects personal income and corporate taxes. Joining four other members, each elected from districts encompassing one-fourth of the state, the controller is the fifth member of the Board of Equalization. This board collects the sales tax, gasoline tax, and taxes on liquor and cigarettes. As in the case of the lieutenant governor, the controller serves on the State Lands Commission. The controller also is a member of a wide variety of commissions and boards dealing with public employee pensions, public construction projects (such as schools, hospitals, and community colleges), and bonded indebtedness. The current controller, first elected in 2006, is Democrat John Chiang, who previously served as a member of the Board of Equalization.

The *treasurer* is the state's banker, with primary responsibility for selling state bonds, investing the state's funds in financial institutions, and paying out state funds when authorized by the controller. The state invests hundreds of *billions* of dollars in various securities, making it a potential major player in the nation's financial markets. Jesse Unruh, the once-powerful speaker of the assembly, held onto the treasurer's job with little opposition from 1975 until his death in 1987, prior to the imposition of term limits. Unruh, who was perhaps the first treasurer to realize just how much clout all that money potentially represented, transformed this formerly obscure position into one of considerable influence and notoriety. The treasurer also serves on some 45 boards and commissions dealing with the investment of public funds and the financing of public projects through the use of bonds. This position's current occupant, Democrat Bill Lockyer, won the treasurer's office in 2006 after serving as attorney general for eight years. Prior to that, he was a long time legislator, including serving as state senate president pro tem.

The *secretary of state* is the chief elections officer, record keeper, and archivist for the State of California. This office is responsible for overseeing the qualification of initiatives, the printing of ballots, the preparation of the voters' pamphlet describing each proposition, and the tabulation of the vote. Corporations, lobbyists, notaries public, and a whole host of other businesses and professions must register with the secretary of state. This office also maintains a registry of vacant appointive positions within state government. Debra Bowen, a Democrat and fourteen year legislator, was elected secretary in 2006 by defeating the incumbent, Republican Bruce McPherson.

The *superintendent of public instruction* (SPI), the one statewide electoral officeholder whose election is, at least officially, nonpartisan, heads the Department of Education and theoretically carries out policies set by an 11-member Board of Education appointed by the governor. The state's assumption of more fiscal and hence policy control over local school districts after Proposition 13's permanent property tax cuts in 1978 and education's emergence as the main policy concern of many citizens increased the spotlight on the SPI. But, in fact, the SPI is not really a superintendent at all; the power of the office is shared with other actors, often with more policy clout and at political odds with the superintendent. For example, the governor and legislature must agree to any changes in the Education Code, and both control the educational budget process. Also, the state Board of Education, whose members are appointed by the governor, maintains formal authority over the state Department of Education, Sacramento's largest bureau-

---

BOX 4.2

Executive Wing Musical Chairs: You Gotta Find a Seat When the Term Limit Music Stops

One side effect of term limits has been changes in the dynamics of executive wing elected office politics. As legislators faced the mandatory end of their legislative careers, the statewide offices beckoned as a way of keeping their political careers alive. This movement from the legislature to executive wing has not stopped; for example, Debra Bowen ran for and won the secretary of state job immediately upon exhausting her 14-year (6 in the Assembly, 8 in the state senate) legislative limit. But more recently, a newer trend, office-hopping *within* the executive branch, has gained momentum.

Prior to the final years of the twentieth century, aspiring politicians generally only held one executive statewide position below governor before seeking the big prize: the governorship itself. But Gray Davis broke the mold when he moved from the controller's office to that of the lieutenant governor before successfully running for governor. Now, jumping from one executive office to another is becoming commonplace. Of the current executive office holders, the following fit into this new mold:

John Garamendi was the first insurance commissioner, leaving that office to serve in the Clinton presidential administration. Upon his return he again won the insurance job. Now he is the lieutenant governor.

Bill Lockyer served his eight-year limit as attorney general, and has now moved over to the treasurer job.

John Chiang served two terms on the Board of Equalization prior to his 2006 election as state controller.

Jerry Brown began his state elective career as secretary of state, back in 1970, then advanced to the governorship in 1974, leaving the office after the 1982 elections. Now he has reemerged as the attorney general.

So what's behind all this office shifting? Term limits. As discussed later, the lower statewide offices are often seen as stepping-stones for the job their holders really seek; the governorship. But term limits on these offices can put a crimp in career plans if those limits come due when the time is not right to run for the governorship. This was the dilemma facing Gray Davis when he was termed out of the controller's job in 1994 and was not yet in a strong position to challenge for the governorship. Without term limits, Davis could have run once again for, and likely won, four more years as controller. With term limits, the only way to keep his career in the political spotlight was to find a new job, in this case, the lieutenant governorship.

The same thing might be said for Bill Lockyer. Once considered a prime candidate for the Democratic governor's nomination in 2006, the then-attorney general opted out of that race, but still had to find a job when term limits ran out on his tenure as that office. Now he is the newly elected state treasurer.

cratic unit and a force of its own. Also included in this mix is the governor's appointed secretary of education, who can serve as yet another prominent voice in the educational policy area. Finally, the approximately 1,000 local school boards have at least some policy-making discretion in their individual districts.

The office of SPI presents a couple of paradoxes. Voters presumably think they are really putting someone in charge of the state's K–12 (plus community colleges) public education system when they elect a superintendent. In fact, they are electing only one cog in the vast educational machinery. Also, as stated, the office is officially "nonpartisan," the only such elected office in the executive wing, meaning no party label appears next to the candidates' names on the ballot. The elections are, however, almost as partisan as those for the other executive offices. For example, in his successful 2002 election to this office, Jack O'Connell, a former Democratic legislator, easily defeated his challenger, Katherine Smith, generally recognized as the Republican alternative. He also easily won reelection in 2006.

With the passage of Proposition 103 in 1988, the elected post of *insurance commissioner* was established. The commissioner is in charge of the State Department of Insurance, charged with regulating most components of the insurance industry. This is a highly charged political area; Republican office holders tend to support the insurance industry against its archenemy, the trial lawyers, who are generally supported by Democratic politicians. The insurance commissioner and Department of Insurance are in the middle of this partisan and high-stakes struggle. Since its creation as an elective position, the office of insurance commissioner has shifted back and forth between Democrat and Republican. In 2006, Republican Steve Poizner replaced Democrat John Garamendi, who in turn won his election for Lieutenant Governor. Poizner, a successful hi-tech entrepreneur who had never held elective office, ran an "independent campaign" that stressed his determination to vigilantly regulate the insurance industry. This approach appealed to independent and even many Democratic voters. In 2010 he will be (with Arnold Schwarzenegger being termed out of office) the only Republican statewide office holder and thus perhaps an important player in the contest for the Republican gubernatorial nomination.

Finally, we come to the *Board of Equalization*. Every ten years when new legislative district lines are drawn, the four Board of Equalization districts, each containing one-quarter of the state's population, or currently slightly more than 9 million residents, must also be mapped out. Candidates run on a partisan basis for these four seats. Once elected, they join the state controller on the board. This five-member board is responsible for overseeing the assessment and administration of property taxes throughout the state, though in most cases it is county assessors who actually do the work. The board also oversees the collection and distribution of sales taxes, which are collected locally but divided between state and local governments (with the lion's share going to the state). Income taxes do not fall under the board's jurisdiction; this revenue program is administered by the Franchise Tax Board, consisting of the director of the Department of Finance, the chairperson of the Board of Equalization, and the state controller. The Board of Equalization, however, does serve as the state's "tax court" for all forms of taxes, including the income tax. Individuals and companies who believe they have been unfairly subject to any state tax, or overtaxed, may bring their cases to the board. The four board members are currently split two to two between Republicans and Democrats, but the addition of the controller, a Democrat, results in a 3-to-2 Democratic edge.

Too Many Elected Statewide Executives?

Many observers of California government argue that there are too many independently elected statewide elected officials, who should be replaced by appointees of the governor.

BOX
4.3

Plural Elected Executive—Voter Choice or Politician Full-Employment System?

With eight independently elected executives, California voters have ample latitude in selecting the leadership of this branch of government. But this plural executive system also creates real problems in terms of executive branch coherence and accountability. In any year, crime and education are at or near the top of citizens' concerns. By electing the attorney general and superintendent of public instruction separately, Californians run the risk of destroying executive wing cohesion in these policy areas and defeating accountability. Who is in charge, and who should be held accountable for policy areas such as public education? Other components of the plural executive—such as the secretary of state, the controller, and the treasurer—oversee technical programs that are little understood by the voters. Ask yourself how many of these offices, such as secretary of state, treasurer, or controller, you understood when you began reading this book. In these cases, how valuable can the right to elect be if voters have no idea about the position the candidates seek? And how effectively can incumbent performance be evaluated?

The "dirty little truth" about most, if not all, of these offices is that they are usually sought after not for their own worth but merely as stepping-stones to "real jobs." Most occupants of these positions are "wannabes" who hope to parlay the name recognition of a statewide office into a successful run for the governorship or the U.S. Senate. Term limits may have made things worse, as every election cycle creates a new group of termed-out lawmakers or state executives looking for a new niche to extend and enlarge their political careers. (Please see Box 4.2 for a discussion of statewide executive office switching.)

Beyond the charade character of many of these statewide electoral positions, they hold a real potential for conflict of interest. Most of these contests are fairly low-key and voters don't pay all that much attention. Nevertheless, any statewide election campaign costs money. But because these offices lack general public interest and understanding, the pool of campaign donors can be quite limited and, in fact, is dominated by those interests and individuals with a material stake in the operations of the office. For example, much of the funding for the treasurer's campaign comes from the bond houses that hope to reap the commissions from handling the state's bond sales. Likewise, insurance companies and trial lawyers have traditionally been heavy contributors to candidates for insurance commissioner, as the policies of this office can directly affect them financially. Individuals and companies with tax cases before the Board of Equalization are not allowed to contribute directly to board candidates' campaigns. But political action committees, including those representing companies and interests with business before the board, are not currently prohibited from such donations. The obscurity of these offices' operations, combined with the narrowness of their campaign funding base, creates a situation fraught with the potential for favoritism, if not outright corruption.

They point to the federal government model, where most of the executive positions corresponding to these statewide elected offices are filled by presidential appointment. In the 1990s, a Constitutional Revision Commission recognized some of the problems with multiple elected executive positions and recommended that the governor and lieutenant governor run on a single ticket and that the elected positions of treasurer, superintendent of public instruction, and insurance commissioner be made appointive by the governor. The commission also called for the abolition of the state Board of Equalization and the assumption of its responsibilities by the Franchise Tax Board (California Constitutional Revision Commission, 1996). As was the case with all the commission's recommendations, the legislature never acted on these proposals.

APPOINTED EXECUTIVES

The remainder of the high-level positions in the executive branch are filled by gubernatorial appointment. The governor's *cabinet* consists of the secretaries in charge of the superagencies in state government, such as Business, Transportation and Housing, Health and Welfare, and Resources. Nested under the superagencies are the various operating departments, such as the Department of Motor Vehicles under the Business and Transportation Agency. Governors also appoint the directors of these departments. Individuals appointed as agency secretaries or department directors are the senior managers in the executive branch, and they usually possess considerable background in the program area they administer.

Members of the governor's *personal staff* are not responsible for managing programs or personnel in the various departments of state government but instead provide the chief executive with close support in the performance of such daily tasks in the governor's capitol office as appointments, media relations, constituent outreach, and legislative relations. In essence, they are the "governor's people," whose sole focus is the governor's political career. Given their unique and personal roles, these individuals do not require senate confirmation. They, as well as the senior executive officials just discussed, serve "at the pleasure" of the governor, which means the governor can fire them.

A wide assortment of more than 400 *boards and commissions* completes the appointed portion of the executive branch. Some of these entities (e.g., University of California Board of Regents, Public Utilities Commission, Water Resources Control Board, State Lottery Commission, and Air Resources Board) are large entities on their own and receive a great deal of public attention. Others, such as the boards that regulate licensed professions (e.g., architects, doctors, nurses, accountants, psychologists, landscape architects, and acupuncturists), are much smaller and escape most public attention. They are, however, closely watched by those constituencies they were created to regulate. Once appointed, commission and board members may not generally be removed by the governor, though the governor can decline to reappoint them, should their term end. (Most of these appointees serve four-year staggered terms, though some, like the University of California regents, serve much longer terms.)

(See Box 4.4 for a discussion of the executive branch's nonelected, nonappointed employees.)

BOX 4.4	**State Employees, Foot Soldiers of the Executive Branch**

Our discussion of state executive branch personnel has been limited to those individuals elected or appointed to their positions. These are clearly the top rung of the executive wing, but they count for only a small fraction of those who actually do the work. We usually think of these latter employees, the "state bureaucrats," as denizens of the state capital headquarters offices. In fact, many are stationed throughout the state, in all its cities and counties.

The great majority of state employees, most of them housed within departments such as Education, Highway Patrol, State Parks, and Health, are part of the civil service, or "merit" system. This system, also utilized in the federal government and most states, was created to minimize political influence on the hiring and firing of public employees and to ensure that the awarding of jobs and promotions was based on appropriate training and performance standards.

Jobs within the state system, or bureaucracy, are filled through a process of testing and interviews, and job designations, responsibilities, and salaries are defined by an elaborate and highly formal system. Employees may be terminated only after a similarly formal process. Getting rid of "deadwood" in the public sector can be an arduous and very time-consuming task.

This last attribute of civil service has been a target of criticism for a long time, though defenders argue that the elaborate job protection serves to insulate workers from political influence. Another area of criticism is the current system's reliance on testing, often pencil-and-paper testing, for hiring and promotion. These screening devices may not always pertain directly to the job in question and may work against minorities who, while competent to do the work, may lack the language skills necessary to score well on the tests.

In all, just over 200,000 individuals, stationed in Sacramento and throughout the 58 counties, work directly for the state. That seems like a lot, and there are plenty of references to the state's "swollen bureaucracy." On the other hand, California's number of state workers per capita ranks 47th among all the states.

THE GOVERNOR'S POWERS

The state constitution establishes specific legal roles and powers for the governor. Among these formal functions, the governor is required to give an annual report to the legislature, to make recommendations for future legislation, to sign or veto legislation, and to submit an annual budget covering anticipated expenditures by the branches of government. The governor has the power to fill vacancies created by death or retirement in a variety of offices (such as U.S. senators, statewide executive offices, and county boards of supervisors) until a successor is chosen in the next scheduled election. The governor may call the legislature into special session to consider a specific issue and is empowered to call special elections between regularly scheduled ones. He or she can embark on executive reorganization plans to restructure the state bureaucracy. Additionally, the governor is the commander of the California National Guard and has the authority to issue reprieves, pardons, and commutations to those convicted of a crime.

Budget and Veto

At the federal level, historically the chief executive must accept or reject bills in their entirety. In California, the governor is similarly limited in regard to regular legislation. For bills involving appropriations, however, including the budget, the governor can reduce or omit spending totals voted out by the legislature (*line-item veto*). The line-item veto may be used only on monetary provisions of bills, and then only to decrease, not increase, legislative appropriations.

When the governor receives a regular bill during the middle of a legislative session, he or she has 12 days to either sign or veto the measure. If the governor does neither, the bill becomes law upon expiration of the deadline. Because the legislature passes a large number of bills when it recesses or adjourns at year's end, the chief executive, during this period, is allowed 30 days to decide whether to sign or to veto measures.

The governor exerts a great deal of influence over the budget. The governor and the Department of Finance consult while developing the initial budget and then hand it to the legislature. Furthermore, it is returned from the legislature for the governor's signature before it can become law. Thus, the governor has the opportunity to structure the original document and the final say as to its shape when completed. While it is being debated in the legislature, the governor's key supporters there can use their influence to ward off drastic alterations. (See Chapter 10 for a detailed discussion of the governor's role as budget maker.)

Both the general and the line-item vetoes may be overridden by a two-thirds vote in each house, although such overrides seldom occur. The reason is the strong partisan caucus solidarity in the legislature. Members of the governor's party will vote against an override even if they voted for the bill the first time through. In effect, as long as at least 14 senators or 27 assembly members of the governor's party hold office, the governor is assured almost "bulletproof" protection against a veto override. The last veto overrides occurred during the administration of Jerry Brown, some four governors ago. Curiously, it happened during an era when Democrats controlled both the executive and the legislature and testifies to the lack of goodwill between the governor and many of his Democratic colleagues in the legislature. Gray Davis did not suffer the indignity of a veto override, but the sour relations between him and many Democratic legislators reminded seasoned observers of the Jerry Brown days. Given the current level of public support for Arnold Schwarzenegger and the presence of the necessary number of Republican legislators, an override of any of his vetoes seems a very remote possibility.

Appointments

The authority to make appointments allows governors to have a broad and lasting impact on state government. Not only does the governor select the leaders of the executive departments, but also he or she decides who will occupy judicial positions as well as those on boards and commissions. Some positions are known as "pleasure appointments," meaning that the occupant serves as long as the governor so desires. Other positions are known as "term appointments," meaning that the occupant serves for a fixed period, protected from removal by the governor. The term of a member of the University of California Board of Regents is 12 years (as are the terms of appellate justices), so the influence of governors can last long after they leave office. As a general rule, the heads of superagencies and departments are pleasure appointments, and the judiciary and the boards and commissions are term appointments.

Roughly 400 appointments must be made at the beginning of a new administration. Thereafter, approximately 2,600 additional appointments will be required as terms expire on boards and judges retire from the bench. A hallmark of the Davis administration was its unhurried approach to filling those positions, leaving many positions vacant for long periods of time.

Depending on the legislation that originally established a given board or department, some appointments require confirmation by the California Senate and some do not. When an appointment requires confirmation, the Senate Rules Committee mails letters of inquiry to various groups in California to obtain reaction to the nominee. The committee holds hearings regarding appointments, and interested citizens are invited to testify on controversial appointees. Nominees are given the opportunity to defend their credentials. After Rules Committee approval, an appointment must be approved by a majority (21 votes) of the full senate. In rare instances, such as appointments to the University of California Board of Regents, a two-thirds majority (27 votes) is required for confirmation.

As is evident in Table 4.1, not all gubernatorial appointments are subject to confirmation. As already discussed, the governor may appoint whomever he or she pleases to personal staff. Governor Pete Wilson's appointment of state senator John Seymour to the U.S. Senate vacancy created when Wilson left that post to become governor did not require any review. Crucially, appellate judicial appointments are confirmed by the Commission on Judicial Appointments, not the California Senate. (See Chapter 5 for a discussion of why this is an important distinction.) Most other

TABLE 4.1 Confirmation of Gubernatorial Appointments	
Type of Vacancy	**Confirmation by California Senate**
Judicial	No
U.S. Senate	No
County supervisor	No
Governor's personal staff	No
Executive departments and superagencies	Yes
Boards and commissions	Yes
Statewide elected executive	Yes*
Board of Equalization	Yes*

Both legislative chambers review confirmation; defeat in one house kills the appointment.

appointments are subject to state senate approval, though governors' nominees to fill vacant constitutional executive positions, such as secretary of state, also require assembly approval. The overwhelming majority of gubernatorial appointments win confirmation, but the few appointments that are blocked understandably garner a great deal of press attention.

Beyond Formal Powers

Formal powers, situational factors, and personal characteristics are interwoven in the performance of the governor's job. The formal powers of the governor are spelled out in the state constitution. However, just how successful the chief executive is in winning passage of his or her legislative package and having budgets approved, vetoes upheld, and appointments confirmed by the senate depends on the situational factors and personal characteristics. Generally, situational factors cannot be controlled by the governor. Rather, they provide the political context within which the governor must operate. Clearly, if a Republican governor such as Pete Wilson or Arnold Schwarzenegger must contend with a Democratic majority in one or both houses of the legislature, much of the governor's energy can be sapped by political infighting. Conflicts between independently elected executives can limit a governor's power; so, too, can budgetary constraints imposed by economic downturns or the initiative process.

Governors also vary in the personal resources they bring to the job. Some are better than others at negotiating political compromise with other Sacramento players. A governor with media appeal can more effectively mobilize public opinion on behalf of his or her political program. Stamina, intelligence, and the proper mix of tenacity and flexibility are highly personal characteristics and another set of keys to gubernatorial effectiveness.

Because the constitutional responsibilities of the governor have remained largely the same over the years, we need to explore the personal and situational factors impacting recent governors to understand how they succeeded and failed in convincing the electorate and the legislature of the wisdom of their agendas. Examining their years as chief executive makes apparent six distinct gubernatorial styles and fortunes.

GUBERNATORIAL CONTRASTS

Ronald Reagan

In the mid-1950s, Ronald Reagan polished the political philosophy that landed him in the governor's seat in 1966 and provided him with a national following in subsequent presidential elections. That philosophy, repeated many times in what came to be called "the speech," was a defense of the free enterprise system in the face of the rising tide of "socialism" that threatened individual freedoms in the United States.

When Reagan challenged Pat Brown's bid for a third term in 1966, he combined this traditional conservative appeal with strong stands on campus unrest (the free speech movement in Berkeley began in 1964) and urban civil disturbances (the Watts riots broke out in the summer of 1965). He also stressed his lack of office-holding experience as a positive, referring to himself as the "citizen candidate," a self-description that would well serve Arnold Schwarzenegger some 37 years later. The result was a landslide victory over two-term incumbent Pat Brown.

Although Reagan campaigned against big government, he was able to do little to drastically curtail governmental spending and services after he became governor. In fact, as opposed to taxation and "big government" as he was, he was forced to preside over an increase in taxes in order to maintain essential services and to balance the budget in the wake of a deficit left by the Brown administration. Like many other Republican governors over the last 40 years, Ronald Reagan's policy agenda was checkmated and his relations with the legislature strained by Democratic control over the state senate and assembly for most of his tenure. Nonetheless, Reagan won reelection easily in 1970, although not as impressively as in 1966.

Like so many governors before Reagan and since, this governor harbored long-standing presidential aspirations. As early as 1968, with less than two years' experience in the governorship, or any other public office, he mounted an unsuccessful challenge against Richard Nixon for the Republican presidential nomination. Not seeking a third term as governor, he left Sacramento at the end of his second term in January 1975 and restarted his quest for the presidency. In 1976, he just barely failed to wrest the Republican nomination from Gerald Ford, the incumbent President. A third run at the White House in 1980 was the charm. He captured the Republican nomination and swept to a comfortable general election victory over the incumbent Democrat, Jimmy Carter. Four years later he was overwhelmingly propelled into a second term, winning 49 of the 50 states.

Reagan's managerial style as governor foreshadowed the style he later adopted in the White House. His approach was to appoint individuals to key executive positions who shared his own "small government," probusiness, antiregulation philosophy and to then allow them to carry out his policies with a minimum of micromanagement. In his later career, he was sometimes characterized as a "9 to 5" president, meaning he did not become involved in the time-consuming detail work of governance but instead provided broad general direction. It was a style he honed as California's governor.

Edmund G. "Jerry" Brown, Jr.

Jerry Brown was, in his way, a product of the 1960s. His very quick rise to the governorship after only four years in a state political office, that of secretary of state, was propelled by the Watergate era's sense of disenchantment with conventional politics and politicians. The time was right for a public figure like Jerry Brown, who combined newness with unconventional ideas and a nontraditional lifestyle. As governor, he flew tourist class, rode in a Plymouth rather than a Cadillac, refused to sign autographs, lived in an apartment in downtown Sacramento rather than the ornate governor's mansion, and went off on an African safari with Linda Ronstadt.

As in his personal style, Jerry Brown "broke the mold" for the way governors typically approach their job. His own political and policy goals defied easy definition. Unlike most Democrats of that era, he was reluctant to commit the state to huge new enterprises, stressing an "era of limits" instead. On the other hand, he was probably the most environmentally oriented governor the state had ever had, a strong supporter of civil rights, and a champion of farm workers in their struggles to unionize and improve their pay and working conditions. Creation of the Agricultural Labor Relations Board to oversee farm labor issues was probably the biggest policy accomplishment of his gubernatorial tenure.

Brown was also an early proponent of "diversity" in filling the top positions in the state's executive and judicial branches. He was the first governor to actively seek out opportunities to appoint women and people of color to cabinet and departmental leadership positions as well as to the state's courts, including the state supreme court.

Brown's organizational style was nothing like that of any other governor, before or since. He was uninterested in formal lines of authority and communication and ignored the "chain of command" in seeking out information and advice. His cabinet meetings, held without benefit of formal agenda, followed no regular schedule but were called anytime—day or night—that the governor had an idea or policy he wished to explore.

Brown (following the pattern established by Ronald Reagan) entered his initial race for the Democratic presidential nomination after only two years in the governorship. His "new spirit" attracted voters, but his entry into the race came too late to stop the nomination from going to Jimmy Carter. After losing the presidential nomination in 1976, Brown easily won reelection as governor in 1978. In spite of his reelection, Brown was already planning a second run for the presidential nomination two years away. Oblivious to what the polls indicated, Brown entered the 1980 presidential primary election, but after inglorious defeats in several states, he quit the race.

Back home in California, Brown's popularity began to wane. Although he served during a time of Democratic majorities in both the state senate and the state assembly, his relationship with the legislature grew increasingly chilly. Many Democratic lawmakers found him indifferent to their party's typical bread-and-butter issues and overly enthusiastic in his embrace of Proposition 13, the property tax reduction measure, once it had passed in 1978. Consequently, he holds the dubious distinction of being the last governor to have suffered a veto override, even though the legislature was controlled by Democrats!

The final blow to his public standing was delivered by a tiny insect. An infestation of medflies posed a threat to the state's fruit crops, and farmers demanded a program of aerial pesticide spraying. Citing health concerns, Brown resisted, creating great animosity in agriculture and reinforcing his image as a flaky visionary. By the end of his term in 1982, when he ran against Pete Wilson for the U.S. Senate, most California voters had had enough of "Governor Moonbeam." He lost that election by five percentage points.

More recently, however, Jerry Brown has reemerged. After a short stint as state chair of the Democratic Party, Brown, who had been hosting a political talk show in the San Francisco Bay Area, was elected mayor of Oakland in 1998, a position he held for eight years. In 2006 he reemerged at the statewide level, winning election to the position of Attorney General.

It could be argued that in many ways the California governorship was a position ill suited for Jerry Brown's personality, goals, and considerable talents. As governor, he was a visionary in a job whose most crucial formal powers relate to control, such as through the line-item veto, rather than broad, creative policy innovation. As a futuristic thinker, Brown was unconcerned with the day-to-day management functions of the governorship. However, the powers of the office are essentially management oriented and are less adaptable to broad, creative policy innovation. He also served at the time of

Proposition 13's passage and the beginning of the "tax revolt," a movement that sharply limited (and continues to limit) options available to politicians and policy makers.

George "Duke" Deukmejian

On January 3, 1983, George Deukmejian was sworn in as California's thirty-fifth governor. In contrast to Jerry Brown's promise of a "new spirit," Governor Deukmejian pledged a pragmatic "commonsense society." Alluding to his predecessor, Deukmejian promised to appoint "a judiciary with a more balanced view" and to change "regulations which have choked off growth and progress." Unlike his two immediate predecessors, Deukmejian came to the governorship with a lengthy track record in elective office, in both the legislative and the executive wings. In his long career as an assembly member, state senator, and finally attorney general, he had consistently carved out probusiness, antitax, and strong law-and-order positions.

The most pressing problem Governor Deukmejian faced in his first term in office concerned the state budget. Although the budget must be balanced when enacted into law, it can become out of balance if anticipated revenues fall short of state spending rates. The 1982–1983 budget, the last prepared by Jerry Brown, fell $1.6 billion into deficit.

During his campaign, Deukmejian pledged he would not raise general taxes, and he rejected even a temporary one-cent increase in the sales tax proposed by Democratic legislators to offset the deficit. Loans from banks allowed the state to meet its obligations for the remainder of the 1982–1983 fiscal year, and these debts were repaid during the next fiscal year.

Deukmejian's margin of victory over Los Angeles Mayor Tom Bradley in 1982 had been razor thin. In a rematch of the contestants four years later, Deukmejian was given another four-year term by a landslide 61 percent majority. Nonetheless, his second term in the governor's office involved a considerable amount of rough sledding. His principal accomplishments were recasting the California judiciary (by appointing two out of every three of that era's state judges while he was governor), keeping his campaign pledge not to raise general taxes, and using his veto power to contain the growth of state government, except in the area of corrections, where he led a very large scale prison construction program. He also suffered two highly visible defeats: one involving his desire to shut down Cal-OSHA (a state agency overseeing worker safety) and the other concerning his attempt to place Dan Lungren in the position of state treasurer, following the death of Jesse Unruh. In the first controversy, the courts ruled that he could not use the line-item veto power to completely dismantle a program that had been legislatively created. In the case of the nomination of Dan Lungren to the treasury job, the state senate refused to confirm.

Without suffering a single override in his eight years as governor, Deukmejian established new records for using general and line-item vetoes. As a mirror opposite of his predecessor, Jerry Brown, Deukmejian saw his role as governor almost exclusively in terms of maintaining control and preventing bad ideas (in his opinion) from becoming policy. And it can be argued that the powers of the governorship are much better honed for this negative agenda. As effective as Deukmejian was in using the powers of office to keep things under control, however, he was faulted for failing to produce positive proposals to deal with the changing needs of California.

Pete Wilson

In the late 1980s, the California Republican Party had a problem. George Deukmejian had announced he would not seek a third term in the 1990 elections, and chances of gaining control of either the senate or assembly were slim to none. Without a Republican governor to checkmate Democratic legislative majorities, the post-1990 legislative redistricting was a likely to be as devastating to Republican fortunes as was the 1980s remapping. Republican leaders, believing, probably accurately, that U.S. Senator Pete Wilson was the only Republican with a chance to win, prevailed on Wilson to give up his Senate seat and run for governor in 1990.

With his gubernatorial victory over Democrat Dianne Feinstein in November 1990, Republicans could heave a sigh of relief. But Pete Wilson was not a "typical" Republican governor, at least not in the George Deukmejian sense. Though both entered the governor's office facing budget deficits, Deukmejian and Wilson represented contrasting views and styles. Most fundamental, Wilson never made the no-new-taxes pledge favored by his predecessor. Deukmejian opposed funds for family planning, whereas Wilson believed in reducing burdens on society whenever possible through "prevention programs." Deukmejian supported the location of pesticide regulation in the pro-grower California Department of Food and Agriculture, and Wilson would suggest moving this responsibility to a newly created environmental protection agency. They also disagreed concerning the advisability of drilling for offshore oil.

Saying that he was endeavoring to spread the pain caused by his inherited deficit, Governor Wilson delivered a budget to the legislature in January 1991 that featured cuts in welfare and school spending but also hikes in automobile registration fees and university fees and new taxes on items such as candy, newspapers, and bottled water. Though some Republicans opposed the tax hikes and some Democrats took exception to the cuts in welfare and education, many legislators of both parties called the governor's first budget a serious attempt to deal with California's fiscal crisis. As in his campaigns for public office, Governor Wilson seemed prepared to sacrifice votes at both ends of the political spectrum to hold the center. The pattern of his early appointments also had a moderate, bipartisan tilt. For example, he appointed a moderate Republican legislator, John Seymour, to fill the U.S. Senate position he had vacated, much to the disgruntlement of more conservative Republicans in the legislature.

These early indications that Wilson's administration could avoid partisan and policy gridlock proved overly optimistic. However, the legislature and governor were able to agree on an overhaul of California's workers' compensation program, a goal that had eluded policy makers for many years. Pete Wilson did win reelection, coming from behind in the polls to comfortably defeat Kathleen Brown, daughter of Pat Brown and sister of Jerry Brown. Like his predecessor, though, most of Wilson's tenure as governor was marked by increasingly bitter struggle with the legislature.

It is fair to say that both situational and personal factors conspired to dash early hopes of a new spirit in Sacramento. Most of Wilson's years in the governor's office were marked by constrained revenues and deep deficits. As a result, annual budget deliberations, which usually ran well past the July 1 deadline, dissolved into protracted partisan stalemates. Wilson's early emphasis on preventive programs, such as prenatal care, was also a victim of the budgetary constraints. As well, like Ronald Reagan and George Deukmejian before him, Republican Pete Wilson had to contend with a legislature that was under constant Democratic control. With his own legislative agenda blocked, Wilson regularly adopted the initiative route for his policy priorities, and many of these propositions, dealing with issues such as illegal immigration, governors' budgetary powers, and labor union use of membership dues for political purposes drove a deeper wedge between him and the legislature's Democratic majority. His very visible and public role on behalf of ending the University of California's affirmative action admissions policy further eroded his centrist, moderate credentials.

In addition to his problems with Democrats, Wilson never enjoyed the full support of the Republican caucuses in the state senate and, especially, in the state assembly. Republican conservatives had distrusted him ever since he supported Gerald Ford over Ronald Reagan for the 1976 Republican presidential nomination, and that distrust was deepened by his pro-choice abortion position and moderate stances on other noneconomic policy issues.

The final factor in the demise of Wilson's hopes to rise above partisan and ideological political warfare was personal: that old friend of California governors, Potomac fever. In his 1994 campaign for reelection, he promised not to seek the presidency during his second administration, but he quickly broke that promise and embarked on a futile run for the Republican nomination. The attempt went nowhere, and he dropped out without seriously threatening the front-runners. Like Jerry Brown before him, failure cost Wilson prestige and support back home. Even though his political career ended in frustration and diminished public support, Pete Wilson could make one claim no other Republican could: he was the last Republican to win a top-of-the-ticket regularly scheduled election until 2006.

Gray Davis

Early in the election season, in the winter and spring of 1998, nobody gave Gray Davis much chance to win his party's gubernatorial nomination, let alone the governorship. Severely underfunded compared to his two Democratic self-financed opponents, Davis continued to plod along, stressing his experience. Ultimately, in a kind of tortoise-and-hare way, Davis caught and passed his two inexperienced, big-spending opponents and won the nomination.

Still, most Sacramento insiders rated him a decided underdog in the general election against Republican Dan Lungren, the state's attorney general, who had breezed through his primary unopposed. Lungren was articulate, energetic, and telegenic. In contrast, pundits joked that Davis's first name was a perfect description of his appeal. True to his style, however, Davis continued to pound away on a few basic points: his own experience (he had served as chief of staff for a governor, in the state assembly, and as both controller and lieutenant governor prior to running for the governorship), his support for education, and his support for a woman's right to choose. He was also greatly helped by the endorsement of law enforcement unions. These endorsements blunted much of Lungren's appeal. Lungren ran a race more attuned to attorney general than governor. While the Lungren campaign cast about for issues that would resonate with voters, Davis continued his highly disciplined, almost unvarying message. Early polls showed Davis in the lead; throughout the campaign he continued to build on that lead, sweeping into office by 20 percentage points.

And what can be said about Gray Davis's performance as governor? The hallmarks of his campaign for the office were caution, safety, moderation, and success. The same can be said for the first two years of his governorship. Although Davis was a prolabor Democrat, his Democratic colleagues in the legislature were consistently frustrated by his threatened and actual vetoes of legislation that might strongly offend business, from whom he was receiving campaign financial support. His approach to budget making was, at least until the appearance of the recall movement, also consistently centrist, avoiding long-term fiscal commitments for social programs favored by Democratic law-makers and their constituencies. Davis's stance on law-and-order issues, such as his parole policies, didn't seem to differ from those of his Republican predecessors either.

On top of these policy differences with other Democrats, Davis's personality, or at least most insiders' perception of it, did not endear him to Sacramento politicians. He was, in this capital city, generally regarded as cold and aloof, and many believed he placed personal political calculations well ahead of any real policy loyalties or goals.

Nonetheless, until 2001, the situational factors surrounding his governorship seemed uniformly positive. The California economy was booming, thus easing the usual budgetary problems. Not surprisingly, given the good economic times, the California public seemed generally content. Davis's safe, centrist, no-chances-taken approach to governance and his popular positions on education reform seemed to be exactly what the public wanted.

The stability of Davis's early years in the governorship was shattered by the energy crisis, terrorist attacks and their threat, war in Afghanistan and then Iraq, economic bust, and a massive state budget deficit. Gray Davis, nonvisionary, cautious, slow moving, and uncharismatic, was not such a good fit for these new, unsettled times. Lacking a reserve of personal popularity and unable to articulate a broad vision of where the

BOX 4.5

Potomac Fever: Is There Any Cure?

Going back to Hiram Johnson, California governors have been particularly susceptible to "Potomac fever," the urge to seek the U.S. presidency. As the state grew and became a polit-ical, cultural, and media center of the nation, it was fairly natural that its governors would be "short-listed" as potential White House residents or, at the least, vice presidents.

But are governors' presidential ambitions good for the state? If those ambitions are fulfilled, the answer is almost certainly yes. A Californian in the White House means many good things for California, just as a Texan in the White House is good news for that state. On the other hand, a governor seeking his or her presidential nomination is going to be spending a lot of time out of state in places like Iowa and New Hampshire. The policy agendas adopted by these governors may be targeted at a national voting audience rather than the most pressing needs of the state. When a governor tries and fails to win the nom-ination, Californians grumble about their "absent" governor. Jerry Brown and Pete Wilson are the latest examples of such failed candidacies. Back home, these disappointed national aspirants found that their state-based support had also eroded.

state needed to be going, Davis was vulnerable to the upsurge of voter anger and frustration that accompanied the end of placid times. By late 2002, Gray Davis's stock of public support was running low, and his relatively narrow victory over a weak reelection opponent in November of that year was, seen in retrospect, a storm warning for the recall disaster that awaited him. Aware of the approaching recall and sensing the need to rally his core constituency, Davis signed legislative enactments he had currently opposed—among them, a bill granting undocumented immigrants the right to apply for driving licenses. This conversion only hardened the public's image of him as a politician who would do anything to win.

"Politics as usual," an acceptable formula when things are going well, becomes a negative rallying cry when voters are frightened and angry. In such times, voters look for big-scale change, even when they can't agree on the nature of those changes. Experience and technical expertise, the hallmarks of Davis's rise to the governorship, lose their political and popular hold. Given this, the recall of Gray Davis, and his replacement by political neophyte Arnold Schwarzenegger, is perhaps less than shocking.

Arnold Schwarzenegger

Governor Schwarzenegger seeks to be a "big-picture" governor, perhaps in the mode of Ronald Reagan. Like his Hollywood predecessor, Schwarzenegger came to the governor's office without having held prior elective office and with a minimum of substantive, insider policy knowledge. What he does best is apply his considerable personal and communication skills (again echoing Reagan) to his broadest goals of political reform, a more "business friendly" set of regulatory policies, and lowered expenditures and taxes. However, Schwarzenegger is not as consistently ideological or partisan as Reagan. His proclamation, following a series of defeats described below, of a "post-partisanship era" is more reminiscent of Earl Warren than Ronald Reagan.

On the other hand, especially in his earlier gubernatorial career, and again like Ronald Reagan, he at times got into trouble going "off script" and speaking off the top of his head. Careless references (such as his characterization of Democratic legislators as "girlie men") may have delighted his hard-core support but also complicated his relationships with other Sacramento politicians whose help he needed. By his own admission, he overstepped in taking on public employee unions and the legislature by sponsoring four ballot initiatives that would have reduced public school teachers' job protections, make it harder for public employee unions to use membership dues for campaign contributions, shift budgetary control and discretion to the governorship, and take the power of legislative and congressional redistricting out of the legislature's hands. Placed on a late 2005 special election ballot, all four went down to crushing defeat, and the governor's support levels plummeted.

Many of these proposals echoed initiatives sponsored by his Republican predecessor, Pete Wilson, and as in the earlier attempts, left the governor isolated. But Schwarzenegger showed himself to be a quick learner and a nimble strategist. In the wake of his special election fiasco, he essentially recast his governorship in the mold of Earl Warren. His very public and even international leadership in the fight against greenhouse gas emissions distanced him from Republican President George Bush, who is not at all popular in California, and established his "green" credentials. His advocacy of some form of universal or at least expanded health care protection and his appointment of a moderate jurist to the State Supreme Court are also moves that increased his support beyond the traditional Republican base. At the same time, he has maintained Republican support by his opposition to tax increases. The wisdom of his new approach was evident in his 2006 landslide reelection, where he collected large majorities in Republican core areas and made inroads into typically Democratic regions.

His prospects for a successful second term depend on several factors. One of them is his ability to generate public support for his policies while at the same time working on the inside with the Democrat-controlled legislature. On the public side of the job, his first months in office were an unqualified success. He succeeded, though in a mirror-opposite manner, in capturing the public's fascination with his lack of conventionality in much the way that Jerry Brown did. His fleet of Hummer megavehicles, his penchant for cigars, and his free and easy, perhaps even glib, tone kept him at the center of media attention. The media's penchant for referring to him simply as "Arnold" indicated they had bought into his breezy style.

But, as with Jerry Brown, there are limits to the politics of personality. The excitement of a new face and style in the governor's office fades as tough issues don't get resolved, and the familiar pattern of policy stalemate sets in. In short, a charismatic governor with innovative proposals still needs to follow through with policy successes. And these in turn require the help of other political actors with their own agendas and goals. Prominent among political skeptics are conservative Republican legislators, who don't buy into his "post-partisan" approach. And as always, circumstances beyond governors' control shape and limit chances for gubernatorial success.

The annual budget process is the clearest case in point. As was true for Gray Davis, governors get credit when economic times are good, and get blamed when the state's economy slumps. But in fact, California's economic well-being is determined much more by global and national economic conditions than by anything the governor can directly control. In good economic years, meaning lots of tax revenue flowing into state coffers, passing a budget is much easier than when revenue slumps in response to economic decline. Californians want their budget passed on time, or nearly so, and both legislative and gubernatorial support levels take a hit when the budget is many weeks or months late. In 2007, the economy was jolted by the housing market downturn, and budget passage was seven weeks late. (See Chapter 10 for a discussion of the budget process.) For a governor whose main appeal is a perceived ability to shake up the system and get things done, the appearance of politics as usual in Sacramento may be particularly deflating.

Nor is there much chance that the governor can claim major success in overcoming California's near-chronic budget problems, at least in the immediate future. The economic fallout from the 2007 southern wildfires have yet to be calculated, but the final figure will be in the billions. And the 2007–2008 budget, although advertised as "balanced," is in reality a deficit budget of perhaps $14 billion, leading into a 2008–2009 budget deficit already projected at $8 billion.

Ironically, part of the dilemma can be traced back to Schwarzenegger's decisions shortly after winning the governorship: he reduced the car license tax and paid off part of the then-existing deficit by selling bonds, with premiums that must be paid now (Walters, 2007). But the broader lesson here is that governors, regardless of their personal strengths, abilities, and popular appeal, are subject to constraints and events (e.g., economic downturns and natural disasters) well beyond their control.

In part, budget struggles represents the long-standing differences between Democratic and Republican policy priorities. In lean budget years, Democrats prefer to maintain social program spending levels even if that means tax increases; Republicans would prefer cuts in those programs in order to avoid raising taxes. Governor Schwarzenegger must contend on this issue with the legislative Democratic majority. On top of this, the Republican legislative caucus, not pleased with his "post-partisan," moderate profile, cannot be counted on to support him up and down the line. Like Pete Wilson before him, Governor Schwarzenegger may be hard pressed to maintain a stable and dependable base of support within the capital's political community.

In short, there are factors that limit or enhance a governor's prospects for success beyond personality. Personal factors are certainly a key ingredient in governors' successes or failures, as evidenced by Gray Davis, but institutional, political, and economic factors also crucially define and limit governors' options. If these other forces are not positively aligned, the long-term prospects for "personality politics" are not very favorable.

SUMMARY

California governors receive national attention, and the promise and lure of the presidency have become a part of the job. Whether that's a good or bad thing is an open question. But flirtations with presidential politics, unless they succeed, tend to complicate a governor's ability to lead back at home. On the job, a governor is equipped with a powerful arsenal of formal powers, among them the line-item and general legislative vetoes and the ability to appoint like-minded individuals to powerful executive and judicial positions. However, the amount of success a governor enjoys will ultimately be determined by her or his personal skills and by situational factors not controlled by the governor. Governors must often contend with a legislature controlled by partisan or ideological opponents as well as a plural executive system that installs other politicians, often political rivals with divergent personal and policy goals, in strategically placed executive offices. And the state of the economy and perhaps the overall governability of this diverse and divisive state are forces that define any gubernatorial administration but exist well beyond its power to control.

REFERENCES

California Constitutional Revision Commission. *Final Report and Recommendations to the Governor and the Legislature.* Sacramento: 1996.
Walters, Dan. "Governor's Milestone Oozes Irony." *Sacramento Bee* (November 18, 2007).

CHAPTER five

THE CALIFORNIA JUDICIARY

Though it has been over three decades since the late Rose Bird served as chief justice of the California Supreme Court, her name recognition among Californians remains relatively high. On the other hand, few Californians could name the current chief justice, Ronald George. Bird and the supreme court she led were front-page political news from the late 1970s through the middle 1980s. Later supreme courts, much less activist and controversial, pretty much dropped off the public's radar screen.

The supreme court's low profile does not mean that all is well with the state's court system. The new problems center not on controversial decisions, as was the case during the Bird era, but on the ability of the system to meet the increasing demands placed on it. The rise in caseloads, the actual number of cases being tried in the courts, has in no way been matched by an increase in the judicial system's productive capacity. As with so many areas in California's public sector, the problem is money or, more accurately, the shortage of it. The result has been clogged court schedules and long delays, generally around two years, sometimes longer, for noncriminal cases. (Because criminal defendants have a constitutional right to a "speedy trial," their cases go to the front of the line.)

The system's inability to hear cases in a timely manner has prompted a partial privatization of the judicial system. Increasingly, private litigants opt to have their cases heard not in public courts but by retired judges in the employ of arbitration services or private firms. These services are not cheap; the ex-judges command fees that far exceed what they were paid as state judges. The new system—politely titled "alternative dispute resolution," and less euphemistically "rent-a-judge"—delivers timely decisions and settlements for those who can afford them.

This two-tier civil case decision system, private and public, raises a philosophical question. Is it right that litigants with plenty of money can get their cases settled quickly while the less affluent have to wait their turn in the traditional public court system?

Meanwhile, the underfunded public court system faces other problems. The crush of criminal cases that many assumed would result from adoption of the "three-strikes" sentencing policy failed to reach the levels predicted by three-strikes opponents, but that situation could change, especially if there is a sharp rise in the crime rate. For example, felony court filings in California superior courts, generally stable or even declining between 1996 and 2002, have started rising again, reaching a 2007 level approximately 15% higher than 1996 (California Judicial Council, 2007). (A fuller discussion of three strikes is presented later in this chapter.) Even when criminal and civil cases get their court date, rounding up jurors poses an increasingly problematic issue. Potential jurors, picked out of voter registration and automobile registration lists, are, in increasing numbers, just ignoring summonses to appear for jury duty. The small stipend paid by most counties is evidently insufficient compensation for the inconvenience of spending a day in court to find out whether one will serve as a juror on a case that may last only hours or may run several days, weeks, or, in the worst scenario, months.

The court system and legislature continue to work on these problems. The state has absorbed more of the operating costs of local courts from the cash-strapped counties. Trial courts have unified in an attempt to create efficiencies of scale and resource allocation in the face of the ever-increasing caseloads borne by the courts. Retired justices who serve in the private court system are now prohibited from also serving as temporary substitute judges in the regular state court system. And there is a major push on the legislature to increase and fund the number of authorized judicial positions. Whether these reforms can match the growing demands on the court system is the major question facing the state's judicial branch.

These fiscal and administrative problems of the court system are not just a source of inconvenience for those whose cases must be heard. For better or worse, courts have always played a part in the political process, and that part is increasing. Courts are "political" because they are called on to interpret and even make public policy through their functions of judicial review and judicial interpretation. In cases of judicial interpretation, courts are asked to decide the meaning of a particular law. For example, a conservative legal group might sue the University of California or California State University system claiming that its minority outreach programs violate the provisions of Proposition 209's ban on racial or gender preferences in hiring and admissions. It would be up to the courts to decide exactly what that proposition allows and prohibits in the name of affirmative action. By deciding what the law really means, courts actually decide what the policy will be.

Judicial review involves a judgment as to whether a law or an action by government is, in itself, constitutional. In 2004, the California Supreme Court was asked to decide whether or not the state's voter-approved law restricting marrige to a man and woman violated the state constitution. If a law such as this is found to be unconstitutional, it is null and void. Only a change in the state constitution itself can then resurrect that law or policy.

In the modern era, courts are increasingly called on to play a political and policy role, for a variety of reasons. A complex society generates complex policy and complex laws that require judicial untangling. Legislative enactments tend to be written with a degree of generality that leaves their interpretation open to question and hence judicial interpretation. Policy gridlock within and between elected institutions leads citizens and interest groups to the courts as a strategy for resolving political and policy conflicts. Finally, California's heavy use of the initiative often results in the enactment of policy that is poorly and ambiguously drafted, as well as constitutionally suspect, again creating the need for judicial interpretation and review.

A CHANGED JUDICIAL SYSTEM

Traditionally, the judicial system was divided into four levels: supreme court, courts of appeal, superior courts, and municipal courts. These latter two court systems tried a variety of legal cases involving alleged criminal behavior (misdemeanors and felonies) and civil matters including disputes between individuals such as divorces, suits for damages arising from automobile accidents, and broken contracts, as well as suits between government agencies and private citizens and organizations. The more serious civil and criminal cases (felonies as opposed to misdemeanors) were tried in superior courts; lesser cases (for example, civil suits involving less money or misdemeanor criminal cases) were assigned to the municipal courts.

The supreme court and courts of appeal remain the same, but local levels no longer use a two-tier court system. Following voter approval of a legislatively proposed constitutional change in 1998, these courts' judges were granted the option of unifying their municipal and superior structures into a single superior court. By 2001, all 58 counties had approved unification; thus, all counties now possess a single, unified superior court, responsible for all cases previously heard in either municipal or superior court.

The superior courts are the workhorses in the system (about 9 million cases are filed with them annually), and it is here that most cases begin and end. Because the superior courts hear the cases first, they have what is termed *original jurisdiction*. These courts are often referred to as *trial courts*, where the two sides present their facts and argue their cases. Depending on the desires of the litigants (in criminal cases, this choice belongs to just the defendant), superior court cases can be heard by a jury or just by the presiding judge. *Appellate jurisdiction* refers to a higher court to which the dissatisfied litigant appeals the verdict, hoping the justices will find an error in the original trial sufficient to warrant a new hearing. In California's new three-level system, then, superior courts are the trial courts, while the courts of appeal and supreme court are the appellate courts. Unlike in superior court, cases at the appellate levels are never heard by juries, but instead by just the justices (usually three at the court of appeal level and by the entire membership of seven in the California Supreme Court).

Superior Courts

Each county has a single superior court, although the number of judges assigned to that court varies widely according to the county's population, and hence caseload. The Los Angeles Superior Court utilizes more than 400 judges, making it the largest trial court system in the nation. Superior courts in the most rural counties consist of as few as two judges. Superior courts are the original venue for all criminal trials, such as the O.J. Simpson and Michael Jackson cases, and practically all civil proceedings, including those that interpret or review the meaning and constitutionality of public policy.

Courts of Appeal

In 1928, the legislature divided the state into five appellate districts, with Sacramento, San Francisco, Fresno, Los Angeles, and San Diego as the district seats. In 1981, the legislature created a new sixth district appellate court in San Jose. These courts have appellate jurisdiction over matters coming out of superior courts within their geographic areas. Appellate court justices usually sit as a panel of three and decide whether to grant a new trial because an error was made in the original hearing. Error here refers not to the facts of the case, as determined by the jury or judge, but rather to legal and administrative questions arising out of the trial. Although everyone is entitled to one appeal, only about half of those eligible contest their verdicts. If the appellate justices determine that the trial judge erred in the handling of the case, then a new trial may be ordered. However, most trial proceedings are upheld. Losers at the court of appeal level have a final recourse, appeal to the California Supreme Court. The supreme court's jurisdiction over practically all appeals is discretionary, however, meaning that it is not required to take up these appeals at all. Only a small percentage of cases appealed to this top rung of the court system are actually heard.

Supreme Court

The California Supreme Court is composed of six associate justices and one chief justice. The majority of the cases that come before the court are appeals from lower courts, although original appellate jurisdiction exists for a limited number of cases dealing with special court procedures and death penalty cases. More than 5,000 cases are appealed to the supreme court from the courts of appeal each year; however, fewer than 10 percent are actually accepted for court review. Cases are accepted only upon the affirmative vote of at least four of the justices. How the court exercises its discretion over the cases it will take up defines its personality. An "activist" supreme court will seek out those cases with broad political and policy ramifications. A less activist court will avoid cases with the potential of overturning current law or previous court decisions.

Once an item is accepted for review, the chief justice assigns the case to a justice for preparation of another recommendation—this time a suggested resolution of the issues contained in the case. This proposed resolution of the case is circulated to all seven justices, who give a preliminary response in agreement or disagreement with the suggested outcome. When four or more justices signify they tentatively agree with the proposal to resolve the issues in the case, the chief justice schedules the item for oral argument. (The practice of writing a proposed opinion before hearing oral argument has led some critics of the high court to argue that the jurists have already made up their minds before listening to the lawyers present the appeal.)

Excluding July and August, the California Supreme Court, which normally meets in San Francisco rather than the state capital, hears oral argument for one week of every month. Unlike trial court proceedings, where evidence may have to be read into the record at considerable length, the oral portion of appellate review is concise. Having read the trial court transcript, attorneys' briefs, and internal recommendations in advance, the justices on the high court know a great deal about a case before hearing oral argument. As a result, appellate jurists tend to interrupt lawyers making oral presentations to ask incisive questions pertaining to the most pivotal points in a case. Soon

---

BOX
5.1

Court Consolidation: Good-Bye to the Muni Courts

In June of 1998, the voters approved a legislatively proposed constitutional amendment that allowed the absorption of all California's municipal courts into their respective county superior courts. Under the amendment, if the majority of a county's superior court judges and a majority of its municipal judges approved, the two courts would be merged as a single county superior court, elevating the former municipal court judges to the new rank of superior court judges. The new consolidated court would assume jurisdiction over all the cases that formerly went to either one of the two courts.

Initially, some doubted whether all or most judges would agree to consolidation, especially those superior court judges being asked to share their position with the heretofore "inferior" municipal court judges. The Los Angeles County courts, by far the state's largest court system, were, in fact, slow to come around. Ultimately, one by one, the 58 county courts voted "yes," and by early 2001, the last remaining municipal courts were absorbed into their superior courts.

Court consolidation was a legislative response to the court system's funding problems and backlog of cases. The theory is that larger court units will enjoy economies of scale and that the availability of many more judges to hear the largest, most complex, and longest-lasting cases (which the old municipal court judges were not empowered to hear) will expedite the process and reduce case backlog. Early reports on court consolidation have been positive; whether the streamlining ultimately works well enough to substantially reduce waiting time for cases to be heard, and hence the demand for private rent-a-judge services, remains to be seen.

---

after hearing oral argument, the seven justices on the high court hold a conference. If the proposed resolution of the case that was prepared prior to hearing oral argument is still favored by four or more members of the court, the justice who prepared the initial resolution of the issues is responsible for writing the majority opinion in the case. Should the majority have shifted away from the initial recommendation as a result of hearing oral argument, the chief justice will ask one of the judges making up the new majority to draft the lead opinion. Once the majority opinion is prepared and circulated among all the justices, dissenting and concurring opinions may be written to accompany the release of the court's decision.

The Bird Court

Until the late 1970s, the California Supreme Court enjoyed a reputation as an independent, professional, and progressive body. It did not shy away from major social issues such as ordering equalization of per-pupil expenditures regardless of the local tax base (*Serrano v. Priest*, 1971) and identifying "reverse discrimination" brought about by affirmative action programs designed to equalize opportunities for minorities and women (*Bakke v. State Board of Regents*, 1976). In 1972 and 1976, the court declared the

TABLE 5.1	California's Court Organization: Number of Courts and Judges (2007)	
Type of Court	**Courts**	**Judges***
Supreme court	1	7
Courts of appeal	6	105
Superior courts	58	1,548*

Includes currently filled plus authorized positions.
Source: California Judicial Council, 2007.

death penalty in the state unconstitutional, although subsequent legislative action restored capital punishment. It was, therefore, an "activist" court.

Although many of these decisions were quite controversial, the supreme court itself did not become a storm center until the effects of Governor Jerry Brown's judicial appointments began to be felt. As discussed in Chapter 4, one of Brown's major priorities was to appoint a more inclusive, diverse set of judges, essentially breaking the older pattern that made the judicial corps an almost entirely white, male enclave. Many of these judicial appointments were controversial, but Rose Bird stood out.

At the time of her appointment as chief justice of the state supreme court, Bird was Brown's secretary of the Food and Agriculture Agency and mirrored the Brown administration's pro-farm-labor tilt. As a result, she entered the job with one set of enemies—agricultural growers—already in place. Her lack of any experience as a judge and the fact that her legal experience came mostly from the criminal defendant side of the justice system while working in the Santa Clara County public defender's office raised the hackles of legal traditionalists and the law enforcement community. Of course, she was young and a woman, two characteristics notably missing among state supreme court justices, let alone among chief justices.

Nothing Bird did during her tenure as the state's top jurist lessened the opposition to her. Rumors that her abrasive style undermined morale among other supreme court justices and court personnel persisted. Her relations with the press were strained, at best. It was the tenor of supreme court decisions under her leadership, however, that resulted in animosity on the part of most of the voting public. Among those decisions that rankled citizens were the approximately 60 cases where Bird and a majority of the court voted to set aside the death penalty imposed on convicted murderers by the trial courts. In her defense, Bird argued that she and her allies on the court were only doing their jobs, dissecting lower-court decisions based on a poorly written death penalty initiative that produced confusion, and hence reversible error, among juries and trial court judges. Her opponents charged her with using her legal position to render a popularly enacted law null and void based on her own philosophical and political preferences. Most voters opted for the latter interpretation. George Deukmejian and all other Republican candidates in the 1986 general election made opposition to three justices up for retention, Cruz Reynoso, Joseph Grodin, and especially Bird, key aspects of their campaigns. Anti-Bird organizations, led by the Victims for Court Reform, spent $8 million to defeat the three. Bird ran her own $2 million campaign, such as it was, through the Committee to Conserve the Courts. The thrust of her message was that the attacks against the justices represented an assault on judicial independence. The opposition focused on the three justices' reluctance to uphold death penalty convictions.

These campaigns raised a basic issue regarding the balance between judicial independence and judicial accountability. If judges are denied additional years on the courts because their decisions run counter to public opinion, then they may well consider public feelings rather than constitutional obligations before rendering some decisions. On the other hand, the public has a right to expect judges to set aside their personal feelings in deciding cases. Another problem presented in the effort to oust Bird, Reynoso, and Grodin concerned the way in which complicated legal issues were reduced to 30-second ads for television. Although judges are political figures, they have no vested constituency to which they can make promises as do other politicians. Judges are prohibited by the canons of judicial ethics from campaigning in a partisan manner or discussing cases. (See Box 5.2 for more discussion on the issues raised by the Bird episode.)

At least in this election, voters had little difficulty in deciding these issues. By a wide margin, they voted not to retain Rose Bird or her two liberal allies on the supreme court. For the first time in the half-century history of the appellate judge retention election system, three judges were summarily removed from the court.

The Lucas and George Courts

When the voters removed Bird, Reynoso, and Grodin, they presented Governor Deukmejian with the opportunity to make three appointments to the high court, including

---

BOX 5.2
Public Opinion and the Judges—How Much Linkage Do We Want?

In the federal judicial system, judges, once appointed, serve for life. The only form of removal is impeachment, generally reserved for those who actually violate the law. But in California, as Rose Bird and two of her high-court allies discovered, judicial job security is not so iron-clad. Unpopular decisions can mean the end of a career.

Some argue that California judges, just like their federal counterparts, need complete independence from the voters if they are going to be able to do their job, which includes upholding the law against popular but unconstitutional ideas and protecting unpopular minorities against a "tyranny of the majority."

Others argue that in a day and age when judges make public policy just like any other politicians, voters should have a right to remove them when those policies consistently deny the public what it wants. Why should judges be insulated from voters just because they wear black robes?

Should California adopt the federal model and grant life tenure to its judges? Should it subject its higher court justices to more frequent elections with actual candidates running against them? Or is the current system of long terms interrupted by retention votes rather than competitive elections about the right mix between judicial independence and judicial accountability?

the chief justice. Deukmejian named Malcolm Lucas, who was already serving as associate justice, to the top position. Lucas and the new members steered the court on a much different route than that taken by the Bird court. In general, the new regime was much less likely to set aside the death penalty, and it was more probusiness than its predecessor. It was also less "activist," particularly in its reluctance to invalidate voter-approved initiatives. On the other hand, the Lucas court was willing, at times, to stake out fairly liberal positions on civil liberties issues.

In 1996, Lucas retired and was replaced as chief justice by Ronald George, who, like his predecessor, had been serving as a supreme court associate justice. In general, the George court's overall direction has been similar to that of its predecessor, which is not surprising, given Republican control of the governorship and hence the judicial nomination power from the time of Rose Bird's departure in 1986 to 1998. By that latter date, only one member of the court, Stanley Mosk, had been appointed by a Democratic governor. Like Deukmejian before him, Wilson appointed Republican lower-court judges with established records as proprosecution, business-friendly jurists. His appointments, however, reflected a good deal of racial and ethnic diversity.

The more conservative, less activist tenor of the Lucas and George courts lowered the supreme court's political profile. This does not mean, however, that these courts always decided cases in a way their appointing governors would approve of or that they were entirely free of controversy. The Lucas court, for example, handed Governor Deukmejian a stinging defeat. When Treasurer Jesse Unruh died in 1987, Deukmejian nominated Dan Lungren to fill his position. His nomination was approved in the state assembly but rejected by the state senate. Citing ambiguities in the wording of the law covering such appointments, Deukmejian argued that the approval of one house was enough. The Lucas court emphatically rejected that argument, thus shutting Lungren out of the treasurer's position.

Nor have post-Bird courts entirely avoided the wrath of conservatives. The Lucas court consistently upheld the right of California women to publicly funded abortions, a policy position strongly opposed by Governor Deukmejian and the right-to-life movement. Nor were Governor Wilson and law-and-order advocates pleased when the George court ruled that judges maintained some discretionary criminal sentencing powers despite the provisions of the three-strikes law. In fact, as the 1998 election approached, the possibility seemed to grow that conservatives would mount a drive to deny retention to two Wilson appointees to the high court because they had voted to overturn a state law requiring parental consent before a minor could obtain an abortion. Ultimately, the movement fizzled, and both were retained by comfortable margins.

On a more positive note, under the leadership of Ronald George, the relationship between the judicial and legislative branches improved considerably. That relationship had deteriorated badly after the Lucas court upheld Proposition 140, the term limits initiative, in language that strongly paraphrased term-limits advocates' attack on the legislature. The legislature struck back in a variety of ways. It refused, for a period of several years, to create any new judge positions, despite the case backlog problem, and it changed the mechanism by which a judge's own performance is evaluated. (This change is discussed later in this chapter.) George set about to heal this rift, and the enhanced cooperation between the two branches is evident in the legislative passage of the court consolidation act and the legislature's newfound willingness to create additional judge positions.

Playing It Safe: Recent Supreme Court Appointments

In late 1982, just before leaving the governorship, Jerry Brown made his last nomination to the state supreme court. As it turned out, that would be the last Democrat appointed for almost 20 years because Republicans occupied the governorship for the next 16 years and Gray Davis was not presented with a high court vacancy until the third year of his term. Ironically, that vacancy resulted from the death of Stanley Mosk in 2001. Mosk had been appointed by Governor Pat Brown way back in 1964.

As discussed in Chapter 4, Gray Davis's gubernatorial style was nothing like that of Jerry Brown, and his lower-court appointments were much safer and less controversial than those of his former boss. When given his first (and only) chance to fill a supreme court vacancy, his choice to replace Mosk was Carlos Moreno, a jurist with experience in both state and federal court systems and a reputation as a solid, moderate jurist. Governor Schwarzenegger has since had the opportunity to make one supreme court appointment, Carol Corrigan, another well-experienced judicial moderate.

Generally, with either Republican or Democratic governors, nominations to judgeships are strongly partisan. It is rare for a Democrat to be named by a Republican governor (although Moreno was originally appointed to the municipal court by Republican Pete Wilson) or for a Republican to be named by a Democratic governor. After 16 years of Republican governors, Democrats who were judge wannabes (practicing attorneys desiring a judgeship and lower-court judges hoping to move up through the judicial ranks) finally had their chance, and it was the Republican hopefuls who were shunted to the sidelines. Under Republican governor Arnold Schwarzenegger, judicial career opportunities have again swung back to Republican attorneys and lower court justices.

JUDICIAL SELECTION

Originally, all judges were elected on a partisan ballot. In 1911, however, party identification labels were dropped from the ballot in an attempt to insulate judges from partisan politics. In 1934, the constitution was changed again to provide for the system used today, whereby appellate court judges are selected via a modified appointment system.

Superior court judges are elected for six-year terms on a *competitive* nonpartisan ballot. Because most citizens vote to retain the incumbent, it is important to realize that once a judge is on the bench, he or she usually will be there for some time. In fact, when a judge is not opposed for reelection, the judge's name does not even appear on the ballot; reelection is automatic. When midterm vacancies occur or when the legislature creates new judge positions, the governor appoints someone to fill the vacancy. Although the election process cannot be dismissed, its relevance is, in the great majority of superior court judgeships, mostly symbolic. More than 90 percent of the present superior court judges were originally appointed by the governor, not initially elected to the bench. And most superior court judges will not face competition in seeking additional terms in office.

The selection process for appellate justices (those in the top two levels of courts) begins with the governor submitting the names of individuals he or she is considering for appointment to the State Bar's Judicial Nominees Evaluation Commission. This commission collects information from lawyers and judges about the suitability of each possible appointee. A confidential report sent to the governor characterizes the potential appointee as either qualified or unqualified. The governor is not bound by the contents of this report, but if the chief executive should proceed to appoint someone who the Judicial Nominees Evaluation Commission found unqualified, the State Bar is free to release its findings on the appointee to the public. This situation occurred just once. In 1996, Governor Wilson nominated Janice Rodgers Brown, a very conservative jurist, to the state supreme court even though she had been rated "unqualified" due to lack of judicial experience. She was nevertheless confirmed by the Commission on Judicial Appointments. Symbolically, when Brown left the California system with a federal judgeship appointment from George Bush, Governor Schwarzenegger replaced her with the much more moderate Carol Corrigan.

Once the governor appoints an appellate justice, the three-member Commission on Judicial Appointments takes public testimony on the qualifications of the appointee. To be confirmed for membership on the appellate bench, the appointee must receive at least two of the three votes of the commission.

Once confirmed, the appellate justice must stand for election at the next scheduled gubernatorial contest. The ballot for this *noncompetitive* or *retention* election asks, "Should Judge X be retained, 'yes' or 'no,' in office?" Thereafter, the justice again appears on the ballot when his or her predecessor's 12-year term of office was scheduled to expire. A justice who survives these two electoral tests finally is ready to serve a full 12-year term. (The elections division of the secretary of state's office clarifies when appellate justices must next face the voters—lest there be any question concerning how much of a particular judicial term has already been served.) Until 1986, when Bird, Reynoso, and Grodin were defeated, no appellate justice had ever been voted out of office in California.

THE JUDICIAL BUREAUCRACY

Besides the courts, three organizations help in the transaction of business in the judicial system. First, the *Judicial Council* is the chief administrative agency in the state court system. The council enacts rules on court procedures and acts as the official statistician and record keeper for activities of the courts. The work of the Judicial Council is eased by the staff support provided by the Administrative Office of the Courts. This agency also monitors court-related legislation and organizes training workshops for trial judges and appellate court justices. The 21-member Judicial Council consists of 15 jurists from all levels of the court system, 4 lawyers from the State Bar, and two state legislators. The chief justice chairs the Judicial Council.

Second, the *Commission on Judicial Appointments* has the authority to confirm or reject gubernatorial nominations to the courts of appeal and the supreme court. This three-member board consists of the chief justice of the supreme court, the attorney general, and a senior appellate justice. Clearly, this procedure is completely unlike that used to fill vacancies at the federal level, in which U.S. Senate confirmation is required. The commission holds public hearings on the nominee, at which time supporters and opponents may express their views. An appellate court justice cannot take office without majority confirmation. At first blush, it appears as if the commission serves as a check against a governor's appointment of unqualified individuals to the appellate courts. However, this appearance is misleading because the state constitution prescribes no qualifications for appointees to the appellate courts aside from membership in the state bar association for ten years. Given the lack of additional criteria, the Commission on Judicial Nominations has in the great majority of cases not considered the political or judicial philosophies of nominees.

Rose Bird owed her confirmation as supreme court chief justice to the commission's tradition of avoiding political/philosophical screening (although one member, the ranking court of appeal justice, did vote no). In his role as attorney general, and hence a commission member, George Deukmejian, on political grounds, voted against some Jerry Brown judicial nominees and doubtless would have voted against Rose Bird had he been attorney general when Brown nominated her. Since that time, however, the commission has been nonpolitical in the way it evaluates potential appellate judges.

This approach leads some critics to label the commission process as little more than a rubber stamp for the governor's nominations to appellate court positions. Thus a number of proposals over the years have recommended either enlarging the commission to include attorneys and private citizens or abolishing it in favor of state senate confirmation of appellate court appointees. Other proposals have called for the requirement that appellate court nominees have prior judicial experience (i.e., previous service on federal or superior courts) before becoming eligible for a position on the appellate bench.

Third, the *Commission on Judicial Performance* monitors the professional demeanor and fitness of the more than 1,500 judges in the state. Until recently, the nine-member commission consisted of five judges from the various judicial levels and four non-judges—two attorneys and two private citizens. However, in 1994, the legislature proposed a constitutional amendment, subsequently approved by the voters, to take majority control of the commission out of judges' hands. The newly constituted commission consists of 11 members, only 3 of whom are judges; they serve with 2 attorneys and 6 public members. The governor, assembly speaker, and Senate Rules Committee each appoint two of the public members. The new law also opens up the commission hearings to public scrutiny. Critics of the old system argued that it is inappropriate to allow judges to dominate a commission in charge of regulating judicial behavior and that the commission resorted to secrecy in order to protect its judicial colleagues under investigation. These "good government" arguments aside, the amended commission can also be understood as part of the ongoing "guerrilla warfare" in the early 1990s between the legislative and judicial branches, sparked by the supreme court's refusal to strike down term limits.

The commission does not act like a "judicial police force"; that is, it does not seek out cases of judges' malfeasance. Instead, it investigates complaints it receives of judicial misconduct. By misconduct, the commission means behavior such as abuse of witnesses or litigants, racial slurs, sexual harassment of court personnel and those doing business with the court, excessive drinking, habitual tardiness, and so on. Misconduct can also include a physical or mental condition that results in a judge being unable to discharge her or his judicial responsibilities in a reasonable manner. The commission does not judge the quality of a judge's decisions. A "wrong decision," as opposed to personal misconduct or disability, is not the subject of commission investigations. If an investigation pursuant to a complaint indicates that the alleged problem is real, the commission has several options. It can issue a private advisory letter or admonishment or a public

BOX
5.3
Judges Behaving Badly: What Was His Honor Thinking?

Judges are among the most respected professionals in our society, and the overwhelming majority of California judges fully deserve that respect. Yet, according to the yearly reports issued by the Commission on Judicial Performance, a small handful of these judges seems to lack the basic judgment expected of any of us.

Physical and verbal sexual harassment, often on the part of male judges many decades older than their victims, is a reoccurring theme. In 2000, a rural county judge was publicly censored, the strongest discipline meted out that year, for physically groping a court bailiff and consistently subjecting her to uninvited and unwelcome verbal abuse of a sexual nature.

In the past, use of race or gender epithets in court has landed judges in trouble, as have patterns of drunkenness on the job; outlandish use of arbitrary power to intimidate court employees, witnesses, and attorneys; drunken driving; and just plain failure to show up for work. One judge was disciplined for slashing the tires of a handicapped van parked in the stall reserved for the judge.

admonishment or censure of the judge. The commission is also empowered, in the severest cases, to actually retire a judge. The commission's most celebrated case occurred in 1977 and involved a supreme court justice, Marshall McComb. The commission investigated complaints that the elderly judge had ceased functioning on the court and found them to be true. McComb was subsequently removed from the supreme court.

Most commission cases and actions are, of course, less high-profile. In 2003, for example, the commission received just over 1,000 complaints but found only about 5 percent of them worthy of further investigation after preliminary review and commenced only 3 new formal proceedings. (Many of the complaints alleged "wrong decision" and hence were not properly subject to further investigation.) Commission action during that year did result in three removals. One of these was for a pattern of traffic ticket fixing; the second was for a consistent habit of humiliating, sometimes in an ethnically prejudicial manner, attorneys and prosecutors; and the third was for illegally hacking into the Motor Vehicles Department computer records to dig up dirt on a driver who had cut the judge off in a traffic incident (California Commission on Judicial Performance, 2004). (See Box 5.3 for further discussion of the Commission on Judicial Performance and the issue of judges' misbehavior.)

LOBBYING THE JUDICIARY

The judiciary is expected to be less politicized than the legislative and executive branches of government. To lessen political influences, judges run on nonpartisan ballots and are immune from being dismissed from their positions by governors, although they can be recalled by the voters. Whereas legislators may frequently appear as speakers before pow-erful groups that want certain bills enacted, judges are prohibited by a code of profes-sional ethics from engaging in any activity that may be construed as a conflict of interest. However, it would be misleading to assume that judges operate in a vacuum free from their own personal biases or outside political pressures.

Groups can attempt to influence the judiciary in several ways. First, they can lobby the governor for the appointment of certain judges sympathetic to their cause. A poten-tial judge's political ideology might not be common knowledge among members of the public, but local bar associations and interest groups usually are aware of a lawyer's position on certain policies such as capital punishment, regulation of business, and environmental quality standards. Furthermore, lawyers belong to organizations that give visibility to their political and social beliefs, such as the Sierra Club, NAACP, cham-bers of commerce, and fraternal lodges. Governors are well apprised of such affilia-tions, which influence appointments to the bench. Law enforcement organizations will write letters to the governor on behalf of a lawyer considered for a court appointment if that lawyer is regarded as a law-and-order proponent. Members of the Sierra Club urge appointment of attorneys who are viewed as environmentalists. Deukmejian's votes against Jerry Brown's three appellate court appointees in San Jose (when the sixth dis-trict of the court of appeal was created) were based in part on critical letters he received from the state's agricultural lobby.

Second, groups can help members of the judiciary when they stand for election. If a sitting judge is challenged at the end of a term or is the target of a recall, interest groups may contribute money, labor, and endorsements to the ensuing campaign.

Third, individuals and organizations who are not parties in a legal suit can file ami-cus curiae briefs in support of one side or the other. These "friend of the court" briefs usually broaden the scope of a lawsuit from a particular case to a general issue that can have a major impact. For example, if the use of a certain pesticide was challenged by farm workers in Fresno, it is likely that agricultural groups and environmentalists would be involved as amicus participants to argue that pesticide regulations should be nar-rowed or broadened, respectively, for the state as a whole. It is difficult to measure the results of amicus activity in legal proceedings; however, it is certainly to the advantage of each side to muster outside support.

Fourth, interest groups can shape the docket of court business by filing "test cases" concerning issues on which they have encountered unfavorable legislative, regulatory, or ballot initiative results. Test cases are a principal vehicle by which courts become policy decision makers.

Fifth, a recent and controversial tactic used to lobby the judiciary is to pack court-rooms during trials. Members of MADD (Mothers Against Drunk Driving) frequently appear in the courtrooms where alleged drunk drivers are on trial or convicted ones are about to be sentenced for injury- and death-related offenses. Their presence is a vis-ible reminder to the judge and jury that many citizens want harsher treatment for con-victed drunk drivers. Increasingly, crime victims or their families are highly visible at criminal trial proceedings.

Influencing the governor concerning judicial selection often involves communica-tion out of public view, similar to inside lobbying of legislators. In contrast, the filing of test cases or amicus briefs is open to public view. Given adequate resources, other groups can respond to an open lobbying effort on a particular judicial decision.

Attempting to influence judicial decisions is one of the more public displays of lobbying power.

THE ADMINISTRATION OF CRIMINAL JUSTICE

The functions of the criminal justice system are to prohibit certain types of behavior, enforce laws and apprehend violators, decide the guilt or innocence of the accused, and punish the guilty. Thus, in order of the preceding functions, participants in the system include the legislators (who pass laws), law enforcement personnel (who enforce the laws and apprehend suspected violators), the judges, district attorneys and defense attorneys (who try cases), and the corrections officials (who deal with those convicted).

In theory, the system is a rational one: Citizens report crimes to the police, who apprehend the suspects; these suspects are then brought to trial in the courts, where the judge and/or jury weighs the evidence presented by the district attorney and the defense attorney before reaching a decision; if found not guilty, the accused is set free; and if found guilty, then he or she is punished in the appropriate manner. However, the criminal justice system operates neither smoothly nor efficiently, in part because of inadequate facilities, low budgets, changing rules, and a lack of consensus about how criminals should be treated. In addition, the criminal justice system is set into motion after a crime has occurred; it can do little by itself to change the social conditions that encourage criminal behavior.

The main responsibility for preventing crime and apprehending culprits rests with some 35,000 municipal law enforcement officers in 500 city police departments in the state. Another 6,000 deputy sheriffs handle law enforcement duties in the unincorporated areas of the state's 58 counties. The California Highway Patrol, with more than 5,000 officers, concerns itself primarily with traffic-related duties on the highways. The 225 state police officers provide security for state buildings, public officials, and visiting dignitaries in addition to doing investigative work on organized crime.

Historically, the legislature and the court system established the rules governing criminal trials, but in this area, as in so many others, the initiative process leaves a large and heavy footprint. In 1982, Proposition 8, the "Victims Bill of Rights," established the right of crime victims to seek restitution from their criminal assailants, required judges to weigh considerations of public safety in making bail decisions, abolished the exclusionary rule regarding illegally collected evidence, cut back on insanity defenses, and allowed the use of a defendant's prior criminal record in court proceedings. In 1990, Proposition 115 changed court procedures in ways that confer advantage to the prosecution over the defense. Its strongest provision, one that limited defendants' rights to those contained in the U.S. Constitution and voided additional rights appended to the state constitution, was struck down by the California Supreme Court. Other initiatives recommended by the legislature and approved by the voters add definitions of "special circumstances" that permit imposition of the death penalty.

The passage of a "three-strikes" initiative in 1994 indicated the continued popularity of get-tough-on-crime policies and the belief that longer sentences will deter criminal activity. Under three strikes, a third "strike"—that is, a third felony conviction—results in automatic imposition of a 25-year-to-life term if any of the three convictions was for a "violent" felony. (The third strike need not be for a violent crime.) The initiative also limited the ability of district attorneys and defendants to plea-bargain down charges so as to avoid the three-strikes rules. Further, the initiative reduced "good-time" reductions in prison sentences, meaning longer sentences even for those not convicted of a third strike.

The impact of three strikes on the court system still remains a matter of conjecture. Almost certainly, a higher percentage of cases will be adjudicated by a full jury trial, given the limitations on plea bargaining and the disinclination of defendants to be convicted of a "strike" felony, especially a third strike. This increased pressure on an already overburdened court system will be avoided only if, over the long haul, three strikes constitutes such a deterrent to crime that many fewer cases are brought to that court system. Since the passage of the three-strikes law, California's crime rate dropped, leading three-strikes supporters to conclude that the new system works. Others, however, cite the strong economy during the last half of the 1990s and note that crime dropped nationwide. In addressing crime and punishment, political rhetoric on both sides overwhelms factual knowledge about the deterrent effect of enhanced sentencing. Are longer prison sentences a significant deterrent to crime, or does the crime rate respond most significantly to economic cycles and/or the presence of more cops on the streets? Given a lack of consensus on this question, it is difficult to argue certainly whether three strikes is worth the costs it creates through longer terms of incarceration. At any rate, because the three-strikes law was a constitutional amendment initiative, it will take a two-thirds vote of the legislature or a successful petition campaign, plus an affirmative vote by the citizens, to fine-tune any problems. For example, in the 2004 general election, California voters were asked to decide whether application of the third-strike penalty should be restricted to cases where the third crime was a violent crime. They responded that no such restriction should be added to the three-strikes law.

Corrections System

California's prison system, formally titled its corrections system, is the state public sector's biggest growth area. In 1980, the system housed 22,500 inmates; 27 years later that total was about 170,000. What was once a relatively inconsequential portion of the budget now accounts for about 9 percent of general fund expenditures. These numbers are the result of politicians' and the public's get-tough-on-crime sentiment, which, in turn, stems from high crime rates and even higher feelings of fear among law-abiding, and voting, citizens. The policy response has been the imposition of longer sentences for convicted felons. In 1977, the state adopted a system of determinate sentencing to replace the old indeterminate system with its wide range of sentence terms. This range was greatly narrowed and term lengths generally increased under the new system. The longer prisoners serve, the more prisoners there are going to be unless tougher sentences result in a proportional drop in the crime rate.

The three-strikes initiative already discussed was passed in the wake of the abduction and murder of 12-year-old Polly Klaas. Her accused assassin, Richard Allen, had previous convictions for kidnapping. The legislature responded with passage of a three-strikes law, but that was superseded by passage of an identical constitutional initiative in November of 1994.

As mentioned, longer terms mean more prisoners unless their deterrent effect significantly lowers crime rates. Certainly, those individuals spending many years behind bars are not out in the street committing repeat crimes. But the three-strikes law means that many prisoners will be held into middle and old age, although the great bulk of violent crime is the work of younger felons. Thus, while the public may be safer for each 25-year-old violent felon behind bars, keeping that same person incarcerated into his fifties and sixties doesn't add much public safety. And keeping a person in prison is no inexpensive matter. Current costs run about $30,000 per inmate per year. An older prison population, because it requires more health care, will be even more expensive.

Three-strikes proponents question these assumptions. They argue that prison projections fail to fully account for the reduced crime rate resulting from the tougher sentencing. They also note that costs for prison construction and operation need to be balanced by the reduced costs—personal, social, and financial—inherent in crime-rate reduction. Again, the key seems to be the deterrent effect of the three-strikes law. At this time, we can say only that the state is engaged in a high-stakes experiment examining the relationship between long sentences and reduced crime rates.

Meantime, the corrections system itself has become the center of controversy. Mistreatment of prisoners is one issue; overcrowding is another. Critics of the system charge that corrections management has lost control of the prisons and that guards all too routinely brutalize inmates. The second target is the California Correctional Peace Officers Association (CCPOA), the guards' union and political representative. CCPOA is a huge money player in Sacramento; its critics believe that it has used its power to extort exhorbitant salaries for its members and to vest them with way too much administrative control of the prisons.

The corrections situation is serious enough that a federal judge has considered taking over the whole system and placing it in some kind of judicially controlled receivership. In response, the legislature and Governor Schwarzenegger agreed in spring of 2007 to appropriate an additional $7 billion to increase the prison system's capacity, decentralize its institutions, and enlarge its rehabilitation programs. Whether the new commitment actually satisfies the federal judiciary, let alone turns the huge California prison system around, remains an open question.

Law-and-order issues are high profile, and California voters continue to use the initiative process to further tinker with crime and punishment policies. Proposition 21, passed in March 2000, is a further "get tough" measure, this time directed at juvenile offenders. Under Proposition 21, penalties for juvenile offenders were increased, grounds for trying and sentencing juveniles through the adult criminal justice system were expanded, and possibilities of granting informal felony probation were abolished. On the other hand, voters took a much different tack just months later in passing Proposition 36 in the November 2000 general election. Proposition 36 sets up a system of rehabilitative treatment, rather than incarceration, for those adults convicted of possessing or using narcotics (though not their sale). But, as previously mentioned, in 2004 voters reaffirmed their tough-on-crime stance by rejecting Proposition 66, which proposed to limit the application of the three-strikes law's enhanced prison sentencing.

In an ironic twist, looming budgetary problems have forced Governor Schwarzenegger to change course on the question of prison term lengths. He established his law and order position by opposing Proposition 66. But in fall 2007, facing a growing budget deficit crisis, he supported early release for 20,000 "non-dangerous" felons currently housed in the state's prison system.

Much of the debate over crime and punishment concerns the relative effectiveness of punishment versus rehabilitation in lowering the crime rate. In 2000, the state's voters seemed to come down on the side of punishment in the case of juvenile offenders generally but took a position in favor of rehabilitation in regard to narcotics use. But then again, one can't expect consistency when a policy area as emotional and complex as crime and punishment is addressed through separate and noncomplementary ballot issues.

SUMMARY

The California judicial system is separate from the branches most citizens consider "political," but it is up to its eyeballs in politics. It is increasingly called on to settle political and policy questions left unanswered by the regular political processes. As well, in their immediate relationship with crime and punishment, courts are involved in one of the state's hottest political arenas. That is certainly the lesson of Rose Bird, who was removed from her chief justice position largely because of her unpopular decisions relative to the death penalty. Her removal also raises questions about the proper balance between judicial independence and accountability to the public.

Another unanswered question concerns the relationship between crime and punishment. Do we decrease the former by increasing the latter? This question is central to the debate over "three strikes." The state embarked on a policy of long criminal sentences on the theory that longer sentences will lead to steeply reduced crime rates. If the theory fails, Californians will be seeing even greater portions of governmental spending allocated to the corrections field. The question has also been addressed, in a contradictory fashion, by the voters' recent decisions concerning juvenile crime and narcotics violations. Given the level of public concern with these and related issues, more law-and-order propositions are likely to appear on future ballots.

REFERENCES

California Commission on Judicial Performance. *Annual Report.* Sacramento: 2004.
California Judicial Council. *Statistical Report.* Sacramento: 2007.

CHAPTER six

LOCAL GOVERNMENTS IN CALIFORNIA

The institutional dilemmas we spoke of in Chapter 1 are nowhere more evident than in California's localities. County boundaries, completely frozen for a century, no longer correspond to demographic and economic realities. The state's general blueprint for municipal government, based on early-twentieth-century reform assumptions, may be ill-suited to the current political and social realities of many cities. Special districts form a bewildering web of jurisdictional and functional domains. And overlaying the various structural problems facing local governments is a chronic shortage of dependable funding.

Local institutions are markedly different from those at the state and national levels. While bicameral legislatures are found at the state and federal levels, unicameral decision-making bodies are the rule at the local level. The relationship between the nation and the states (federalism) provides at least some degree of sovereignty and independent legal status to the states. However, local governments are, legally, creatures of their states without independent legal status. Thus, the state-local relationship is unitary, not federal. Local ordinances may not conflict with state statutes, just as state laws may not violate federal statutes. While states maintain broad areas of legal discretion not controlled by federal policy, states are free to preempt any area of local jurisdiction they see fit. For example, California's state government could preempt the policy area of rent control, thus preventing local governments from enacting any rent control ordinances. In addition, the clear separation of the executive and the legislative branches found at the state and national levels is not evident at the local level. The multimember boards, councils, and districts elected at the local level usually carry out both executive and legislative functions.

The electoral arena in local government differs as well. Unlike the partisan contests at the state and national levels, localities conduct nonpartisan elections. Whereas the upper levels of government feature legislative races from *districts*, it is still common at the local level to elect council members and trustees *at large*—that is, candidates seek votes throughout the entire geographic area administered by that local government instead of just a portion of it. Recall campaigns (see Chapter 9) are more common at the local than the state level. Term limits are a reality at the state level, but they are less common in local politics.

The number and variety of local governments creates both cooperative and contentious interactions among the many jurisdictions. The cost of expensive services may be shared by several localities through joint powers authorities (JPAs). And it is common for school districts and cities to locate parks and schools adjacent to each other. Such cooperation enables students to more easily engage in athletic programs. Moreover, a new school gymnasium could be jointly funded by the school district and city, thus allowing for adult league utilization in the evenings and weekends outside of regular school hours.

Conversely, local governments can become intense rivals. The city of Los Angeles has been engaged in protracted legal battles with the counties of Inyo and Mono over the aqueduct which transfers water from those eastern counties into the big city. Cities strenuously compete with each other to lure auto malls into their jurisdiction and thus capture a share of the sales tax these malls generate.

Sometimes the struggle is between different jurisdictions within the same locality. Dissatisfied with the performance of schools within their communities, mayors in cities such as Oakland, Sacramento, and Los Angeles have challenged the autonomy of school boards by attempting to increase their own authority over school governance. Although the courts have generally rejected these direct mayoral incursions into school politics, mayors have succeeded in running slates of candidates to replace incumbents on local school boards.

Aside from their unique structural attributes, local governments are crucial to the quality of life enjoyed by everyone in California. Land use, air quality, crime levels, traffic congestion, and K–14 education are but a few of the matters dealt with by local jurisdictions. Although we intend to devote considerable attention to the structural alternatives that are open to local units, it is important to understand that several other factors besides governmental structure contribute to the quality of life in a locality. For instance, decisions by industries to locate in (or to relocate away from) a certain area profoundly impact a locality's employment rates, revenues collected, housing values, and overall fiscal and economic health. Local governments may try to attract and to retain businesses by offering incentives such as tax breaks or subsidized services, but a business's choice to come, stay, or leave is fundamentally a private decision. The role of community influentials (leaders in the realms of society, culture, and the media) likewise is central to the character and development of localities.

In addition to these private influences, an area's dominant political and social outlook (its political culture) helps shape and define the scope and direction of local government. Some communities are eager to attract new businesses and residents, others are content to provide minimal services to their citizens, and still others strive to enhance the cultural and recreational life of the community through investment in parks, symphonies, and other amenities. Some localities, such as many college towns, reflect a preference for liberal politicians and policy and a tolerance of alternative lifestyles. Others—for example, many rural communities—are dominated by conservative preferences for low taxes and traditional moral standards. Keeping in mind industrial leadership, community influentials, and political culture, lest we overestimate the significance of local political institutions, let us now turn to the structures of local governments in California.

COUNTY GOVERNMENTS

When California was granted statehood in 1850, 27 counties were created. Shortly after the turn of the century, the original boundaries were redrawn to provide for 58 counties (see Figure 6.1). Although this number has not changed for a hundred years, contentment with the existing lines is far from universal. Many areas, both urban and rural,

FIGURE 6.1   California's 58 counties.

have witnessed or are witnessing movements to split off a segment of an existing county to form a new jurisdiction. Los Angeles County is the most notable recent target.

Thus, it may seem surprising that no actual changes in county lines have occurred in an entire century. Part of the reason is that the rules are stacked against those seeking to secede and create new counties. Not only must the voters in the area breaking away from an existing county approve a separation, but also the voters residing in the *entire* county must consent. Although majorities were obtained in some proposed new counties, the voters countywide nixed these separations.

California counties vary as much in size as they do in their economies, politics, and geographic setting. San Bernardino County, the largest in the United States, is 46 times as large in area as Santa Cruz County. Indeed, San Bernardino County is larger than three of the New England states combined. Alpine County, which borders on Nevada, south of Lake Tahoe, has a population of slightly more than 1,100, whereas Los Angeles County is the most populous, with approximately 10 million residents, which would make it the ninth largest *state.* That's a "population gap" ratio of 10,000 to 1. Of all 58 counties, the 10 most populous contain almost three-quarters of all the state's residents. By contrast, the 10 smallest counties account for less than one-half of 1 percent of the state's population. In fact, the smallest 29 counties, half the total county number of 58, are home to barely 3 percent of all Californians (California Department of Finance, 2007).

Despite vast intercounty differences in terrain, size, economy, and population, the 58 county governing structures are not particularly distinctive. County governments, like other local governance units in the state, derive their operating authority from the state. The state constitution recognizes two types of counties: general law and charter. General law counties follow state law as to the number and function of elected officials in the county. The 13 charter counties may establish governing structures and arrangements that better suit their particular needs. Charter status also conveys revenue advantages in permitting more tax flexibility. San Francisco's charter is the state's most unique, in that it establishes a consolidated city/county government, one of the few in the nation. Counties in California are responsible for vital record keeping functions, such as births, deaths, marriages and property ownership records. Because San Francisco is both a city and a county, Mayor Gavin Newsom attempted to use county authority in ordering the records staff to perform same-sex marriages in 2004. The California Supreme Court ruled, however, that this was an overreach for even a charter county, and voided the same-sex marriage licenses issued under the mayor's orders.

A general law county can become a charter county if a majority of the residents vote accordingly. The more populous counties, such as Los Angeles, Alameda, and San Diego, secured charter status because of their need to serve large constituencies. Some exceptions are notable, of course: Orange County is a general law county in spite of its high population, whereas Tehama County, with a little more than 55,000 residents and ranking thirty-fourth in population in the state, is a charter county.

In both general law and charter counties, the main governing authority is the board of supervisors. These 5-member boards (11 members in San Francisco) wield both legislative and executive authority; that is, they pass laws (called ordinances at the local level) and oversee most of the departments charged with implementing those laws. Board members are elected for four-year staggered terms by districts within the counties. As agents of the state, counties in California are required to provide their residents with the following services, in addition to those related to keeping the aforementioned vital records: hospitals and mental health clinics, voter registration and elections, courts and jails, drug prevention and rehabilitation, probation and juvenile detention, accuracy of weights and measures, social welfare and homeless programs, and tax collection for all local governments in the county. The boards can provide additional services as allowed by county budgets and voter approval.

Land-use decisions traditionally fall within the responsibility of local governments in California and, arguably, are the most crucial decisions that the locals must make. Boards of supervisors are responsible for making these decisions with respect to county areas outside city limits, and the issues raised in the process can be quite divisive when those favoring development square off with those trying to slow or stop it. Supervisorial elections are sometimes referenda as voters choose between candidates who are "slow growth" and ones who are "pro-development." The county's political culture and disposition will often determine which side has the upper hand. Local decision makers increasingly must also factor in the revenue consequences in making their land-use policy decisions.

In addition to the boards of supervisors, the other major elected county officers include the following:

- *Sheriff*: Responsible for law enforcement in unincorporated (noncity) areas, maintains the county jail, and serves as county coroner.

- *District attorney*: Prosecutes on behalf of the county and represents the county in legal suits.

- *Auditor, treasurer, assessor, and tax collector*: Collects revenues and disburses county funds.

- *County clerk*: Maintains county documents and supervises elections.

- *Superintendent of schools*: Responsible for county schools.

Most of the state's counties employ an appointed *county administrative officer*, who is responsible for implementing board policies and coordinating county services. Boards of supervisors also appoint the *county welfare director* and the *county health officer* as well as members of advisory commissions. Commissions on the status of women, human relations, and planning report to the board on topics ranging from discrimination to zoning changes. New advisory boards and commissions may be utilized as the county voters desire. These boards and commissions are excellent avenues for citizen input. Residents can demonstrate their interest in and knowledge of issues at commission and board of supervisors meetings. Because many positions on the commissions are filled by appointment, they represent an opportunity for local residents to influence policy guidelines and to begin careers in politics.

MUNICIPAL GOVERNMENTS

All cities are located in a single county and may not stretch across county lines (although not all counties contain incorporated cities). Fundamental differences separate county and city governments (the latter officially called municipal governments), In the first place, it is a great deal easier to create a new city than it is a new county. An unincorporated area wishing to incorporate as a city must first get approval from its

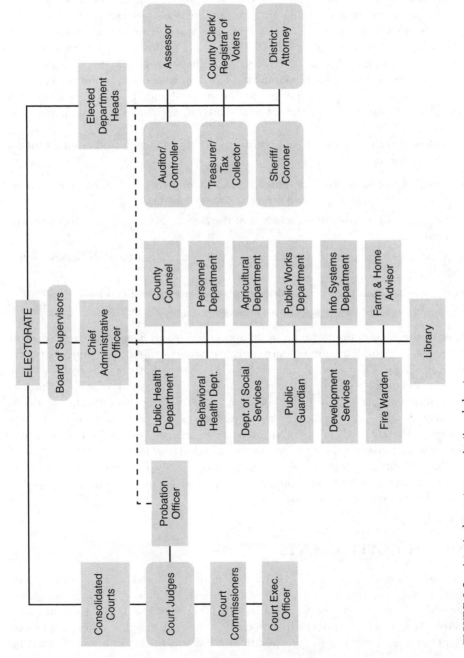

FIGURE 6.2   A typical county organizational chart.

Local Agency Formation Commission (LAFCO). The incorporation vote is limited to those living within the limits of the proposed new city. However, if a new city wants to detach or secede from an existing city, a dual majority is required in the newly proposed city as well as citywide. When San Fernando Valley attempted to form a new city by detaching from the City of Los Angeles in 2002, the citywide vote blocked the idea by a two-to-one vote.

Cities and counties differ in more ways than just their modes of creation. Whereas counties must carry out certain state laws in areas such as public assistance and health, cities are less encumbered by state mandates. Citizens choose to establish a municipality (from unincorporated county territory) when they wish to collect additional taxes to pay for services over and above those provided by county government. In other words, cities deliver services their residents request, not programs ordered by the state. Counties and cities also differ in terms of their financial health. Most of the money expended by counties is transferred to them by the state and national governments, whereas cities are more self-sufficient financially. Budget shortfalls in Sacramento and Washington, D.C., result in squeezed and trimmed transfers allocated to the counties.

More than 80 percent of California residents live within one of the state's 478 incorporated cities. The remainder of the population is located in the unincorporated areas of the counties. As counties are divided into general law and charter status, so too are cities. Some 109 of the more populous cities have charters, which, as is the case with counties, permit them greater structural latitude than they would have under the general law plan.

The Progressives' Vision for Municipal Government

The structures and processes that define local governance, like so many elements of California's public sector, were profoundly shaped by the vision of the early-twentieth-century progressives. Progressives held the following beliefs about local government:

1. Local government should be nonpartisan; parties and partisanship have nothing positive to contribute to local affairs.
2. In fact, local governance ought not be "political," or combative, but rather consensual.
3. Local governance is properly concerned with the creation and distribution of public services, and hence should be directed by standards of efficiency, not by politics.

Nearly a century after California's progressive era, these tenets still define most local governmental structures as well as the way most Californians think about local government. For example, California law mandating local nonpartisan elections is perhaps the strongest in the nation. Candidates for any office below that of state legislator may not be identified by party on the ballot. The law also prohibited parties from endorsing or supporting local candidates and prohibited candidates from referencing their party in their campaign materials. These latter prohibitions, except for the nonpartisan ballot, were struck down by the courts in the 1980s and early 1990s. Still, few instances occur of official party involvement in local elections or candidates' use of a party label in their campaign literature and publicity.

Progressives perceived strong city mayors as a threat to their vision of a nonpartisan, nonpolitical local governing system. Indeed, in the early twentieth century, big-city mayors were often political kingpins and thus at the heart of the political party machines so offensive to progressives. In response, progressives favored weak mayors and strong city managers. Their alternative, called the *council-manager* system, is used in about three-quarters of California's incorporated cities and is almost universal among cities smaller than 100,000 in population. In this scheme, the mayor is not elected separately but rather is a city council member voted mayor by the city council itself. The mayor's powers are ceremonial: wielding the gavel at council meetings, cutting ribbons to commemorate the opening of new local businesses, and handing over the "keys to the city" to returning local heroes.

In this system, mayors are not in charge of the day-to-day city departmental operations. That task is performed by the *city manager,* a professional formally trained in the administration of local government. This position, again arising out of the progressive movement, was traditionally considered "nonpolitical." Technical expertise, not political skill, is the strength that city managers were supposed to bring to the job of running local government. City managers are not elected; instead, they are appointed by and serve at the pleasure of the city council.

At-large elections are the final ingredient in the progressives' blueprint for municipal government. The five council members (including the mayor) serve staggered four-year terms upon being elected at a citywide rather than a district election. If, for example, two council seat terms are ending at election time, those seats will be filled by the top two vote getters from throughout the city.

Taken together, these processes result in an overall plan that is faithful to the progressives' beliefs about local governance. Political parties are entirely removed from the picture, and the mayor is unlikely to become a center of political power. Instead, much of that power is wielded by the appointed city manager, whose authority derives from technical expertise rather than political clout. Finally, at-large elections for council members represent the search for a community-wide consensus as opposed to the divisiveness of a district-elected council whose members see their role as representing their district's particular agendas rather than advancing broader community-wide needs.

Again, this system is in use in the great majority of municipal governments up and down the state. However, these arrangements, as well as the assumptions that sustain them, have not been immune to criticism, especially recently. This argument will be taken up later when we discuss structural controversies surrounding local government.

SPECIAL DISTRICTS

The most numerically prevalent form of government in the state is the special district, such as the mosquito abatement, cemetery, airport, fire, air pollution, transportation, flood control, and water districts. The establishment of special districts must be approved by the Local Agency Formation Commission and the residents within the proposed district. Some 5,000 such special districts, in addition to approximately 1,000 school districts, have been established throughout the state to provide services not made available by cities and counties. Unlike other types of local governments, special districts are unique in two respects: (1) most are concerned with only one area of service, although some multipurpose community service districts perform a variety of functions; and (2) special districts create their own boundaries, which are permitted to transcend city and county lines. Thousands of single-purpose districts, each with distinct borders, create a jumble of local jurisdictions.

Special districts initially were established to provide services that voters wanted; however, fiscal inflexibility can result from the proliferation of single-purpose jurisdictions. Although general-purpose governments (cities and counties) may shift spending priorities between their many functions, it is unlikely that a special district with a surplus of funds will transfer resources to another strapped special district.

Special districts, like all forms of government in the state, are required to conform to the state constitution and Government Code in terms of their operating authority. School districts, a type of special district, derive their authority from the Education Code. The operating revenues for special districts originate from the property tax or from special fees imposed, such as landing charges for private planes at an airport.

REGIONAL GOVERNMENTS

Because modern problems such as air quality and water contamination pay no heed to local boundaries, it has been necessary to establish regional bodies in an effort to cope with such issues (see Figure 6.3). Some of these regional institutions are *advisory* in nature, and some possess strong *regulatory* powers. Councils of government (COGs) are examples of the former. Counties, cities, and special districts may voluntarily join a COG to discuss mutual problems and make recommendations for the member governments to follow. The Association of Bay Area Governments consists of 8 counties and 89 cities. The Southern California Association of Governments is made up of 6 counties and 175 cities. The Sacramento Area Council of Governments has 4 counties and 15 cities within it. The San Diego Association of Governments involves some 14 cities, while the county initially opted not to join this COG. These regional bodies provide useful forums for sharing information. However, they lack enforcement power, and the member units are free to ignore their suggestions. As a result, COGs have not been highly successful in addressing difficult issues.

Regional governments of a regulatory nature are becoming more common in California. The San Francisco Bay Conservation and Development Commission (BCDC) must approve any waterfront development in the bay. Designed to stop the bay from being filled in by construction projects, BCDC has actually increased the amount of open water in the bay by some 625 acres. The 27 member agencies in BCDC include the U.S. Environmental Protection Agency, the Army Corps of Engineers, the State Lands Commission, the California Resources Agency, and city and county officials from jurisdictions bordering the bay. The California Coastal Commission (CCC) is empowered to grant (or withhold) permits for all development within the coastal zone (generally 1,000 yards from the shoreline). The CCC has improved public access to beaches, protected scenic views, and restored some wetlands. The 12-member CCC is appointed by the governor and the state legislature. Not surprisingly, local governments resent their loss of control over land-use decisions in the coastal zone. The CCC exemplifies state preemption over local objection.

Protecting the environment in the Lake Tahoe basin has proven especially difficult and contentious. The federal government rejected requests to create a national park at Lake Tahoe because much of the basin already had been logged or was privately owned.

FIGURE 6.3   Air quality districts.

Some sixty three streams flow into the lake from the surrounding region. Each stream is a potential source of sewage, fertilizers, pesticides, fuels and lubricants, ash from wild-fires, and erosion from building sites.

Given these very real threats to the purity and clarity of Lake Tahoe, California and Nevada entered into a bi-state compact to oversee development in the basin. The result-ing Tahoe Regional Planning Agency (TRPA) was ratified by the U.S. Congress in 1969. TRPA encompasses two California counties (Placer and El Dorado) and three counties in Nevada (Washoe, Carson, and Douglas). The TRPA governing board consists of seven persons each from California and Nevada, plus an appointee named by the U.S. president.

The 2007 wildfires in the Tahoe basin gave rise to criticisms of some of TRPA's regulatory decisions. In order to limit erosion into Lake Tahoe, the agency prohibits removal of trees over 6 inches in diameter from private property without a permit. It has been argued that the limit should be raised to 14 inches to enhance homeowners' ability to clear fire-defensible space around their structures. But the wildfire and ensuing policy controversy is broader than a disagreement as to how best to avoid erosion runoff. The more basic and politically charged question is whether forest area urban development ought be allowed in the first place, especially since firefighters are not confident about the prospects of saving houses located in heavily wooded terrain.

Parts or all of four counties (Los Angeles, Orange, Riverside, and San Bernardino) make up the South Coast air basin. Pollutants emitted from mobile and stationary sources make the air in this basin the worst in the United States. The South Coast Air Quality Management District (SCAQMD) is empowered to regulate emissions by businesses, local governments, and private citizens. The 12-member board of SCAQMD (selected by city governments in the air basin) is endeavoring to enforce new air quality standards that will require significant alterations in residents' lifestyle. To reduce emissions from idling automobiles, SCAQMD is fostering mass transit, ride sharing, flexible working hours, and cleaner fuels. Excessive emissions from oil refineries and from ships purging their holds of pollutants result in stiff fines.

However, the work of Air Quality Management Districts throughout California will become more complex in the coming years. AQMDs traditionally have been responsible for curbing the emission of harmful particulates. With the legislative enactment of AB 32 in 2006, California must, by 2020, reduce its emission of greenhouse gases (such as carbon dioxide) by 25%. This mandate will require a major effort by AQMDs, as well as cities, counties and other state agencies, to inventory and then reduce these emissions. And of course, as critics of tough emission controls like to point out, California's attempts to reverse global warming will not accomplish anything unless other states and nations follow suit. However, it is the position of Governor Schwarzenegger and his mostly Democratic allies in the legislature that California ought to be setting the right example. The governor's 2007 participation in an international conference on the issue is the public part of this lead by example strategy.

The state's responsibility for the success or failure of regional government is undeniable. The state legislature established BCDC, CCC, TRPA, and SCAQMD. If local governments and COGs feel their powers usurped by these regional regulators, they can turn their wrath on the state government that brought these agencies into being. The extent to which the legislature and governor protect the jurisdictional integrity of these entities, or bow to local constituent power, will determine the long-term viability of regional government in California.

THE STRUCTURAL DEBATES

California is a radically different place today than it was during the progressive era, let alone when the current basic constitution was written some 130 years ago. Even though just about everything else has changed, those constitution writers of the 1870s and progressives from the early twentieth century would still recognize the basic structures of local government. In this realm, nothing has changed.

County lines are a perfect example of institutional stability, or stagnation, depending on your point of view. Alert motorists might note that county boundaries often are placed in the middle of rivers or along mountain ridge lines. One hundred years ago this demarcation strategy made abundant sense: rivers and mountains were formidable barriers to travel and communication, and thus logical places to divide one county from another. Today, those rivers are easily spanned by multilane bridges and those mountains routinely crossed by roads and highways. Obstacles to communication across geographical barriers have been reduced in even greater measure. Yet county lines remained unchanged, even as the state itself underwent massive change.

As already discussed, California consists of a few counties with huge populations, and many counties that are, for the most part, empty. These extremes raise issues of responsiveness and efficiency. A purported central virtue of local government is its responsiveness to individual needs, providing citizens face-to-face, nonbureaucratic access to the political system. But can this value be captured by counties whose populations equal or even dwarf that of the entire state at the time those county lines were drawn? Los Angeles County is, of course, the most salient example of massive local government. Is it even realistic to call a jurisdiction containing 10 million residents "local"? With 2 million residents in each of just five supervisorial districts, isn't it time for the board of supervisors in Los Angeles County to be expanded in size?

At the other end of the scale, are citizens' needs effectively served by counties that are too small to enjoy efficiencies of scale and that have painfully small and narrow economic bases? Most of the counties in California's rural, mountainous regions were shaped by geographic barriers. Although no longer barriers, these features continue to define dozens of counties, some with population numbers lower than those reported during the 1850s gold rush era.

Municipal governmental structures have also come under critical scrutiny. Most of the larger cities have moved away from the progressives' council-manager system. Their mayors, in varying degrees, tend to be elected separately and to hold additional powers such as budget making, veto power over council-passed ordinances, and control over city departments. Significantly, as the power of mayors increases, the power of city managers declines. As well, most larger cities elect council members on a district basis, not at-large. The progressive vision of a unified, consensual, and nonpolitical approach to local decision making never "fit" as well with large city governance, where constituents are more diverse and the needs for political leadership more pressing.

Now the question is whether progressive theories still fit the realities of medium-sized cities. For example, about 95 percent of all California cities still employ the at-large mode of city council election, but that practice has come under sharp attack by local reformers and some members of the state legislature. Advocates of at-large elections believe that officeholders chosen in this manner are more likely to represent the interests of the whole rather than those of a neighborhood. At-large voting does not prohibit two or more qualified candidates who happen to reside near each other from serving together on the city council, and the best qualified should serve regardless of where they live. At-large voting eliminates one more problem with district elections: that of incumbents drawing the districts, with the potential for gerrymandering.

Proponents of district elections counter that the at-large approach permits all officeholders to reside in the same area of a community, frequently the most affluent neighborhood. District elections encourage face-to-face canvassing by candidates walking one district; effective campaigns may be waged with less money than is the case with at-large races. Reduced financial outlays in district campaigns encourage a broader spectrum of citizens to run for office. District elections give residents the sense that a particular officeholder is "their representative" in case they should need to lodge a complaint or request government services. District elections are seen as one way of increasing minority representation, especially in cities in which a racial or ethnic minority tends to be concentrated in residential areas that can be encompassed within a council district. The U.S. Department of Justice may even require adoption of a district system when it finds that voting patterns are polarized along racial or ethnic lines, resulting in minorities being shut out of council seats.

Further, in order to give voters more information about local candidates, it is possible to change county and/or large city elections to partisan contests. Given the phenomenon of "shadow partisanship," why not print the party label next to a local candidate's name on the ballot? Whatever the merits of this argument, abolishing or softening the current local nonpartisanship system would be a tall order. The current system is constitutionally mandated, meaning a legislative constitutional amendment, or initiative constitutional amendment would be required. It's hard to imagine the legislature taking such a step, given the state's weak party ethos (discussed in Chapter 8). And are there any organized interests or individual deep pockets willing to expend the money for signature gathering and the necessary very expensive campaign to convince a skeptical electorate to bring political parties into local elections?

Another structural choice facing California's cities is the extent to which they rely on strong city managers or rejuvenated mayors. In the former case, the appointed city manager has the power to appoint department heads, to propose the city's budget, and to negotiate land-use matters with major developers. Proponents of the strong manager arrangement believe that municipalities need professional, not political, administration. Although many council members are part-time public servants who have other forms of gainful employment, cities require full-time experts to manage their day-to-day affairs. Managers who are isolated to an extent from political pressure are capable of managing municipalities in the most efficient and businesslike manner.

Opponents of strong manager systems argue that appointed officials are inherently less accountable to the public than are elected ones. Mayors are more visible than managers, and the public is more likely to know where a mayor stands on the issues. Salaries are increasing for council members and mayors, and elected city officials are spending more and more time at their public work. In large cities such as Los Angeles, council members actually are paid more than state legislators. In short, elected officials in some cities are becoming full-time participants in municipal governance.

It is generally true that big-city mayors, such as those in San Diego, Sacramento, San Jose, Oakland, and Fresno, have recently received voter approved increases in their powers. Should they gain the ability to propose budgets, appoint department heads, and veto local ordinances passed by city councils, such as has long been the case in San Francisco, they can become formidable players in local politics. Time will tell whether stronger mayors were really a good idea. If the urban landscape of these cities benefits from sound development decisions, the move to strong mayors will have been vindicated. If not, perhaps the expert "nonpolitical" managers of municipal government should have been left in charge.

In addition to county lines, district/at-large, and mayor/manager issues, several fundamental structural questions involve the consolidation of existing government units. As anyone who has seen the word *unified* on the side of a school bus might guess, many small school districts in California have been consolidated in the past in hopes of improving services and saving money. Consolidation can occur in many forms. Similar types of government units (e.g., school districts or tiny counties) can be merged to achieve greater economies of scale. It is also possible to consolidate dissimilar government units. For example, following the model of the City and County of San Francisco, two different sorts of government entities can be brought together into one unit. A proposal to consolidate the city and county governments in Sacramento was put before the voters in November 1990, but it was defeated.

It is also possible to consolidate different special districts or to join such districts with general-purpose governments like cities and counties. Proponents of consolidation argue that it makes no sense to have one agency make land-use decisions about the location of housing, another authority make transportation policy, and still another body set air quality standards. Because the development of housing determines commutes and the lengths of these commutes impact air quality, a consolidated government entity ought to be empowered to make coordinated policies in all these areas. Eliminating elective offices, however, is no easy matter.

THE LOCAL FISCAL CRUNCH

The structural issues and debates surrounding local government are nothing new, and the arguments are likely to be around for some time to come. The urgency of these structural dilemmas, however, pales in comparison to the seemingly permanent resource shortages that afflict local governments, especially in the eyes of local office-holders. If one were writing a history of local government finance, June of 1978, when Proposition 13 was passed, would be the watershed date. Proposition 13 changed a great many things throughout the state, but its most direct and immediate impact was on local governments. It froze the tax rate on real property at 1 percent and rolled back the assessed valuation of property on which that rate is levied to 1975 property values. Moreover, that assessed valuation, subject to only moderate inflation-based increases, was frozen in place until the property in question changes ownership. At that point, the property is reassessed at the sale price, but the new owner is then guaranteed that assessment level until the property is resold.

Historically, property taxes were set, collected, and spent by the local governments; they were the source of financial independence for the locals. Proposition 13's immediate impact was a 57 percent reduction in property tax revenues. At the time of Proposition 13's passage, the state government was enjoying a large surplus and was able to backfill most of this revenue shortfall with state funds. Subsequently, the new funding relationship created two serious problems for local governments: with increased state financial support of heretofore local programs, state control over these programs also increased. Then, when the state encountered its own fiscal problems, support for those local programs dwindled. In fact, during the state deficit years of the middle 1990s, the state began scooping up portions of counties' property tax revenues to help meet its school funding requirements under Proposition 98.

In short, since the passage of Proposition 13 in 1978, local governments have encountered programmatic and financial risk; when the state's financial picture is bright, it is able to backfill revenue losses felt by the locals, but at the cost of reduced local discretion and program control. When finances are bad in Sacramento, the money spigot dries up. Currently, real doubts that the state will have the ability to bail local government out make that second risk even more acute. Ironically, though local governments' revenue picture is cloudy, demands for local governmental services have not abated. In 1994, eight counties asked the state for a supplemental payment in order to fund their normal operations. In that same year, Orange County was forced to declare bankruptcy.

Of all the local governments, counties were hit hardest. The great majority of their operations are mandated by the state. The mandates keep coming, but the money doesn't always follow. In fact, as already discussed, sometimes the flow goes the other way. And with the continuing state budget uncertainty, counties face the specter of new state raids on their remaining property tax revenues.

Coping with Fiscal Woes: The Locals Get Creative

City governments, perhaps not quite so afflicted, owe their relative insulation to the fact that fewer of their activities and programs are state-mandated. Still, the money shortage felt throughout all levels of local government has resulted in changed policies, priorities, and strategies at the city level as well. Fees for service are now the local government rule. Except for the most basic services, such as public protection, increasingly you pay for what you get from local government. This issue raises serious equity problems. Where do we draw the line between what is a "luxury" that recipients should pay for and what is a "basic service" that all residents should enjoy regardless of their ability to pay? (In some cases, residents are charged for services they decidedly would prefer not to have. Individuals locked up in county jails can now be charged for their "lodging.")

Local money worries affect all sorts of issues, including land-use planning. "Fiscalization of land-use planning" is the catchphrase for the new reality. When cities, as well as counties, make zoning and development decisions, they must factor in the revenue consequences, perhaps to the detriment of balanced planning. Housing development, for example, may be good social planning, given the state's shortage of affordable housing, but it is bad for the revenue stream because increases in property tax from new housing are limited under Proposition 13 and subject to state appropriation. In addition, new houses, meaning more people, create further expensive demands on local services. Even encouraging new, environmentally clean, manufacturing enterprises presents a mixed fiscal bag because plants and factories pay local property taxes, but the individual and corporate income taxes generated by manufacturing go directly to the state (and national) coffers, not to the host local government. Instead, the biggest payoff for local governments lies in major retail centers, malls, and "big-box" consumer outlets. A portion of the sales tax collected stays with the county and city in which it is collected. Thus, from a revenue perspective, a mall may make much more sense than new housing, new job-creating factories, or more green space. But these malls, warehouse-sized retail outlets, and automobile rows may make no sense from a balanced land-use perspective, however.

Incorporation is another strategy employed in the search for dollars. For each dollar purchase subject to sales tax, 1.25 cents go to the local jurisdiction(s) in which the tax is collected. If the purchase takes place in an unincorporated portion of the county, the entire local take goes to the county treasury. If the transaction takes place in an incorporated city, however, a full cent out of the local portion remains in that city. Imagine a fairly rural county with an unincorporated area that contains an auto row. That area is the source of a lot of sales tax revenue. People living in that immediate area may be tempted to incorporate in order to capture that tax money, but in doing so, they leave the rest of the county more strapped for tax revenues. Recall from the earlier discussion that incorporation votes require only a majority from citizens within the proposed new city limits, not the approval of the other county voters. In response to this problem, current law now requires that, as part of the incorporation process, new cities must negotiate a financial agreement with their county that compensates the county for lost revenues.

The Commission on Constitutional Revision, as well as others, points out that the ultimate solution lies in freeing local government from its current level of state control and providing it with a stable revenue base. In fact, the first goal depends on the second. It is much less clear how to accomplish them, however. The most likely strategy is a revitalization of the property tax as a revenue source for the locals, which, in turn, would require a revamping, if not repeal, of Proposition 13. To date, neither politicians nor voters show much inclination to lead this charge.

SUMMARY

In terms of citizen contact, local government is "where the rubber meets the road." It is also the provider of services that citizens most value. But local governments are in real trouble. Many local boundaries don't make much sense in the modern context. For example, county lines have not changed in a century. Are 58 counties still necessary? Does a county of 10 million (Los Angeles) make sense? What about a county of 1,200 (Alpine)? Is it time to consider regional approaches to problems that are regional in origin and solvable only through regional efforts? Other structural problems require attention as well, as Californians question the relative benefits of at-large versus district elections and the relative strengths and weaknesses of city manager and strong mayor systems.

Recently, however, these questions paled against the fiscal realities facing local governments. Proposition 13 provided property tax relief that was sorely needed, but it also put local governments at the mercy of the state government. This situation is less than ideal when the state's own financial house is in order, but it is nearly impossible when the state can't pay its own bills. Local governments have adopted a variety of strategies to cope with the new fiscal realities. Some of them, however, such as the emphasis on fees for service and the fiscalization of land-use planning, have created a whole new set of public policy problems.

REFERENCE

California Department of Finance. *California Statistical Abstract.* Sacramento: 2007.

CHAPTER *seven*

INTEREST GROUP POWER IN CALIFORNIA

Due to its sheer size, complexity, and variety, interest group activity in Sacramento defies easy definition or characterization. As government grows, so does its impact on all sectors of society. The "stakes of the game" involved in Sacramento politics increase along with the breadth and depth of modern governmental influence and power. Policy decisions made in Sacramento almost inevitably create winners and losers somewhere in the state. Should big-box warehouse-style retail outlets be prohibited from selling food products? Should employers be required to provide employee health care benefits? How strictly should agriculture's use of pesticides be regulated? Should local card clubs be allowed to expand their gambling options in order to better compete against Native American casinos? Should patients be allowed to sue their health maintenance organizations for alleged medical malpractice? Should undocumented immigrants be allowed to apply for a driver's license? Should Internet buying be exempt from the sales tax levied on over-the-counter retail purchases? The questions go on and on, but one constant remains: most policy issues attract specialized "audiences" with a direct stake in the way those issues are decided. When these audiences become organized for purposes of political persuasion, they can properly be called *interest groups*.

More than 2,400 organizations employ individuals to represent their interests in Sacramento, ranging alphabetically from the Academy of California Adoption Lawyers to a company called Zurich North America (California Secretary of State, 2007). A listing of a few of their categories (the secretary of state uses a total of 19 classifications) conveys the richness and complexity of organizational representation in the state capital: agriculture, education, entertainment/recreation, finance/insurance, government employees, health, labor, legal, manufacturing, oil and gas, professional/trade, transportation, and utilities.

Power, however, is not equally shared among all these groups. Nor does the size of a group's membership alone indicate the extent of its power. In fact, smaller, tightly knit organizations usually enjoy more political clout than large, mass-based groups lacking strong internal organization (Olson, 1965). In addition, groups representing high-prestige individuals and occupations, such as medical doctors, lawyers, or bankers, are more likely to receive a sympathetic ear from public officials than are representatives of low-prestige groups, such as welfare recipients. The presence or absence of strong opposition also affects any group's power. In addition to these determinants of group influence, two remaining factors stand out: organizational cohesiveness and financial resources. The more unified a group is, the more likely it is to act decisively in the political sphere. Individuals will not devote their time, talent, and monetary support to a group unless they are firmly committed to its goals. The development of consensus within a group spurs members' donation of money and effort to the organization. With a strong financial base, groups are in a position to hire skillful leadership and to engage in all forms of political persuasion. After discussing these various techniques used by pressure groups in California, we will assess the power of major interests in the state.

INFLUENCING STRATEGIES

One of the more remarkable aspects of interest group politics in California is the amazing flexibility and adaptability of these organizations in the face of changing political conditions. Political reforms come and go, but the power of interest groups in the state is not altered significantly. The blow suffered by political parties during the progressive era enabled organized interests to fill a political void that they have not relinquished to this day. As will be discussed in Chapter 8, some of the restrictions placed on political parties in the early twentieth century were removed in the late 1980s. Nevertheless, interest group power today is too well entrenched in California to suffer diminution of influence. The key to the central role played by pressure groups in California is their varied and creative use of many forms of political action. Some of these strategies are aimed at decision makers in Sacramento, while others target public opinion, or the "grass roots."

Campaign Contributions

In attempting to place "friends" in office, interest groups may donate money to election campaigns, offer the services of campaign volunteers, endorse candidates and ballot measures, supply free publicity in group publications, and provide free "in-kind" services such as use of office space and telephones. A central fact of political life in California is that election campaigns are expensive. The highest-level statewide races (for governor and U.S. senator) now cost around $50 million, and legislative campaign expenditures exceeding $1 million are not uncommon. Do huge campaign expenditures guarantee electoral success? Not exactly, provided that the opposition is able to spend similar funds. But if one campaign can spend a lot of money while the other campaign cannot, the outcome is pretty much certain. The meaning is clear: winning a competitive election at the statewide or legislative level requires a great deal of political money.

Aspirants for these political offices must either expend huge personal fortunes or seek large-scale campaign contributions from wealthy individuals or, more typically, well-heeled interest groups. In 1994, U.S. Representative Michael Huffington took the former route, spending approximately $29 million of his own money in an unsuccessful U.S. Senate race against Dianne Feinstein. Four years later, airline mogul Al Checchi spent even more of his personal fortune in an unsuccessful bid to capture the Democratic Party's gubernatorial nomination. But while the use of personal money may be on the rise, most candidates rely primarily on interest group donations to fund their campaigns.

From the standpoint of an interest group donor, a generous campaign contribution constitutes a rational "political investment." Such a donation can help elect a candidate who shares that group's overall view or policy goals, thus providing a friendly playing field in Sacramento. In addition, groups known as big contributors are more likely to receive a friendly hearing from officials concerned with building electoral war chests for reelection or elevation to higher office. Some campaign money does come from individual donors and from candidates themselves or their families, but interest groups represented in Sacramento are the predominant source of election funds in California. (An extended discussion of campaign finance and attempts to regulate it can be found in Chapter 9.)

Appointment Politics

With so many areas of California life involving government regulation of one form or another, groups endeavor to win appointment for their friends to a wide variety of state regulatory boards, commissions, and agencies. Because these bodies make decisions of crucial importance to those they regulate, the politics and predispositions of those who sit on them are of great interest to organized groups. Appointments to the Agricultural Labor Relations Board and the Coastal Commission are high-priority items for farmers, farm workers, developers, and conservationists. Utility companies have vital interests in the decisions rendered by the Public Utilities Commission, and commercial and recreational fishers have a stake in the policy priorities of those appointed to the Fish and Game Commission. Nor are economic interest groups the only ones concerned with whom the governor nominates to boards, commissions, and departments. With the recent controversies over affirmative action in higher education, groups and individuals on both sides of the issue closely monitor the philosophies of gubernatorial nominees to the University of California Board of Regents and the California State University Board of Trustees.

For the great majority of such nominations, approval or rejection of the governor's choice is the responsibility of the state senate. Some of that chamber's most bruising fights occur when opposing economic or philosophical interest groups square off over a controversial nomination.

Lobbying

Because this topic is examined in detail later in this chapter, we simply say at this point that many types of people attempt to influence decision makers, or apply pressure to them, in many sorts of ways. Some lobbying occurs in Sacramento and some is aimed at the grass roots. Some lobbyists are required by state law to register with the secretary of state and some are exempted from registration. Some lobbyists are considered to be professionals and some are not. In short, *lobbying* and *lobbyists* are terms that cover a broad range of individuals, strategies, and legal and organizational relationships.

Public Relations and Media Campaigns

Apart from having friends in positions of power, it is advantageous to have popular opinion behind a group's goals. Public attitudes may be influenced by either paid or free means of communication. Besides promoting specific products, advertising is used to sell political ideas and to improve the image of a particular group. Such public relations campaigns are not explicitly political. That is, they generally do not talk specifically about the organization's political or policy goals but instead attempt to paint a more general, positive picture of its activities in hopes that enhanced public popularity will translate to greater receptivity to its political needs by elected officials. Lumber interests' televised blurbs—emphasizing their concern for and love of the environment and stressing that trees are a renewable resource—are an example of an interest group attempting to reshape general public opinion. Public relations firms also are hired to plan campaigns to reach the public through the so-called free media. Advocates for a group's viewpoint are scheduled to speak on radio and television talk shows, messages are prepared for dissemination through public service announcements over the electronic media, and packets containing information supporting a group's position are sent to newspapers with the aim of creating editorial support for the organization. California Common Cause is a good example of an organization that lacks the funds to use paid media but makes effective use of free media to disseminate information to the public and to put pressure on elected officials. This organization is known for publicizing the amounts of money donated to campaigns by affluent interests and for calling attention to any decision methods (i.e., agendas, hearings, and votes) that are not open or accessible to everyone with a stake in the issue.

Initiative, Referendum, and Recall

Despite efforts to influence government officials and to place sympathetic persons in public positions, groups still may not obtain the policies they seek. When confronted with this predicament, an interest group may attempt to circumvent officeholders entirely or to have them removed by employing ballot propositions or recall procedures. Not all direct appeals to the electorate are successful by any means, but enough are to make the alternative of bypassing uncooperative elected officials a viable option for many interest groups. This opportunity for political organizations is discussed at length in Chapter 9.

Legal Action

When a legislative enactment, an executive order, a ballot initiative, or a regulatory decision goes against a group's wishes despite the use of the foregoing methods of influence, an organization may file a lawsuit to impede implementation of the decision.

When Proposition 103 (car insurance rate reduction) was passed by the voters in November 1988, insurance companies stymied its implementation for years by filing numerous legal actions. More recently, opponents of Proposition 187, the successful 1994 initiative that sought to deny educational and social services to undocumented immigrants, prevailed on the courts to enjoin its implementation. Opponents of strict political campaign contribution limits have been generally successful in convincing the courts to void ballot initiatives that put limits on such donations. On the other hand, attempts to cancel the imposition of term limits and the prohibition against certain forms of affirmative action were rebuffed by the courts. Both sides of the gay rights and same-sex marriage issue have gone to the courts on behalf of their policy agendas. Win or lose, legal action has become a staple of interest group activity in an era where great complexity as well as increasing overlap between state and federal constitutional and statute law creates confusion and conflict that courts are asked to settle. (See Chapter 5 for a discussion of the courts' role as policy maker.)

Protest

Hiring lawyers, lobbyists, and media consultants takes money, and many groups cannot afford to retain the services of such hired guns. For organizations lacking deep pockets, protest actions can be one of the few options available—in addition to donated or pro bono legal services. Environmentalists draped huge banners from the roof of the state capitol, college students marched on Sacramento to oppose fee hikes, and, during the budget impasse of 1990, disabled persons in wheelchairs blocked the entrance to the governor's office to protest proposed cutbacks in state services. Motorcyclists jammed Capitol Mall in roaring protests of the state's mandatory helmet law.

It is doubtful, however, that many legislators are moved to change their vote by a chanting crowd outside the legislative hall or on the lawn below their office. In fact, the real "target" of the protests is usually the media, especially television. A lively rally may earn a few seconds of air time on the afternoon and evening news shows: free television in place of the public relations programs whose costs remain beyond the financial reach of many interest groups. Groups experienced in the art of protest politics stage their rallies early in the day, so that their demonstrations can be filmed in time to be edited for that afternoon's and evening's news shows.

LOBBYING IN CALIFORNIA

According to the Political Reform Act of 1974, a lobbyist in California is anyone paid to communicate with state elective officials or their staffs, provided that a "substantial portion" of his or her activity is for the purpose of influencing legislative or administrative action. What is a substantial portion? The Fair Political Practices Commission, the body created to enforce the act, ruled that activity is substantial when either (1) a person earns $2,000 or more a month to influence officials or (2) a person is paid less than $2,000 per month but directly contacts state officials on at least 25 separate occasions in any two consecutive months. Most persons meeting the preceding criteria must register as lobbyists with the secretary of state. The net effect of this legal definition of lobbying is that persons who are not primarily paid to communicate are not lobbyists in the eyes of the law.

Therefore, a corporate executive, a union leader, or a school principal who infrequently (less than 25 times in two months) communicates with legislative and executive officials need not register as a lobbyist. Nor does the current law require registration of the hundreds of state bureaucrats whose main function is to lobby the legislature on behalf of their departments and agencies. Usually called "legislative liaisons," these individuals perform tasks almost identical to those we associate with lobbyists. (See Box 7.1 for a discussion of the wide variety of interest group and lobbying activity in Sacramento.)

Because negative stereotypes persist about lobbyists, registered lobbyists often refer to themselves by other titles. We see businesses called California Advocates, Commmon Interest Advocates, and Platinum Advocates, as well as firms with "Governmental Relations" or "Public Relations" in their business names. But despite their widely held negative image, lobbyists, in fact, perform the necessary and constitutionally protected function of relating the views and the information of the groups they represent to decision makers in government. However, lobbyists and lobbying campaigns do not come free. Generally, the more a group has to spend, the bigger and more polished its lobbying effort is likely to be.

No specific degrees or credentials are required to become a lobbyist. Some would-be lobbyists master an issue area while working in an industry or profession and subsequently represent that group in the state capital. Other lobbyists were formerly in elective or appointive positions in government. Some two dozen former legislators are now registered lobbyists in Sacramento. Robert Monagan was speaker of the assembly before heading the lobbying operation for the California Manufacturers Association for many years. George Steffes was Governor Reagan's legislative aide before opening his

---

BOX 7.1

California's Interest Group Constellation—Diversity at Work

Whatever a person thinks about the influence of lobbying on the political system, Sacramento's lobbyists represent an exotically diverse group of interests. Among those represented by paid lobbyists are egg producers and energy producers, acupuncturists and adult entertainment producers, utility companies and undertakers, bankers and bail bondsmen, medical doctors and motorcyclists, and just about every other interest conceivable.

Many groups represent economic interests, but good government and "cause groups," such as those representing both sides of the abortion and gay rights issues, also abound. Local governments and associations of state and local officials, both appointed and elected, also are heavily represented at the capitol. Virtually no bills are introduced in the legislature that are not important to some interest group with a lobbyist in Sacramento.

Does this mean that all interest groups are created equal? No. As discussed later in this chapter, financial and organizational resources are invaluable weapons in fighting the interest group wars. But the number and variety of represented interests do attest to the richness of this state's economic, occupational, social, and philosophical diversity. They are also an indication that what state government does is of importance to just about every Californian.

own lobbying firm. Numerous legislative staffers have left government employment for presumably greener pastures representing clients in the capital. Term limits have, and will continue to, cut short legislators' careers. These limits also create much more uncertainty and insecurity among legislative staff. As a result, Sacramento's lobbying corps is likely to be more and more impacted by legislative members and staff moving "across the street" to join the third house.

Sacramento's lobbying corps, once overwhelmingly male, now includes an almost 40% female contingent, and women lobbyists now represent some of the state's most powerful interests and biggest lobbying firms. On the other hand, Latino/Latina, Asian-American, and African-American presence in the lobbying community in no way comes close to reflecting these groups' share of the state's population, and in fact lags behind their relative numbers in the state legislature.

Rise of Mega-Lobbying

In years past, the conventional means of categorizing advocates consisted of determining whether an individual lobbyist represented one interest or several clients. Individuals representing one large business or one professional group usually were called either in-house lobbyists or association lobbyists. Advocates who, on the other hand, were retained by a multiplicity of diverse clients were referred to as contract lobbyists. An individual contract lobbyist might represent as many as five or ten clients.

Plenty of individual practitioners still operate in Sacramento, but as Table 7.1 indicates, the past four decades have witnessed a dramatic increase in the number and importance of lobbying firms, which have become the dominant lobbying power in Sacramento. The largest firms employ a stable of lobbyists and maintain dozens of individual accounts. For example, one of the largest lobbying firms, Nielsen, Merksamer,

TABLE 7.1	Consolidation of Lobbying Operations in Sacramento				
	1975	**1981**	**1989**	**1997**	**2007**
Number of lobbyists	627	605	798	1,041	981
Number of organizations represented by lobbyists	673	814	1,361	1,944	2,408
Client/lobbyist ratio	1.07	1.34	1.70	1.87	2.45
Number of lobbyists with more than one client*	116	159	299	413	523
Percent of lobbyists with more than one client%	18.5%	26.3%	37.5%	39.7%	53.3%
Number of lobbying firms with more than one lobbyist	6	16	71	91	105
Number of lobbying firms with more than ten clients	8	18	38	54	74

*Defined as lobbyists working alone who represent more than one client and lobbyists working in multilobbyist firms that represent more than one client

Source: California Secretary of State, Directory of Lobbyists, Lobbying Firms, and Lobbyist Employers (Sacramento: various years).

Parrinello, Mueller & Naylor, employs (as of 2007) nine lobbyists and represents more than 60 interest groups. Its varied list of powerhouse clients includes American Airlines, Apple Inc., California Pharmacists Association, Genetech, Motion Picture Association of America, Johnson & Johnson, Philip Morris, and Los Angeles County.

Individual lobbyists (with fewer clients) may be able to provide more personal attention to the needs of their clients than is the case with lobbying firms, where any account is just one among many. On the other hand, the megafirms have the ability to devote several lobbyists to one issue, should the need be pressing enough and the client wealthy enough to afford the extra service. And, typically, the large, heavily staffed lobbying firms can also provide research and other services such as public opinion polling on behalf of their clients' political agendas.

Aside from the differences already mentioned between firms and individual practitioners, two matters are worth noting. First, the larger the number of clients represented by a firm, the greater the likelihood that some of the clients might be on opposite sides of the same issue. Such conflicts can happen to individual practitioners, but they are more likely to occur when a firm represents dozens of clients. Firms attempt to avoid such client conflicts by exercising care when accepting new customers. If such care is not sufficient to avoid problems, lobbying firms attempt to reconcile the differences among their clients or advise certain customers to retain other representation for the issue in conflict.

Second, the more numerous the clients, the more numerous the campaign-contributing interests represented by the lobbying firm. Some time ago this issue of lobbyists representing multiple campaign contributors was a recognized problem among political reformers.

> When Clay Jackson (25 clients) lobbies you on something that is important to him, you are not simply talking to one of his employers. You are relating to Clay Jackson, who has the campaign financing resources of ten or twenty significant players. (Kushman, 1988b)

Note that this observation was made at a time when 25 clients constituted a very large lobbying firm. And the object example, Clay Jackson, was later indicted and convicted of bribery in an FBI sting operation and sentenced to federal prison.

Now that firms representing twice as many clients are common in Sacramento, what is the impact of their "bundled contribution" clout on policy making? And how crucial is this factor in the increasing tendency of wealthy interest groups to sign on with the largest lobbying firms?

These questions are not meant to imply that lobbyists, working individually or as part of a lobbying firm, are part of a sinister, hidden "big money conspiracy." Nor should they be taken to mean that the vast majority of lobbyists are not honest and ethical. As earlier mentioned, lobbying is an integral and necessary part of the policy-making process. And unless we want to restrict public officeholding to the very rich, campaign contributions from interest groups are absolutely necessary in a state in which it is so expensive to run for the legislature and there is no public funding for campaigns. But as will be discussed later in this chapter, a merging of wealthy interests, campaign contributions, and megalobbying operations is worth noting and requires concerned attention.

Inside Lobbying

Inside lobbying is partly communicating information and partly cultivating friendships. Lobbyists give drafts of bills, amendments, speeches, and regulations to decision makers. In addition, they transmit information on proposed policies' costs, economic ramifications, and social and environmental impacts to public officials. Along with materials bearing on the substance or merits of the issue at hand, lobbyists provide procedural and political information. They advise lawmakers concerning the appropriate vehicle—a bill, a resolution, or control language in the state budget—for a specific matter, and they may be of assistance on parliamentary rules. Lobbyists provide political intelligence that is extremely useful to decision makers, concerning who opposes and who supports a measure, both inside and outside of government. Lobbying organizations prepare precise head counts of votes at various points along the legislative process to assist authors carrying their bills and to find out where more work needs to be done.

Even seemingly minor bits of information ultimately may have political uses, so sophisticated lobbying operations have files of several types. *District characteristic files* can be maintained to assist lobbyists in determining how a given legislator's constituents will react to a bill. *Personal data files* can be kept on public officials. Is the decision maker a pilot or a hunter? Is the public servant the parent of a physically challenged child? Does someone in the family have a drug problem? Or is a family member a schoolteacher or other type of public employee? Such background material may aid a lobbyist in finding a sympathetic ear in government. *Topic or issue files* contain information on specific areas used to provide decision makers with ample justification to support a measure on its merits alone. It may be necessary for lobbyists to stress different points with different officials. Finally, though such information may or may not be placed in a file, competent lobbyists make mental notes about the most effective way to gain access to particular officials. Perhaps approaching a decision maker through his or her staff, through a particular legislator, through the director of an executive department, or through a respected person in an interest group or political party is preferable to contacting the official personally.

Having a thorough understanding of the issues and an in-depth knowledge of the personalities of the key decision makers, lobbyists serve as guides through the complicated labyrinth of the governmental process. The unwritten code of lobbyists is well known to registered advocates in Sacramento. Trying to undo a decision is most difficult, so lobbyists endeavor to be as timely as possible in their communication. The accuracy of presentations is crucial because political allies should never be embarrassed by repeating incorrect information. As the saying goes in the capitol, "Credibility is like virginity—once you lose it, it's tough to get it back" (Kushman, 1988a).

The term *lobbyist* misleadingly suggests that advocates communicate with public officials in hallways and corridors. A bit of last-minute input is conveyed in the halls outside meeting rooms, but far more information is delivered outside public view. Lobbyists make sure that officials receive written communication concerning their clients' positions on issues pending decision. Telephone conversations and private visits are used to follow up position letters. Lobbyists are free to testify at committee hearings held by the California legislature, but many advocates decline this opportunity because they are confident that the votes are already in place for their clients' positions. Some time ago the importance of early, private communication was underscored by these still-relevant comments of a former legislative staffer:

> My college textbooks had emphasized that a legislature's real work is not accomplished on the floor, but in committee. But I observed very few instances where thoughtful substantive change occurred either on the floor or in committee. Rather the formal hearings merely reflected the gritty negotiations that actually took place beforehand. . . . One of the most striking aspects of legislative decision making is that the basic, formative decisions which shape a major program are made before the formal legislative process ever begins. (BeVier, 1979, pp. 102–103, 218)

The other main aspect of inside lobbying traditionally centers around the cultivation of friendships. Despite the limitations on lobbyists' spending that are discussed at the conclusion of this chapter, it is still possible for lobbyists to meet with public officials on golf courses, on tennis courts, or in exercise clubs. Provided that proper disclosure takes place and the registered lobbyist does not pay the bills, representatives of interest groups may socialize with public officials. In the not-too-distant past, personal friendships with lawmakers could be a crucial part of a lobbyist's influencing tactics. But this statement is likely no longer so true. Term limits, adopted in 1990, shortened legislative careers and thus disrupted the durable networking ties that lobbyists enjoyed. To the extent that an "old boys' network" once was a key to lobbying influence, the realities of term limits have forced advocates to adopt new and less personal influencing styles and strategies.

Though known primarily as communicators, some registered lobbyists really are closer to being coordinators. Much of the lobbyist's time today is spent coordinating the activities of others—e.g., managing an association or coalition, finding appropriate witnesses to testify at hearings, and organizing grassroots input to decision makers—rather than communicating face-to-face with government leaders.

Lobbyists' activities can be characterized as "offensive" or "defensive" legislative lobbying. Some interests are mainly concerned with changing existing laws and relationships through the passage of legislation; others struggle to maintain the status quo by defeating proposed legislation. Although practically all groups find themselves from time to time in either position, certain kinds of interests, such as successful licensed occupations (for example, medical doctors and architects), usually are on the defense. Other organizations may be seeking to enhance their position or reform current conditions. Thus, groups such as the California Chiropractic Association (wishing to expand chiropractors' legal scope of practice) and California Common Cause may be more active in sponsoring legislation. In the wake of legislative staff cuts mandated by Proposition 140 in 1990, organizations sponsoring legislation took on more of the burdens once shouldered by legislative staffs (such as lining up witnesses for bills). And the task of choosing legislative authors for favored bills has become complicated following the departure of many longtime legislative experts who could be counted on to lend their prestige and expertise to bills that bore their name.

Outside Lobbying

Whereas inside lobbying is largely performed by Sacramento-based lobbyists, outside lobbying is usually accomplished by persons who volunteer their time, although lobby-

B O X 7.2	**Political Clout and the Private Utilities: Public Relations to the Rescue?**

California's private power utilities have long been major money players in Sacramento politics. For example, Edison International, parent company of Southern California Edison, spent $2.5 million on its lobbying operations during the 2005–2006 period. Pacific Gas and Electric Company (PG&E) spent $2.4 million on its influencing program. (Utilities lobby both the legislature and the Public Utilities Commission.)

As of 2007, PG&E utilizes the services of one in-house lobbyist and three separate lobbying firms (including the aforementioned Nielsen, Merksamer, etc.), while Edison employs four lobbyists directly and hires the services of four different lobbying firms. Not surprisingly, some of the lobbying firms employed by the two utilities are among the largest in Sacramento.

However, even the biggest lobbying campaigns have their limits if the political tides are not running right. If an interest group suffers from a negative public image, its access to and influence on elected officials also suffer. Especially in the aftermath of the 2001 energy crisis, utilities are unpopular with many Californians, and that likely complicates their attempts to cultivate positive relationships with Sacramento decision makers, since few politicians would like to be labeled "pro-utility" at this point in time. Significantly, PG&E responded to this problem by commencing an aggressive public relations program in an attempt to bolster its standing among California voters.

ists may help coordinate these efforts. As discussed earlier, registration with the secretary of state as a lobbyist is required only of those for whom policy influence is a career. Bankers, teachers, farmers, and real estate brokers, among others, lobby in Sacramento periodically and need not register. Outside lobbying takes two basic forms: letter-writing campaigns and personal visits. Each form may come in several variations.

When organizing letter writing to a government official, it is best if letters are individually written instead of appearing to be form letters. Specificity is crucial. The recipients of letters should be asked precisely what they like and dislike about given bills or regulations. Officials should be asked pointedly what their positions are on particular items, allowing them less opportunity to respond in a vague manner. Letters from a legislator's home district are thought to have more impact than those from other constituencies. Letter writing can be undertaken by a small number of influentials (the rifle approach), by the general membership of an interest group (the shotgun approach), or by the public at large as a result of newspaper ads (the grapeshot approach). However broad or narrow the source of letters, it is important to maintain control over the content of the correspondence and to ensure those letters refer to the current wording of the legislation in question.

Personal contact with officials likewise may be undertaken by the few or the many. Interest groups with established *key contact* systems assign carefully selected members the responsibility of cultivating and later communicating with particular officials. The California Association of Realtors developed a Legislative Tree program that identified real estate brokers who have personal, professional, fraternal, or other ties with officials so that these contacts may be exploited (Lofland, 1982, pp. 33–34). Individuals belonging to the same social and religious organizations as a given lawmaker are used as key contact persons. The California Medical Association (CMA) utilizes physicians in each legislative district to personally contact local representatives. Skillful use of key contact members is a good tool for organizations whose membership includes effective communicators willing to engage authority figures such as state legislators. But what works for an organization of doctors or bankers may not work as well for organizations representing members who lack education and polished communication skills.

One of the unanticipated consequences of term limits is a higher premium on *grassroots lobbying.* The constant turnover of legislators under term limits has probably reduced the effectiveness of the "old-style" lobbying, which relied on advocates' long-term relationships with legislators who were key players in specific policy fields. With legislators moving in and out of the assembly and senate more quickly, they have less chance to develop as key players with whom lobbyists can develop such relationships. Without this inside edge, lobbying operations may find it more expedient to use their group members to lobby as many individual legislators as possible.

However, it would be a mistake to assume that these changes have somehow evened out the struggle for influence and power. Remember, it is the best-organized and re-

PHOTO 7.1   California Correctional Peace Officer Association memorial and office building. Symbolism and political muscle make correctional officers one of Sacramento's most powerful interest groups. (*Department of Government, California State University, Sacramento*)

source-rich groups with articulate and self-confident memberships that can most effec-tively engage in grassroots lobbying. This new emphasis may also be one of the reasons why lobbying firms are replacing single lobbyist operations in Sacramento. These firms are best able to provide the multilevel services, including organizing grassroots campaigns, that interest groups now require for their portfolio of policy-influencing strategies.

If inside lobbying and key contacts are insufficient, an interest group may engage in *crowd lobbying*. A group's members may be mobilized to appear in Sacramento on an emergency basis timed to influence a specific decision or on an annual basis to remind government officials of the group's presence. Swarms of people in the capitol for a one-time event may or may not be effective depending on the level of preparation and coordination they display. Planning, coordination, and control are vital ingredients of a successful crowd lobbying strategy. A close student of crowd lobbying has concluded that "the larger the swarm, the less the likelihood there was of prearrangement and the greater the degree of confusion, milling, abrasive contact with officials, and the likeli-hood of people wandering off and sightseeing in and around the Capitol" (Lofland, 1982, p. 26).

Because legislative hearings are often postponed and rescheduled, it can be diffi-cult to effectively time an emergency mobilization. Alternatively, organized groups may decide to hold their annual meeting in Sacramento. One aspect of an annual gathering might be a Legislative Day. At such an event, group members are briefed by their lobby-ists concerning pending issues and then meet with public officials at prearranged appointments. Groups also may hold receptions or dinners honoring legislators at which officeholders sit with group members from their districts.

Size is not everything in crowd lobbying; style of operation is just as important as sheer numbers, if not more so. Groups lacking competent inside lobbyists cannot count on legions of outside lobbyists to rescue their case in Sacramento. Given the careful planning that is needed to make crowd lobbying work, groups hiring capable registered advocates to lobby inside are the ones most likely to exert effective outside pressure as well. Grassroots lobbying complements inside lobbying; it does not replace it.

MONEY AND POWER: THE SACRAMENTO CONNECTION

In Sacramento, nearly 1,000 registered lobbyists (and, remember, many who lobby are not registered) represent more than 2,400 organized interests. In sheer number and variety, interest group activities mirror the state's size and diversity. None of these fac-tors should be taken to mean, however, that interest group power is so widely dispersed. Most key elements of an organization's political program—experienced and effective lobbyists, well-organized membership infrastructure, generous campaign contributions, and effective public relations—are expensive. Over a two-year period spanning one leg-islative session, California interest groups spent more than one half *billion* dollars on lobbying state officials. This figure is, however, not at all evenly divided among all inter-est groups. The top ten individual business spenders, less than 0.5 percent of all groups attempting to influence government, accounted for more than $25 million, or about 6 percent, of all lobbying expenses (Robertson, 2005). The more an organization can afford to spend, the more potent its political program is likely to be. Moreover, organizations with a well-educated, articulate, and prestigiously positioned membership are better situated to exercise grassroots influence through membership telephone and letter-writing campaigns. Thus, it is no surprise that the largest political-influencing operations in Sacramento tend to represent those interests and individuals who also have the most social and economic power throughout the state.

Although some successful interest groups do not expend a great deal of money in Sacramento, it seems logical to assume that "more is better" in terms of the relationship between the money spent to influence and the degree of influence enjoyed. For example, an organization able to pay top dollar for its lobbying corps can purchase and maintain experienced, top-flight representation. Less well endowed organizations may not enjoy the same advantage; they may instead rely on younger, less experienced lobbyists and more volunteer help. Turnover in their lobbying staffs may also be much more rapid. In addition, money buys the research capabilities and organizational networking to back up the efforts of lobbyists. On a surface, but not necessarily trivial, level, a visitor to Sacramento could compare the lobbying office locations, equipment, and furnishings of the best-funded interests with those of organizations without huge financial resources to get a sense of the advantages money can purchase.

Nor does the money connection end here. These same best-funded interests are also among the state's leaders in campaign contributions. For example, the California Teachers Association, number one on the lobbying expenditure list, sits at, or very near the top of the campaign contribution list in election after election. And to complete the picture of the merger between the big campaign and big lobbying spenders and the megalobbying firms, many of the biggest spenders on lobbying and campaign contributions are represented by the largest lobbying firms.

TABLE 7.2	The Best Influence Money Can Buy? A Sample of Interests Spending at Least $1 Million Per Year on Lobbying Operations
Organization	**Lobbying Expenditures***
California Teachers Assn.	$11,670,000
Western States Petroleum Assn.	$6,650,000
California Chamber of Commerce	$5,564,000
Consumer Attorneys of California	$2,906,000
California Hospital Assn.	$2,816,000
California Manufacturers Assn.	$2,699,098
Edison International	$2,587,000
Pacific Gas & Electric	$2,401,000
California Medical Assn.	$2,369,000
California Nurses Assn.	$2,061,000

Note: Expenditure totals are for the period of January 2005 through December 2006.

Source: California Secretary of State, 2007–2008 Directory of Lobbyists, Lobbying Firms, and Lobbyist Employers (Sacramento: 2007).

INTEREST GROUP POWER: GOOD FOR THE POLITICAL SYSTEM?

The very big spenders clearly are also some of the largest economic interests in the state. Table 7.2 lists some, though hardly all, of the interests that can and do spend at least $1 million per year on lobbying. While there is a good deal of variety in such organization types, all are recognized as very politically influential. Conversely, interests with less economic power are limited to less costly influencing strategies. But should that relationship concern us?

Defenders of interest group politics point out that interest groups can also serve to protect the rights and interests of minorities against "the tyranny of the majority." Because interest group success is based more on internal cohesion and membership solidarity than on mere organizational size, intense minorities can prevail against the apathy or opposition of larger but less intense majorities. Mothers Against Drunk Driving (MADD) affords such an example. Founded by families of victims of drunk drivers, MADD was able to utilize the energy and tenacity of its membership to force the legislature to adopt much more severe sanctions against convicted drunk drivers.

Finally, interest groups afford citizens a form of political representation beyond that of their elected officials. It would be the rare citizen indeed whose entire set of policy preferences was perfectly represented by his or her district's elected state senator and assembly member. Interest groups afford another avenue of persuasion and influence in Sacramento. For example, a voter whose priority issue is environmental protection may be "represented" in Sacramento by pro-development legislators; a citizen adamantly opposed to legalized abortion could live in a district that elects pro-choice advocates to the legislature. In either case, at least in terms of these specific issues, these citizens' priorities will not be supported by their district's elected representatives, but they can be given an organizational presence in Sacramento by interest groups such as the Planning and Conservation League and the National Right to Life Committee.

However, even as we recognize that interest group activity is not inherently evil, we could still argue the undesirability of *undue* group influence, which, at least in the eyes of many state political observers, is the reality in California. In fact, California has long been known as a strong interest group state. First, the historical legal and organizational weakness of the state's political parties (discussed in Chapter 8) is the reason most often cited for California's strong interest groups. In essence, interest groups moved into a power vacuum created by the enfeeblement of political parties. A second, not completely unrelated aspect of state politics is the tremendous expense involved in running for office in the Golden State (discussed in Chapter 9). Expensive campaigns usually require massive infusions of interest group money in the form of campaign donations. As already discussed, such donations purchase access and influence for the interest group in Sacramento. And California's "direct democracy" processes, especially the initiative, are ideal vehicles for interest group power (see Chapter 9). Finally, the size, complexity, and diversity of the state may thwart the creation of inclusive, broad-based policy and political positions and instead encourage a politics based on a set of more narrow, interest group–dominated agendas.

Concerns with the prevalence of interest group power in California politics generally fall into three categories. The first focuses on governmental deadlock. When interest groups' power within their issue areas amounts to a virtual veto over new policy, government's ability to create responsive and effective policy is short-circuited. For many years, California labored under a workers' compensation system that failed to effectively serve the needs of either business or workers. Despite virtually no disagreement that the system was badly flawed, reform attempts were regularly defeated by the veto power held by one of the three key interest group players—insurers, employers, and workers' compensation attorneys. This logjam was finally broken, yet many similar policy areas, such as tort reform and medical insurance, remain stalemated. In these areas where competing interest groups dominate, no one group possesses the power to push through its desired changes, but each can prevent the enactment of the other's agenda. Absent the power and ability of elected officials to push through change over interest group opposition, the result is policy stagnation.

Policy stagnation caused by a standoff between competing interests is one problem caused by interest group–dominated politics. A second variant of the problem arises when vast disparities exist in resources commanded by groups that compete over policy questions. Landlords and renters, farmers and farm workers, and medical doctors and other health care providers are three pairs of interests that compete over certain policy areas. But these opponents clearly differ in terms of the monetary and organizational resources available to them. Hence, big discrepancies also characterize the variety and quality of influencing modes and strategies they can utilize. To the extent that interest group politics decide the policy winners and the policy losers, the rich and established interests prevail over those interests that are not rich and not already comfortably established. In turn, policy decisions reinforce and widen the gap between the "haves" and "have-nots."

The third area of concern engendered by interest group politics deals with corruption, both in its reality and in the public perception of its prevalence. The vast majority of lobbyists are honest representatives who abide by the law; most campaign contributions are delivered legally and are fully and voluntarily reported. A U.S. Department of Justice sting operation that led to the successful prosecution of several Sacramento politicians, legislative staffers, and lobbyists was newsworthy because, compared to politics in most states, California politics are relatively "clean." At times, as the convictions demonstrated, interest group agendas and politicians' personal and political ambitions lead to illegal activity, but this scenario is far from the norm in Sacramento. On the other hand, the political money used by interest groups to enhance their influence and access and by politicians to protect and advance their electoral careers does play a central role in state politics. This evaluation is common knowledge among those who participate in or who write about and study Sacramento politics. Increasingly, it is also assumed by the general public. A political process perceived to be corrupted by political money will continue to lose the public's trust, support, and participation. Interest group politics, the primary generator of political money, thus bear some of the blame for the increasing alienation between California citizens and their government.

REGULATION OF LOBBYISTS AND INTEREST GROUPS

California's basic regulations governing the activity of lobbyists in Sacramento were written in the wake of two scandals. First, California voters approved the Political Reform Act (PRA) in June 1974 at the height of the Watergate episode in Washington,

D.C. Second, the electorate passed Proposition 112 in June 1990, some six weeks after the sentencing of former Senator Joseph Montoya following his conviction for extorting money in exchange for his legislative votes. Technically, Proposition 112 dealt more with restrictions on legislators and legislative staff than on lobbyists, but the provisions of this legislative constitutional amendment altered the working conditions under which lobbyists operate.

The PRA of 1974 requires lobbyists to register with the secretary of state every two years at the beginning of each new legislative session. Registration includes providing a list of all of a lobbyist's clients, from which a directory is prepared. In addition to registering, lobbyists must file quarterly reports disclosing how much they personally received in salary and expenses, as well as how much they spent on particular government officials. The PRA also prohibits *registered lobbyists* from giving gifts (including food and beverages, travel expenses, or anything else of value) in excess of $10 per month to any legislative or administrative official. Note that the $10 limit applies only to registered lobbyists, or fewer than 1,000 people in the entire state. Members of pressure groups (other than their officially registered lobbyists) do not have to abide by this $10 limitation. The PRA does prohibit nonlobbyists from giving more than $250 in gifts per calendar year to each decision maker. Campaign donations are not considered to be gifts under the law.

Even though the PRA directly changed lobbying styles through its entertainment limitations and reporting provisions, it failed to shut off the money connection between interest groups and elected officials. Beyond campaign donations, untouched by the 1974 law, interest groups—although not their lobbyists—were allowed to pay honoraria (speaking fees) to officeholders, to retain lawyer legislators as legal counsel, to put elected officials on salary as political consultants, to provide lavish travel arrangements for state officials, and to employ public decision makers the day after they leave state service. An explicit exchange of money for a vote is an illegal bribe. Through 1990, however, it was perfectly legal for a grateful group to offer a high-paying job to a state official immediately upon his or her retirement from state government—in the eyes of some, little more than a deferred bribe. Financial ties such as these gave the appearance of impropriety, even if actual illegality could not be proven.

When the U.S. attorney and the FBI began what were to be successful cases against public officials, the leaders of the California legislature realized the need to stop the erosion of public confidence in their houses. Legislators drafted and passed a constitutional amendment that altered many of the financial practices that had existed for decades. This measure was placed on the ballot as Proposition 112 in June 1990. The voters approved the measure, which prohibited or restricted many questionable practices. The new restrictions included a prohibition on interest group honoraria payments to elected officials and a one-year "cooling-off period" during which recently retired legislative and executive branch officials cannot be employed to lobby their former governmental branches. Finally, Proposition 34, passed in November 2000, prohibited lobbyists (though not their employers) from making campaign contributions to officials whom they also attempt to influence on behalf of their clients.

Both the 1974 and the 1990 reforms were aimed at some of the most flagrant examples of favor buying, undue influence, and individual officials' questionable practices. But as discussed in Chapter 9, reformers attempting to regulate campaign finance, the most crucial source of interest group influence, have endured a series of partial, temporary victories that were soon wiped away by the courts.

SUMMARY

The number, variety, and energy of political interest groups in California are impressive. Equally impressive are the many tactics and strategies they use in their attempts to influence the state's public policy. It would be a mistake, however, to assume that interest group power, as dependent on monetary and organizational resources as it is, is anywhere close to evenly dispersed throughout society. As the song tells us, "Money can't sing or dance." But it can speak quite clearly and effectively to elected officials who make California's public policy.

This problem, as well as other concerns about the effects of interest group politics on the state's public sector, have historically not been effectively addressed, despite California's strong reform tradition. In fact, some "reforms"—such as the weakening of political parties and the establishment of the initiative, referendum, and recall—whose target were the special interests—ironically enhanced interest group influence over public policy.

REFERENCES

BeVier, Michael. *Politics Backstage: Inside the California Legislature.* Philadelphia: Temple University Press, 1979.

California Secretary of State. *2007–2008 Directory of Lobbyists, Lobbying Firms, and Lobbyist Employers.* Sacramento: 2007.

California Secretary of State. *Campaign Expenditures.* Sacramento: 1999.

Kushman, Rick. "The Business of Lobbying: Part I." *Sacramento Bee* (February 14, 1988a).

Kushman, Rick. "The Business of Lobbying: Part II." *Sacramento Bee* (February 15, 1988b).

Lofland, John. *Crowd Lobbying: An Emerging Tactic of Interest Group Influence in California.* Davis, CA: Institute of Governmental Affairs, 1982.

Olson, Mancur. *The Logic of Collective Action.* Cambridge: Harvard University Press, 1965.

Robertson, Kathy. "Wide Range of Players Spend $422 Million to Steer State Their Way." *Sacramento Business Journal* (February 5, 2005).

CHAPTER eight

POLITICAL PARTIES AND MEDIA: LINKING THE PUBLIC TO THE PROCESS

Interest groups, political parties, and news organizations all serve to link Californians to their government. However, each is distinctive. Interest groups seek to attain benefits for their specific membership. As discussed in Chapter 7, groups need not encompass huge numbers to be effective. In fact, many of the most successful are quite narrow in terms of their goals and their membership, and they tend to be homogeneous or exclusive in character. Political parties and news organizations, on the other hand, serve a much wider and more heterogeneous audience. Because their paramount goal is electing their candidates to office, political parties are open and inclusive by nature, continually trying to attract a majority of voters. Akin to parties, news organizations endeavor to maximize their circulation and their educational objectives so their appeal is to the mass public, or least an identifiable segment of that mass public.

In addition to the breadth of their focus and their inclusiveness, these linking mechanisms differ in the extent to which they are accountable to the public. By shifting their vote to candidates of another party or by utilizing another source for the news, voters and news consumers can hold political parties and media organizations accountable for their actions. In contrast, it is difficult to compel accountability of an interest group unless one is a member of the group, and then perhaps only if one is a member of the group's leadership corps.

CALIFORNIA AS A WEAK PARTY STATE

Political parties consist of three separate segments: the *party in government*, meaning party members holding elective positions; the party organization, referring to those individuals who work (either as paid employees or volunteers) for the party but who do not hold office; and the *party in the electorate*, or the groupings of individual voters who consistently support the party on election day. The main source of strength for California parties is their party-in-government sector, particularly in the state legislature. The state senate and assembly are organized along party lines, and these party lines serve as the main dividing lines on issues. In fact (as discussed in Chapter 3), many citizens believe that legislators and the legislative process are overly partisan.

By contrast, the party-organization and party-in-the-electorate segments of the Republican and Democratic Parties are much less powerful. Unlike the party organizations in "strong party" states, California's party organizations lack the power to determine, or even have much influence over, party nominations to elective office. California voters demonstrate a strong inclination to ignore party labels, especially for top-of-the-ticket elections, such as for governor or U.S. senator. If one motto summarized state voter disdain of party loyalty, it would be "I vote for the best candidate, not the party label." Weak party loyalty among voters and weak party organizations are exactly what the progressives of the early twentieth century hoped to achieve through their political reforms of the 1909–1915 era. Major portions of that reform legislation were much later nullified by the courts. But, ironically, the progressive spirit of antipartyism is alive and well today, despite the court-imposed demise of key components of its statutory and constitutional structure. What follows is a description of this legal attack on California's political parties mounted by the progressives a century ago.

1. *Local Nonpartisanship.* A key reason for weak parties in California is the nonpartisan nature of local elections. Consider the number of offices filled by partisan elections as opposed to those filled by nonpartisan elections. The partisan races for seats in the U.S. Senate (2), U.S. House of Representatives (53), state legislature (120), state executive positions (11), and U.S. president and vice president (2) total a mere 188 contests in which the party label is attached to candidates. Conversely, more than 19,000 officials in the judicial, local government, and special district arenas are selected through nonpartisan elections. With party labels not legally allowed on the ballots for thousands of local contests, a firm foundation for political parties at the grassroots level is missing. With parties on the sidelines in local politics, interest groups (e.g., merchant organizations, teachers' unions, and service clubs) recruit and support candidates for city, county, and special district offices. In the absence of parties at the local level, press endorsements take on more importance. In addition, the absence of strong local party organizations means that even candidates for higher partisan offices must look to nonparty sources of grassroots organizational support.

2. *Ban on Preprimary Endorsement.* From 1913 to 1987, the state elections code forbade official party organizations at the state and local levels to "endorse, support, or oppose, any candidate for nomination by that party for partisan office in the direct primary election." For 74 years following the progressive era, official party bodies were silenced in primary campaigns. Even though this prohibition on preprimary endorsements was lifted on constitutional grounds in 1987, the advantage that interest groups in California developed in terms of endorsing

and bankrolling candidates is likely to persist. And given the antiparty sentiments of many voters, it's an open question as to whether primary election candidates would be much helped by a party's official stamp of approval.

3. *Party Organizational Restrictions.* Language in the elections code formerly required
   that state party chairpersons serve only a two-year term and that they not be
   allowed to succeed themselves. The party chairperson once was required by state
   law to alternate every two years between persons from Northern and Southern
   California. These legal provisions inhibited the development of effective party
   leadership in California. The elections code also instructed the state party when
   to meet, where to meet, and what its composition would be. Although these
   restrictions on party organization were lifted by the ninth U.S. Circuit Court of
   Appeals in 1987 (and affirmed by the U.S. Supreme Court in 1989), California's
   backwardness in matters of party development is an ongoing fact.

4. *Cross-filing.* Cross-filing, also adopted by the progressives, allowed primary election candidates to enter as many party nomination contests as they saw fit. For
   example, a Republican candidate for state senate would, obviously, run in the
   Republican primary contest, but that person could also enter the Democratic
   primary, or any other party's primary. It was thus possible, and, in fact, quite normal in legislative races, for a single candidate to capture both parties' nominations, especially because the actual party affiliation of the candidate was not dis-
   closed on the primary ballot. The effect was to further blur party identification
   of both officeholders and voters and, when candidates won both primaries, to
   remove partisanship from the general election, since both party nominees were,
   in fact, the same person. Cross-filing was abolished by the legislature in 1959.

5. *Direct Democracy.* California, like about half the states, possesses the direct democracy devices of initiative, referendum, and recall. Direct democracy (another product of the progressive era) runs counter to strong parties. Should persons elected
   to state and local offices not be responsive, interest groups may bypass these public
   officials by using initiatives to make public policy or by using referenda to undo
   laws with which they disagree. Interest groups may also attempt to remove officeholders through the use of recall. Having invested considerable effort in electing
   their nominees to office, political parties are undermined by the possibility of their
   officeholders being either circumvented by the initiative process or removed from
   office by recall. Direct democracy provides interest groups with a useful means by
   which to threaten or ignore party officials in government.

California's progressives are long since deceased, as are many of their legal attacks
on the parties. But their spirit lives on in the Golden State, as evidenced by recent ballot
measures aimed at further reducing the role of the parties. In 1996, state voters
approved a new style of primary election, the blanket primary, to replace the existing
closed-primary system. Under the old closed-primary election system, voters were given a
ballot corresponding to their party registration. For example, a voter registered to vote
as a Democrat was given a ballot listing only Democratic candidates for the various
offices. And only registered Democratic voters could take part in that party's primary
election. A registered voter who claimed no party affiliation, one who "declined to state,"
could not participate in any partisan primary contests. In 1996, voters approved
Proposition 198, which gave the state a blanket primary. Under the blanket system, all

voters, regardless of what, if any, party they claim on their voter registration, are given the same ballot. This ballot contains the names of all the candidates from all the parties for each of the contested offices. For each office, the leading vote getter for each of the parties receives that party's nomination and thus appears on the general election ballot. What that means is that an aspirant for a major-party nomination—say, the Republican nomination for state assembly—need not just appeal to her own party members for votes. Instead, she could outpace the other Republican candidates for that office by receiving strong voter support from independents and registrants from the other parties.

Strong pro and con arguments can be made for the blanket primary. One of its certain and intended effects, however, is to weaken the ties between candidates and parties and between voters and parties. One can assume that the progressives would have heartily approved the substance of Proposition 198's blanket primary and the spirit of the voters who supported it, but the U.S. Supreme Court was much less impressed. Citing political parties' right of free association under the U.S. Constitution's First Amendment, the Court in 2001 nullified California's blanket primary. It was back to the drawing board for the state legislature, which had to develop a new primary election system in time for the March 2002 primary elections. The legislature's response was to reimpose, with some modifications, the old closed-primary system. Not to be deterred, the state's antiparty forces qualified yet another primary election system, the nonpartisan primary, for the November 2004 ballot. At that election, voters rejected this proposed change, despite its endorsement by Governor Schwarzenegger. But, given continued strong public disenchantment with both major parties, future assaults on the closed primary can be expected. (See Box 8.1 for a description of the various primary systems that California has utilized or considered.)

 BOX 8.1

Primary Election Options—What Are They, and Why Does It Matter?

There are at least five possible primary systems that states may adopt; their choice is crucial to the role parties play in the selection process.

1. *Closed Primary.* In this system, voters are provided a primary election coinciding with, and limited to, their party registration. For example, a registered Republican voter is automatically given the Republican ballot, containing only the names of candidates for the Republican Party nominations. Those voters who do not specify a party of registration, the decline-to-state voters, may not participate in any partisan primary elections. From 1909 to 1998, California operated under a closed-primary election system.

2. *Modified Open or Hybrid Primary.* When, in 2001, the U.S. Supreme Court invalidated California's newly created blanket primary (described in option 4, below), the legislature was required to quickly create a new system in time for the 2002 election cycle. The legislative response was to reenact the old closed-primary system, at least for all voters registered with a party. Decline-to-state voters, however, were given the right to choose any party's ballot, so long as that party had voluntarily agreed to allow the decline-to-state registrants to participate in its primary.

BOX 8.1	**Primary Election Options—What Are They, and Why Does It Matter? (*continued*)**

(The Democratic Party currently accepts their participation while the Republican Party does not.) This system is currently in place for California.

3. *Open Primary.* Like the closed primary, each party has its separate ballot, containing only the names of candidates for that party's nomination. But voters are allowed to request and receive any party's ballot, regardless of their party registration. California has never utilized this system, although it has been adopted by about half of the other 49 states.

4. *Blanket Primary.* In this system, there is only one primary election ballot form, which contains the names of all candidates for all parties' nominations for all offices. Voters are free to pick and choose among various candidates in all the parties' nomination contests. Voters' party registration or preference, if any, is irrelevant to the ballot they receive.

5. *Nonpartisan Primary.* Proposed to and rejected by the voters in the November 2004 election, the nonpartisan primary essentially removes political parties from the nomination process. After the primary election (whose ballot follows the blanket-primary format), the two leading vote getters for each office advance to the November general election ballot, even if those two candidates are from the same party. In effect, this system consists of two "general elections," the first to reduce the field to two candidates and the second to actually fill the office by selecting one of the two. The general election candidates are not considered, at least officially, as party nominees, although their partisan affiliation appears on the general election ballot.

Option 1 is the most "party friendly," as it is premised on the notions that the nomination process is a political party process and that participation in a party's nomination process should be open only to adherents of that party. Options 4 and 5 are the most antiparty, as they place no limits based on party registration on voting participation and range of primary election choices. The nonpartisan primary goes even one step further than the blanket primary by, in effect, ending the idea that candidates get on the general election ballot through nomination by their party.

Clearly, how citizens judge the relative merits of these primary election options depends on how big a role they wish political parties to play. Those who favor a strong role cite the potential of parties to act as a counterweight to the power of private interest groups and the fact that strong, tightly organized parties can present clear-cut choices to voters. On the other hand, as discussed in Chapter 3, many believe that too much partisanship, perhaps the result of the closed-primary nomination of senate and assembly candidates, has stymied policy compromise and is to blame for legislative stalemate. However, blanket and nonpartisan primaries, based on the "best candidate, not the party label" philosophy, are not without their own shortfalls. If candidates for nomination must reach all voters, as opposed to only their own party registrants, the cost of primary election campaigning is likely to go up. And if party labels no longer play an important role in determining general election winners, political incumbents, who already possess name recognition, and the rich and famous will enjoy even greater electoral advantage.

Beyond California's own antiparty environment, political parties nationwide are experiencing difficult challenges. Changes in campaign technology (radio, movies, television, and now the Internet) make it easier for candidates to mount personalized campaigns instead of running as one member of a party slate. Computerized direct mail and electronic communications permit candidates (provided they have the money to afford these expensive strategies) to reach voters without benefit of a party apparatus. Finally, although political parties can and do raise money for their candidates, campaign contributions and independent expenditures by private interests dwarf those of the parties.

Party Rank and File: Instability as the Norm

About 22.8 million Californians are over the age of 18 and eligible to vote, and out of this population, a little more than 15.7 million are registered to vote. As of 2007, about 76.7 percent of these registrants are registered as either Republican (34.2%) or Democrat (42.5%), while the rest either decline to state a party preference or are enrolled with one of the minor parties. In fact, both major parties have witnessed significant declines in their percentages of registered voters. In 1970, a scant 5 percent, or just 1 in 20, were registered as anything but Republican or Democrat. By 2007, this figure had more than quadrupled to 23.3 percent, or almost one in four. The principal source for this change was not growth in minor-party membership but rather a steady and steep increase in the number of registrants who decline to state any party preference. Almost one in five registered voters now declines to state, and this number is growing (California Secretary of State, 2007).

This trend indicates a growing number of voters do not have strong or consistent ties to either major party (also a nationwide trend). Consequently, Republican and Democratic electoral fortunes are subject to rapid fluctuation; a good election night this year isn't much of a guarantee that, two years later, partisan tides will not be running in a different direction. For example, the 1994 election results seemed to indicate that the Republican Party was on the verge of becoming the dominant party in California. The party held onto the governorship and captured the positions of treasurer, insurance commissioner, and secretary of state, all previously held by Democrats. Most striking, the party also claimed a majority in the state assembly, the first such Republican legislative majority in nearly a quarter century.

But this Republican tide was as short-lived as it was spectacular. Two years later Bill Clinton easily carried the state and, further down the ticket, Democrats regained control of the assembly while maintaining a comfortable majority in the state senate. And in 1998 Democrats scored a landslide gubernatorial victory, comfortably held onto their contested U.S. Senate seat (reelecting Barbara Boxer), and took over the attorney general's office for the first time in eight years. Democrats also recaptured the position of treasurer, an office they lost in 1994, and maintained their control of the lieutenant governorship and controller's office. By 2002, Democrats had scored a clean sweep of all statewide offices. Moreover, prior to very small gains made in 2002, Republican membership in both houses of the legislature continued to drop toward the one-third level.

But was 2002 the bottom of Republican decline? In the aftermath of the great 2003 recall election, Democratic Party leaders had good reason to worry. Democrats, in control of the policy-making processes in both the legislative and the executive wings between 1999 and 2003, were plausible targets of voters' wrath when things, such as the budget deficit, went badly wrong. And as demonstrated by Schwarzenegger's easy 2006 reelection, a Republican with the right personality and policy positions is capable of sweeping the state.

Nonetheless, the statewide elections of 2004 and 2006 would seem to indicate that the Schwarzenegger phenomenon has not yet translated to increased Republican strength up and down the ballot. In 2004 Democratic presidential candidate John Kerry easily defeated George Bush in California despite his 3% loss nationwide; Democratic U.S. Senator Barbara Boxer won a landslide reelection in 2004 as did her Democratic colleague Dianne Feinstein in 2006. Republicans currently claim just a single statewide office (insurance commissioner) other than governor, and Democratic majorities in the state senate, state assembly, and U.S. House of Representatives delegation have remained constant.

However, California voters' party attachments are not all that deeply rooted; supposed solid party majorities can disappear over any two-year electoral cycle, especially if the "out" party candidates capture the lion's share of the growing independent voting bloc As the Schwarzenegger campaign demonstrated, in a state in which the media are all-important, party affiliation is no sure determinant of political success, especially in headline statewide contests.

On the other hand, the Republican Party does face certain hard choices as it attempts to translate the broad appeal of its governor into broader electoral gains. We shall return to a discussion of sources of Republican strength and weakness after a brief look at California's "other" parties.

TILTING AT WINDMILLS? CALIFORNIA'S MINOR PARTIES

Consumers of mainstream media political news are probably hardly aware that California offers alternatives to the Republican and Democratic Parties. But, in fact, the state currently recognizes four "official parties" in addition to the big two. Such official recognition permits a party to hold primary elections at public expense and guarantees the winners of those primary contests a spot on the general election ballot. For a potential new party, achieving official recognition requires registering into the new party a number of qualified registrants equal to 1 percent of the total votes cast in the last regular gubernatorial election (about 89,000 based on turnout for the 2006 election) or soliciting petition signatures equaling 10 percent of the last vote for governor (about 890,000). Once qualified, a party must meet both of two criteria in order to be guaranteed funding for its primary election and automatic inclusion on the general election ballot:

1. Maintain enough party registrants to equal at least 1/15 of 1 percent of all the state's registered voters (currently that number is about 12,000).

2. Receive at least 2 percent of the general election vote for at least one of its statewide candidates at the gubernatorial election.

The last forty years have witnessed both the birth, and extinction, of several minor parties in California. The Peace and Freedom Party and American Independent Party, both initially qualified in 1968, represented mirror opposites on the 1960s issues of civil rights and Vietnam. Peace and Freedom advocated an immediate cessation of the war and a strong civil rights position, while the American Independent Party adopted polar opposite positions on these issues. Peace and Freedom lost its official status at the end of the twentieth century, only to regain it in time for the 2004 elections. (See Box 8.2 for a description of the fall and rise of Peace and Freedom and the extinction of two other minor parties (Reform and Natural Law).)

The Libertarian Party joined the minor-party ranks in 1979. Libertarians espouse minimal or no governmental intervention in the economy or in the private lives of

BOX 8.2

A Perilous Existence: Life and Death for California's Minor Political Parties

As a result of the 1998 elections, and for the first time since 1962, the ranks of qualified parties were reduced. Both the Peace and Freedom Party and the Reform Party failed to gain at least 2 percent of the vote for any of their statewide candidates. As a result, in order to maintain their official qualified status for the 2000 election, these parties had to produce the requisite number of party registrants or ballot signatures required for initial certification. The Reform Party was able to meet this requirement, but Peace and Freedom, with an enrollment of less than 70,000, fell short. However, after a brief disappearance, Peace and Freedom, through a registration drive, was able to win back official recognition. In the meantime, the Reform Party, endangered in 1998, finally succumbed after the 2002 elections. The Natural Law Party lost its certification in the wake of the 2004 elections. The American Independent Party failed to reach the 2% vote threshold for any of its statewide candidates in 2006, but maintains more than enough registrants to keep it off the minor party endangered list.

What happened to imperil these parties? For Peace and Freedom, the addition of new parties (Green, Reform, and Natural Law) perhaps spread the protest vote too thin. This minor-party "overcrowding" hits the Peace and Freedom Party most directly because it shares a good part of its natural constituency with one of the newcomers, the Green Party. Peace and Freedom survived, but just barely, the 2006 election because one of its candidates got 2% of the vote in the race for insurance commissioner.

Internal dissension explains the demise of the Reform Party, which was formed by and based on the presidential candidacies of Ross Perot in 1992 and 1996. With his departure, the party split in two between its moderate and conservative factions, and when none of its statewide candidates received at least 2 percent of the 2002 election vote, the Reform Party was, unlike four years earlier, unable to mount the effective registration drive necessary to save it from oblivion. The disappearance of the Natural Law Party might be explained by the difficulties faced in attempting to make a connection between the precepts of a not widely understood philosophy and lifestyle to political issues in the minds of most voters.

citizens. More recently, the Green, Reform (no longer officially recognized), and Natural Law (also subsequently disqualified) Parties further swelled the ranks of California's minor parties. The Greens, connected most closely in the public mind with Ralph Nader's 2000 presidential campaign and Peter Camejo's 2003 and 2006 campaigns for governor, are mainly concerned with environmental issues and, in particular, emphasize the concept of sustainability rather than consumption of natural resources. The Reform Party, titled Independent Party in most other states, was the invention of Ross Perot and was built around his presidential bids of 1992 and 1996. Reform's main policy issues, mostly oriented to federal questions, are governmental structural changes such as a Balanced Budget Amendment, campaign finance reform, and congressional term limits. The party also adopted a strong anti–free-trade stance. Finally, the Natural Law Party advocates the practices of transcendental meditation and their application to public policy—for example, holistic approaches to education and health issues. The Natural Law Party was officially recognized in California in 1995.

Beyond these officially qualified, or formally qualified parties, languish even smaller parties that have yet to qualify. This group includes, among others, the Citizens Party, the Socialist Action Party, and the God, Truth and Love Party. Because they are not ballot qualified, these parties must choose their candidates through caucus or convention rather than publicly financed primary elections, and their nominees do not automatically qualify for the general election ballot. Their placement on the ballot requires a petition drive to amass signatures totaling 1 percent of all registered voters, or about 170,000. All told, registration for the four qualified minor parties does not total even 5 percent of the state's registered voters, and the unqualified, "miscellaneous" parties together account for less than 1 percent of registrants. The voters declining to register with any party at all, the decline-to-states, now represent almost 19 percent of all registrants.

Why Do Minor Parties Keep Trying?

The success of the Republican and Democratic Parties is gauged by how they do at election time; electing their candidates to office is their primary focus. This goal does not define minor parties, who receive virtually no general election voter support. For the adherents of these parties, the ideas for which they stand make party activity worthwhile. Minor parties, less concerned with appealing to the broad majority of middle-ground voters who determine election winners, tend to adopt stronger, more ideologically "pure" positions. They can also raise issues that the major parties, fearful of general voter backlash, would just as soon avoid. For example, the Libertarian Party, true to its principles, advocates the decriminalization of most drug use, a position way "too hot to handle" for the Republican or Democratic Party. By sticking to their principles, even if it dooms them electorally, minor parties may force issues and ideas onto the public agenda. Parts of their programs, albeit in watered-down form, may even ultimately be adopted by one or both of the mainstream parties. Finally, in close elections, the number of votes drawn by minor-party candidates can help determine the major-party winner. Votes cast for Libertarian or American Independent candidates would otherwise likely go to the Republican candidate; hence, they sometimes help elect Democrats. Conversely, Green Party votes can nudge a close election into the Republican column, as Al Gore discovered in his loss to George Bush by a whisker-thin margin in the 2000 presidential election.

If, as already indicated, many Californians are unenthusiastic about the major parties, why do the minor parties do so poorly on election day? One reason is that these parties tend, in their programmatic and ideological purity, to be seen as extreme, thus failing to appeal to centrist voters not happy with the major-party choices. Also, the fact that minor parties are perceived to be weak tends to perpetuate that status because voters who may be attracted to their programs are nonetheless unwilling to "waste" their votes on candidates with no chance of winning. For the same reason, minor-party candidates, with little chance to tap into sources of major campaign funding, are reduced to low-key electioneering. Finally, California, like the rest of the nation, employs the single-member-district method of electing legislative representatives. This format means that for a minor party to elect one of its own to the state legislature, it must secure an outright victory in one of the state's 120 legislative districts. This order is a tall one, given the lack of funding and general sense of futility that drag down minor-party candidacies. A system of proportional representation would almost surely enhance the fortunes of minor parties. Under such a system, a party that receives, say, 5 percent of the total vote would be entitled to an equivalent ratio of legislators—in this case, six. Under this scenario, minor parties could establish a public and authoritative presence in Sacramento and perhaps build up their ranks.

Given the way the rules of the game are stacked against minor parties, the 1999 election of a Green Party candidate, Audie Bock, in a special election for an Oakland district assembly seat, was a major upset. But in 2000, the Democrats made a concentrated effort to recapture this seat, which had been considered safely Democratic. They easily deposed Bock, who ran for reelection as an independent rather than as a Green, restoring the major-party monopoly over all 120 legislative seats. As of 2007, all of California's partisan offices (totaling 186) in the U.S. Senate, House of Representatives, state legislature, and state executive wing were held by either a Democrat or Republican.

MAJOR-PARTY VOTERS: WHO ARE THE REPUBLICANS AND DEMOCRATS?

Relative Republican and Democratic strength among various population subgroups varies from election to election based on the individual candidates and the types of issues on voters' minds. However, some general patterns in the two parties' support are usually consistent. Breaking down the California electorate by race and ethnicity indicates that Anglos are the group most likely to vote Republican, while African Americans are most strongly Democratic. The state's Latinos tend to vote Democratic, even more so in recent elections. Women are more likely than men to support Democratic office seekers. Generally, those voters in higher income brackets lean toward the Republican column, though this tendency is muddled by the fact that the San Francisco Bay Area, California's richest region in terms of personal income, is also the state's strongest bastion of Democratic voter support.

A county-by-county analysis of top-of-the-ticket elections from 1990 through 2006 reveals sharp regional partisan differentiation throughout the state. Rural counties, especially inland rural counties, are overwhelmingly Republican, though their impact on statewide election outcomes is reduced to near nothing by their small populations. The six highly populated southern counties, with the hugely crucial exception of

Los Angeles, are, in terms of relative percentages voting Republican or Democratic, the second strongest source of Republican support. But because this region has a major share of the state's population, it is here that Republican candidates need to roll up large numerical majorities to offset usual Democratic pluralities in Los Angeles County and the San Francisco Bay Area. One factor that favors Democratic candidates is the higher voter turnout rates in the Bay Area, which reduce the political impact of the south state's population bulge.

Of California's 58 counties, relatively few can truly be called bellwether or closely representative of the state as a whole. In fact, California could be characterized as a series of mostly one-party counties. As Table 8.1 indicates, only nine of the fifty-eight counties show Republican/Democratic vote percentages that fall within 5 percent of the statewide totals; instead, the majority of counties vary by much larger percentages, whether in the

TABLE 8.1	County-by-County "Top-of-the-Ticket" Partisan Voting Comparison, 1990–2006*		
County	Times Voted for Democrat	Times Voted for Election Winner	Average Percent of Democratic Vote vs. State Average
San Francisco	16 of 16	13 of 16	+27.3%
Alameda	16 of 16	13 of 16	+19.2%
Marin	16 of 16	13 of 16	+14.8
Santa Cruz	16 of 16	13 of 16	+13.1
San Mateo	16 of 16	13 of 16	+12.3
Sonoma	15 of 16	14 of 16	+8.1
Los Angeles	16 of 16	13 of 16	+7.9
Santa Clara	14 of 16	15 of 16	+7.8
Contra Costa	14 of 16	15 of 16	+7.1
Mendocino	14 of 16	15 of 16	+6.1
Yolo	15 of 16	14 of 16	+5.8
Solano	13 of 16	16 of 16	+4.7
Monterey	14 of 16	15 of 16	+3.2
Napa	14 of 16	16 of 16	+2.4
Humboldt	13 of 16	16 of 16	+0.1
Lake	13 of 16	16 of 16	0%
Imperial	12 of 16	15 of 16	−0.4%
San Benito	11 of 16	14 of 16	−0.5
Sacramento	12 of 16	15 of 16	−2.5
Santa Barbara	9 of 16	12 of 16	−4.3
Alpine	8 of 16	11 of 16	−6.0
San Joaquin	8 of 14	11 of 16	−6.7
Merced	8 of 16	11 of 16	−6.9
Ventura	5 of 16	8 of 16	−8.0

TABLE 8.1   (*Continued*)

County	Times Voted for Democrat	Times Voted for Election Winner	Average Percent of Democratic Vote vs. State Average
Stanislaus	6 of 16	9 of 16	−8.1
San Diego	5 of 16	8 of 16	−8.3
San Bernardino	6 of 16	9 of 16	−8.7
Del Norte	4 of 16	7 of 16	−9.1
San Luis Obispo	4 of 16	7 of 16	−9.8
Riverside	4 of 16	7 of 16	−10.2
Fresno	3 of 16	6 of 16	−10.3
Tuolumne	2 of 16	5 of 16	−10.4
Mono	4 of 16	7 of 16	−10.5
Trinity	3 of 16	6 of 16	−11.9
Amador	2 of 16	5 of 16	−12.8
Nevada	2 of 16	5 of 16	−12.9
Butte	2 of 16	5 of 16	−13.0
Kings	2 of 16	5 of 16	−13.0
Calaveras	1 of 16	4 of 16	−13.5
Siskiyou	1 of 16	4 of 16	−13.9
Mariposa	2 of 16	5 of 16	−15.0
Plumas	2 of 16	5 of 16	−15.1
Placer	1 of 16	4 of 16	−15.8
El Dorado	0 of 16	3 of 16	−15.9
Orange	0 of 16	3 of 16	−16.2
Yuba	0 of 16	3 of 16	−16.6
Sierra	1 of 16	4 of 16	−17.2
Madera	1 of 16	4 of 16	−17.7
Tulare	0 of 16	3 of 16	−17.8
Lassen	1 of 16	4 of 16	−18.1
Inyo	0 of 16	3 of 16	−18.1
Tehama	1 of 16	4 of 16	−18.2
Kern	0 of 16	3 of 16	−19.4
Colusa	0 of 16	3 of 18	−19.7
Shasta	0 of 16	3 of 16	−20.0
Sutter	0 of 16	3 of 16	−21.1
Modoc	0 of 16	3 of 6	−22.1
Glenn	0 of 16	3 of 16	−23.0

*Gubernatorial elections: 1990 Wilson/Feinstein; 1994 Wilson/Brown; 1998 Davis/Lungren; 2002 Davis/Simon.;
Schwarzenneger/Angelides. U.S. Senate elections: 1992 Feinstein/Seymour, Boxer/Herschensohn; 1994 Feinstein/Huffington;
1998 Boxer/Fong; 2000 Feinstein/Campbell; 2004 Boxer/Jones; Feinstein/Mountjoy. Presidential elections: 1992 Clinton/Bush;
1996 Clinton/Dole; 2000 Bush/Gore; 2004 Bush/Kerry.*

Source: California Secretary of State, Statement of the Vote (Sacramento: various years).

Republican or Democratic direction. In short, most counties are predictably Republican or predictably Democratic in terms of their major-election voting behavior; based on their very consistent record over the last quarter century, well over two-thirds of the counties, including most of the largest counties, can be called "lock" or safe bet counties, falling into either the Republican or Democratic columns long before their votes are actually counted. Thus, even though California has historically been a competitive state in terms of party support, that competitiveness results from a rough balancing out of essentially one-party regions rather than even competition throughout the state.

In the wake of a series of elections from 1990 through 2006, some observers wonder whether that rough balance point had not tilted permanently or semi-permanently in the Democratic direction. Of the 16 top-of-the-ticket regularly scheduled elections in this era (presidential, U.S. Senate, gubernatorial), 13 were won by the Democratic candidate. And a single Republican candidate, Pete Wilson, accounted for two of the Republican victories. Save for one two-year period in the assembly, Democrats enjoyed unbroken majorities in both houses of the legislature over that same period. George W. Bush's failure to carry California in 2000 marked the first time since 1880 that the Republican presidential candidate won the national election but failed to carry this state, and 2004 saw an exact repeat of this pattern.

Again, Table 8.1 provides a picture of the current Republican dilemma. In the most rural areas of the state, Republican support has never been higher. Even in George W. Bush's double-digit losses in 2000 and 2004, this area delivered solid majorities to President Bush. The problem, from the viewpoint of Republican strategists, is that the huge percentage majorities racked up by the party in rural counties are more than off-set by the declining levels of Republican voting strength in the suburbs, and especially in Southern California. In 2004, Los Angeles County alone delivered a voting edge of more than 800,000 to John Kerry, a number that dwarfs the combined populations of the rural Republican counties.

Moreover, a sharp drop-off occurred in Republican support in the other Southern California counties that traditionally delivered large Republican vote margins. Orange, Riverside, San Bernardino, Ventura, and San Diego Counties all supported George W. Bush. But their vote pluralities were much reduced from what Republicans must garner to have any statewide chance of victory. In fact, these counties combined did not come close to offsetting Kerry's Los Angeles County margin, let alone his over 1 million vote plurality in those counties adjacent to San Francisco Bay. The 2004 U.S. Senate race between Barbara Boxer and Bill Jones followed the same pattern, though it was more pronounced. In this case, Republican Jones failed to even carry three of the five southern suburban counties, while absorbing a drubbing in Los Angeles County and the San Francisco Bay Area. The result was a 2.4 million vote loss, despite his victories in most of the state's mountain and agricultural counties. Two years later, Democrat Diane Feinstein won an even more lopsided reelection, carrying all but one of the Southern California suburban counties (Orange County was the exception) and racking up a winning margin of over 24%.

Many short-range factors contributed to recent California Republican woes. These include Bill Clinton's popularity (and the unpopularity of both Bushes) in the state, internal wrangling within the Republican organization, and less than ideal Republican gubernatorial and U.S. Senate candidates and campaigns. But beyond these immediate factors, some observers, both Republican and Democrat, blame the policy stances with which the Republican Party has come to be identified over the decade. In fact, those very issues that play so well in the rural reaches of the state may cost the party dearly in the more crucial urban and suburban areas.

One of those issues is handgun control and Republican opposition to it. In earlier decades, the death penalty question was the defining element in the law-and-order debate. Democrats, associated with opposition to capital punishment, paid a heavy electoral price. Currently, gun control occupies center stage in voters' concerns over law and order, and this time, especially in the suburbs, it is Republican candidates who have paid the electoral price. Embracing the right-to-life side of the abortion question and opposing stem cell research also probably cost the Republican Party suburban votes.

Earlier in the decade, Republicans were hopeful of increasing their support levels among California Latinos, a growing part of the electorate. But the party's endorsement of ballot propositions prohibiting social and educational services to undocumented immigrants, banning affirmative action, and ending bilingual education (Propositions 187 of 1994, 209 of 1996, and 227 of 1998) seems to have enlarged and consolidated Democratic strength amidst this increasingly crucial bloc of voters. More recently, the opposition of many Republican politicians to any form of "amnesty" to undocumented immigrants has further weakened Republican claims on Latino electoral support. Lack of Hispanic support for Republican candidates creates an approximate 6% overall deficit for GOP candidates before the votes of other groups are counted. Unless Republicans can increase their appeal to Hispanics, whose share of the total electorate is growing, this deficit will only grow deeper.

However, as we were forcefully reminded in October 2003, nothing is permanent in California politics. Democrat Gray Davis, a 20-point victor in his 1998 run for the governorship, was just five years later the victim of the state's first successful statewide recall. His replacement, Republican Arnold Schwarzenegger, has a chance to reinvigorate his party's electoral fortunes. Opinion polls indicate that his general policy stances, conservative on economic issues but moderate on social issues, sit well with a majority of the state's voters, solidifying his Republican base while attracting independent and even some Democratic voters. Voter identification of these positions with the Republican Party generally, as opposed to just Schwarzenegger, might be the key to its long-term renewal.

ELECTORAL ACTIVISTS

The party activists who prompt the party rank and file to vote are of two types: official and unofficial. Official party organizations were highly regulated by state law from 1913 to 1987, whereas unofficial party bodies were regulated to a far lesser extent. The titles of the official organizations, their membership, the selection of their officers, and the time and place of meetings of their party units were all provided for in the state elections code. The names, composition, leadership, and meeting arrangements of unofficial party bodies were not determined by state law. Official party units were not allowed to "endorse, support, or oppose" candidates in party primaries, but unofficial party organizations engaged in precisely such activities. With the restrictions on official party organizations having been lifted in 1987, the distinctions between official and unofficial party organizations are no longer so significant.

The main elements of the official parties are the state central committees and the county central committees. The state central committees for the two major parties carry out quite similar responsibilities, but they differ somewhat in composition. The official state committees may undertake the following activities:

- Conduct campaigns for party nominees,
- Raise funds for party nominees,
- Consent to the use of the party's name by organizations using such labels to solicit campaign donations,
- Register new rank-and-file party members,
- Monitor pending legislation in Sacramento,
- Research the records of opposition party candidates,
- Pass resolutions on behalf of the state party,
- Draft and approve a state party platform, and
- Elect the officers of the state party.

A series of federal court rulings in the late 1980s and 1990s were important in that they expanded the functions and organizational independence of California's political parties. Citing First Amendment protections, the courts first voided state law prohibiting parties from endorsing candidates in partisan primary elections, thus allowing the parties to recommend candidates vying for their nomination in those primaries. The courts also ruled that state laws prescribing and limiting parties' internal organization (such as the two-year limitation on state chairpersons' tenure) were invalid. The final decision allowed parties to endorse candidates in nonpartisan elections as well, despite a state constitutional prohibition on such endorsements approved by state voters in 1986.

While these court decisions created a much wider field of permissible activity for the official state and local party organizations, that power remains underused. Preprimary endorsements of candidates for the parties' nomination are the exception rather than the rule. And most county political organizations have been equally reluctant to endorse candidates for legislative or local nonpartisan offices.

When the courts voided state law limiting the length of service of state party chairpersons to two years, the Democrats promptly revised their bylaws to extend the term of their party chair to four years, with the possibility of multiple terms. For example, Art Torres has served as chairperson of the State Democratic Party since 1996. Democrats also moved to professionalize party organization operations and personnel. Republicans were not as quick to take advantage of the less restrictive organizational options provided by the court decisions, which some observers believe played a role in the party's recent electoral problems. It was not until late 2001 that the party ultimately began to professionalize its rules and operations.

The new century's first decade may witness an increase in the role and saliency of the party organizations. Two factors are at work here. The Republican and Democratic Parties' caucuses in the legislature effectively smothered party organization power by taking control of campaign finance and the selection of candidates at the district level. Term limits, however, weakened the continuity and power of those legislative caucuses, especially in the state assembly, leaving room for a reassertion of the party organizations' role. Second, new campaign finance laws have limited the power of legislative party caucuses to raise and disburse campaign funds to raise and, at least nominally, transferred that power to the party organizations. However, whether, in fact, party organizations will actually increase their power significantly remains a matter of conjecture.

STRENGTHENING THE PARTIES: COULD IT, AND SHOULD IT, BE DONE?

Many political scientists and other observers have long lamented the fact that California is a weak party state, and some have attempted to launch party revitalization movements in the hopes of enhancing the parties' role and power. Their arguments for strong parties are based on the following assumptions:

- If party labels rather than individual candidate personal campaigns are the main focus of elections, interest group contributions to individual campaigns become less crucial, leading to less interest group influence over elected officials. (See Chapter 9 for a discussion of the role of campaign money in politics.)

- Elections based on clear differing policies between political parties, rather than on personality contests between individual candidates, provide voters with clear choices on the policy direction of the state over the next electoral cycle. Voters could see that their votes really effect what government actually does.

- Political parties seek to enlarge their support among average citizens, since their success or failure on election night depends on their number of voters. Interest groups, on the other hand, do not always need large numbers of rank and file supporters to succeed. (See Chapter 7 for a discussion of the sources of interest group influence.) Thus, party-based politics is more "democratic" than interest group–based politics.

- Under a party-based political system, average citizens would come to see that their vote now really counted, since policy decisions would be tied to election results. Hence, many more potential voters would become actual voters, thus increasing political involvement and participation.

Based on these arguments, a number of steps could be taken to increase the power of political parties in California. The voting ballot might be reconfigured to encourage straight-party (not split-ticket) voting. (The current "office bloc" ballot, which makes it more difficult to vote a straight ticket, was another progressive reform.) Selected local government offices, perhaps county supervisors as an example, might revert from nonpartisan to partisan offices. The number of executive positions covered by civil service might be reduced by a small percentage to give party officeholders more appointments to dispense to party activists. But given the antiparty mentality that defines many, if not most Californians' political outlook, the likelihood of these ideas being adopted is remote.

Another approach is to increase the clout of political parties in California by building on the recently bestowed right of the parties to endorse candidates before primary elections take place. Colorado election law provides an example of this approach. In that state the parties hold caucuses of party members prior to the primary election. The candidates receiving the most caucus votes are listed first on the later primary election ballot. Candidates receiving less than 30% of the caucus vote do not even appear on that ballot unless they can garner a certain amount of signatures. The idea here is that candidates who have the support of party activists (those who show up at the caucus meetings) are given an advantage in the primary elections that officially determine the parties' nominees.

Colorado law also strengthens the parties through partisan, rather than nonpartisan election of county officials. Even at the local level below that of county, party endorsements of and support for city office candidates is common-place, even though those contests are officially "nonpartisan." And in the case of certain local and state partisan offices, the party organizations are allowed to fill vacancies created by the death or resignation of the current officeholder.

However, as promising as some of these proposals might be from the perspective of those who wish for stronger parties in the state, their acceptance faces an uphill battle. California has, beginning with the progressive era early in the twentieth century, a long antiparty tradition. As already stated, "Vote for the candidate, not the party" is a core value deeply ingrained in the state's political ethos. And it should be noted that the easing of legal restrictions on the parties was the work of the federal court system, not California's citizens or their elected representatives. As the overwhelming vote to establish the blanket primary and the increasing number of decline-to-state voter registrations indicate, most Californians would likely prefer that parties become even less, not more, important.

Finally, there are indications that California is not out of touch with the rest of the nation in terms of its antiparty spirit; there are many citizens in many parts of the nation who seem to be looking for candidates that take a pragmatic, problem-solving approach, as opposed to a partisan approach, to public policy issues. Again by example, even in "strong party" Colorado, fully one-third of registered voters are signed up as "unaffiliated" rather than as a Republican, Democrat, or member of a minor party.

THE POWER OF MEDIA—THEN AND NOW

There is broad agreement that media occupy a strategic political position. In a state of over 36 million, let alone a nation of 300 million, a very small percentage of people have direct, everyday, face-to-face, contact with governmental offices, politicians, and the political process. Their knowledge of politics is, therefore, crucially dependent on links or intermediaries. Media are the most important component of this linkage; but how clear, full and accurate a picture do the media offer? And in what ways have the role and power of media changed since the middle of the twentieth century?

Before the arrival of television and its mass consumption in nearly every home, newspapers were the dominant source of political information. In California, newspaper owners and publishers were dominant forces. Newspaper publishers and journalists were a main force behind the rise and political success of the Progressive movement early in the 20th century. Later, In 1934, newspaper magnates Otis Chandler of the *Los Angeles Times*, William Randolph Hearst of the *San Francisco Examiner*, and William Knowland of the *Oakland Tribune* dedicated their news and editorial pages to a concerted, and successful, attack on the gubernatorial candidacy of Upton Sinclair (Mitchell, 1992). In the next decade, the Hearst chain of papers was a leading voice calling for the relocation of Japanese Americans after the attack on Pearl Harbor. In the

PHOTO 8.1   Media magnets—Arnold Schwarzenegger and Maria Shriver, California's "first couple," display a formidable blend of celebrity and bipartisan appeal. (*New York Times*)

late 1950s, press power was a crucial factor in forcing Governor Knight to not to seek reelection but instead run for the U.S. Senate. According to one source, the political editor of the *Los Angeles Times* essentially blackmailed Knight with the threat of exposing scandal in his administration if he refused to give up the governorship (Halberstram, 1979, pp. 265–66).

In addition to campaign involvement, news organizations shape public decisions both by actual reporting and editorializing and by the mere threat to publicize events. Few Californians have the chance or inclination to observe state politics directly and independently. Too much goes on during any one day for any person, regardless of her diligence, to follow. It is the news organizations that fill this vacuum. They are our primary source of information and, perhaps even more crucially, the determiners of what we perceive as "news" and as "politics." On any given day, print and electronic news media are in possession of much more information than they have time or space to convey. In deciding what is printed or screened, they decide the shape and content of the citizens' political world.

Covering the Capital—Lightly

How much newspaper coverage voters receive about state politics depends on where they live and what papers they read. Los Angeles is a long distance from Sacramento, but the *Los Angeles Times* maintains a stable of accredited reporters in its capital bureau. The *Sacramento Bee* also provides extensive coverage of state politics in its "hometown." But in most areas and for most papers, coverage is much sketchier. Most of the other large-circulation metropolitan dailies rely on just one or two capital correspondents.

Smaller newspapers utilize their own resources to cover state politics only when a distinct "local angle" is involved. Rural, small-town, and suburban dailies rely heavily on the wire services for their state politics stories.

From a statewide perspective, commercial television news coverage of Sacramento is virtually nonexistent. At one time, major city stations kept their own staffs in the capital, but there is no longer permanent television coverage save for local Sacramento stations. On those occasions when out-of-town stations want to cover the capital, they rely on the local outlets or send a crew on a temporary basis. This lack of coverage was partially offset by the arrival of the nonprofit California Channel, which has, since 1990, provided cable television coverage of general legislative sessions, legislative committee hearings, important addresses such as the governor's State of the State speech, and proceedings of the California Supreme Court. The California Channel, whose principal source of support comes from other cable stations, reaches a potential audience of approximately 5 million homes.

The lack of pervasive and consistent print and electronic news coverage of state government presents something of a chicken-and-egg dilemma. Commercial news outlets are, after all, a business, and they have concluded that the "market" for state politics is not very big. On the other hand, lack of coverage further depresses knowledge and, ultimately, interest, thus further reducing demand. In a state as big, diverse, and complex as California, citizens are dependent on the media for information. Lacking this information, how can we expect them to understand the state's public life, let alone effectively participate in it?

Although both print and electronic reporters are accredited with the same organization, newspaper and television correspondents work under significantly different conditions. Television news thrives on good visuals, its equipment is much more intrusive than pencil and notepad, and it has the potential to do live coverage. However, news reports read on television are a great deal shorter than newspaper accounts, and the sheer number of print reporters in the state capital overwhelms the number of representatives from the electronic media. Californians with the highest levels of interest in politics rely far more on the print media for their news than they do on television. Just the reverse is true of individuals with low levels of interest in state government.

Access to Newsmakers

The members of the Capitol Correspondents Association have different levels of access to the various parts of state government. Much legislative activity is open to reporters, but correspondents are not allowed to cover certain important meetings. Floor sessions, committee hearings, fiscal subcommittees, and conference committees are open to the press. On the other hand, meetings of the legislative party caucuses, party leadership gatherings, and meetings of top legislators with the governor are closed to the press corps. The executive branch is much less accessible than the legislature. The correspondents attend the State of the State speech, delivered by the governor each January, as well as periodic press conferences and bill signings held by the state's chief executive. However, the press does not have access to the governor's cabinet meetings, the daily gatherings of the governor's senior staff, any of the meetings at which the governor's budget is prepared, any of the deliberations concerning major gubernatorial appointments, or any of the discussions in the governor's office regarding the use of general or line-item vetoes.

With respect to the judiciary, reporters may listen to the submission of evidence at trial court proceedings and to the oral arguments made before appellate courts. But the right of the electronic media to provide live coverage is subject to limitation and revocation by the presiding judge, and these are often invoked. Journalists may not listen to jury deliberations or to the conferences held by appellate jurists where they discuss cases and make their decisions on them.

Even though they are both considered private associations under the law, political parties are more open to press coverage than are interest groups. Though it is true that legislative party caucuses are off-limits to the press, annual party conventions and party primary elections receive a good deal of attention from journalists. Conversely, meetings of lobbyists and their interest group clients are not open to reporters.

Complete access would bring state government to a standstill. For example, confidential meetings are necessary if detailed information about the strengths and weaknesses of a potential high-level appointee is to be communicated to the governor. Or when the governor and legislative leaders meet privately to negotiate the annual budget or a major policy bill, they are able to be more flexible in search of consensus if correspondents can't reveal the contents of their discussions to the public. However, care must be exercised with the privacy-produces-results argument; excessive use of it may deny specific interests and the general public their right to know.

Beyond attendance at meetings, correspondents can access a vast quantity of information available under open records and public disclosure statutes. The sources and amounts of campaign donations, the types and values of gifts given to politicians, and the sorts of financial assets possessed by state and local officials are all public information. Reporters from the *Sacramento Bee* produced some eye-popping articles concerning the salaries of legislative staffers and university administrators—all from readily available documents filed with public agencies. It would be beneficial to the public if more journalists acted on the maxim "All good stories begin in the library."

What Is Newsworthy?

Gaining access to news and newsmakers is one problem the media face. Defining what should be covered is a whole other matter. What guidelines do reporters use in selecting among events? Because most members of the press see themselves as serving the public, incidents with a wide impact on the population are considered newsworthy. Professional pride, if not concern for the financial health of their news organization, leads journalists to try to beat the competition to what is new, unique, unusual, and sometimes sensational. Correspondents focus on what is controversial, especially when the public may need to participate in the resolution of the issue. The public and private lives of celebrities are considered news by most members of the press. For instance, just prior to the 2003 recall election date, the *Los Angeles Times* broke the story alleging that Arnold Schwarzenegger had groped women at movie and television locations throughout his acting career.

When these general guidelines are insufficient to determine what is news, additional criteria are employed. As an example, a great many candidates run for office in primary and general elections. Instead of expending time and space on aspirants who have no chance of election, reporters cover the "serious" candidates. These newsworthy politicians are selected on the basis of the amount of money they have raised and their standing in public opinion polls. But in making these necessary decisions, the media become part of the process rather than "objective" outsiders merely reporting on it. For example, using the amount of money raised as a criterion for a "serious" candidacy reinforces the importance of money-raising in the electoral process. Lacking such a stamp, a deserving but underfunded candidate will likely remain unnoticed and, hence, a "not serious" candidate. Furthermore, both convenience (i.e., the time and place an event is scheduled) and the habit of using established sources help determine what news is. In the interest of maintaining access inside government, reporters may decide that news is what their sources say it is. Television correspondents' judgments about newsworthiness, of course, are influenced by the quality of visuals related to events. For even the most fair-minded reporter or editor, choosing what is news will always be an art rather than a science. And the nature of those decisions will always carry political consequences.

A Creative Tension?

Members of the capital media have something of a love-hate relationship with the individuals and offices they cover. On the one hand, they depend on the information and insights that political officials provide them. On the other, they must always be aware that these same officials "spin" the information to put themselves and their programs in the best possible light. Legislators, executive branch officials, and political candidates hire speechwriters, media consultants, and public information officers for this purpose. These operatives and their employers love to see their press releases passed on unrevised to the public as the "news." But good newspeople know that they need to dig deeper and go beyond the official line. In doing so, of course, they risk the anger of those officials whose information is a source of their livelihood. At its best, the relationship between the media and public officials probably should be characterized as one of "creative tension."

The press does exercise restraint or self-censorship in some areas. For years, reporters voluntarily withheld from the public information about alcoholism, other drug abuse, and adultery involving high-ranking officials. Many journalists regard these subjects as sensationalism rather than legitimate news and do not believe that these matters deserve coverage unless it can be shown conclusively that such behavior adversely impacts job performance. But as the media treatment of the transgressions of Bill Clinton, and, more recently, Arnold Schwarzenegger indicates, this line between "public" and "private" is increasingly blurred.

Journalists' efforts to inform the public and to serve as watchdogs have aroused the ire of politicians on occasion. But rather than regarding the friction between the press and politicians as dysfunctional, it may well be that the public is best served by one powerful institution challenging another. Columnist Dan Walters of the *Sacramento Bee*, who has been in his share of confrontations with powerful leaders, thinks that criticism of the news media should be worn as a badge of honor. According to Walters, speaking of his often less than cordial relationship with the former assembly speaker, "If Willie Brown is upset by the way the Capitol press corps is performing of late, it means that the political press is having some impact" (Walters, 1985).

Editorial Influence

The media, especially newspapers, also play a participant role through their editorial policy. Editorial decisions as to the treatment, placement, and timing of stories can reflect the political orientation of publishers and editors. For example, for many years clear differences separated the way the "news" was treated by Sacramento's two main newspapers, the liberal Democratic *Sacramento Bee* and the conservative Republican *Sacramento Union*. Sacramento Valley residents who read both papers prior to the *Union*'s demise must have often wondered, given the papers' news placement and emphasis policies, whether they were reading about the same world in those two papers' news accounts.

On the other hand, editorial pages are where readers expect to encounter opinion and bias. This explicitly "political" part of a newspaper carries opinion rather than "straight news." Though editorial endorsements are especially influential in local races, where information about candidates is scarce (St. Dizier, 1985), politicians at all levels eagerly seek the blessing of editors. A newspaper's summary of candidate endorsements and positions on ballot measures usually appears on the editorial page a few days before the election. An earlier study of the *Santa Barbara News Press* found that 39 percent of its readership generally carried the newspaper's summary of endorsements directly into the polling booth on election day (Gregg, 1965, pp. 536–537). Still, it seems likely that endorsements are much less influential in those candidate races and ballot initiatives where the public has other "cues," such as partisan identification and large-scale campaign advertising. For example, *Sacramento Bee* support for Democratic candidates has not prevented a steady movement of its voting readership into the Republican column.

California 2004 Presidential Vote in National and Western State Perspective

Percentage of Vote for Kerry
California: 54%
Highest: Massachusetts, 62%
Lowest: Utah, 26%
National overall: 48%
Other Western States

Washington 53%	Arizona 44%
Oregon 53%	Montana 39%
New Mexico 49%	Idaho 30%
Nevada 48%	Wyoming 29%
Colorado 47%	Utah 26%

SUMMARY

Californians' distaste for political parties, a distaste that goes back to the beginning of the twentieth century, is a central part of their political culture. And given the continuing attempts to diminish the role of political parties, this antiparty feeling is not likely to fade away. Nonetheless, Republican and Democratic candidates dominate state elections, and for many decades, California has been, in terms of the partisan balance, a very competitive state. But this balance is the product of offsetting regions of Republican and Democratic support rather than an even division of party strength throughout the state. Republicans rely on huge majorities in the suburban portions of Southern California as their main vote source; Democrats depend on rolling up large majorities in Los Angeles and in the San Francisco Bay Area. However, recent elections have engendered concern among Republican strategists that the balance had shifted toward the Democratic Party. If suburban support for the Republican Party continues to erode, the small number of voters living in the increasingly Republican rural areas of the state cannot come close to making up this shortfall. On the other hand, given the rapid pace of changing partisan fortunes in California, not to mention the unpredictable impact of the "Schwarzenegger factor," it is too soon to conclude that the Republican Party cannot emerge from its current political decline. In fact, recent trends and events indicate that California's long tradition of opposition to strong political parties, be they Republican or Democrat, is still intact.

REFERENCES

California Secretary of State. *Report of Registration, January, 2007.* Sacramento: 2007.

California Secretary of State. *Statement of the Vote.* Sacramento: various years.

Gregg, James E. "Newspaper Editorial Endorsements and California Elections: 1948–62." *Journalism Quarterly* (Autumn 1965).

Halberstam, David. *The Powers That Be.* New York: Alfred A. Knopf, 1979.

Mitchell, Greg. *The Campaign of the Century.* New York: Random House, 1992.

St. Dizier, Byron. "The Effect of Newspaper Endorsements and Party Identification on Voting Choice." *Journalism Quarterly* (Autumn 1985).

Walters, Dan. "Press Drawing Criticism?" *Sacramento Bee* (November 17, 1985).

CHAPTER nine

ELECTIONS IN CALIFORNIA

Elections are the hallmark of democracies. Voting allows Californians to select the men and women who will occupy public office, and it permits the electorate to govern itself through initiatives and referenda. On election day, every voter has an equal say. The vote of the richest voter in town can be canceled out by the vote of the poorest. But this hardly means that money does not play a crucial role in electoral politics and, as will be discussed throughout this chapter, California elections are particularly subject to the influence of the dollar. Whether it be giving a fee to workers for each new voter they register, paying signature gatherers to qualify ballot measures, commissioning voter surveys by pollsters, purchasing mailers to be sent to voters, creating and maintaining an effective Web site, or buying television time, the role of money is pervasive in California elections. In top of the ticket campaigns (president, U.S. senator, and governor) the importance of party labels has been diminished by candidate-centered campaigns featuring professional managers and media consultants. Businesses profit handsomely from campaigns; companies offering election assistance are a growth industry in California.

This chapter begins with a profile of the California electorate, proceeds to an analysis of the state's "direct democracy" provisions—the initiative, referendum, and recall—and concludes with an examination of the various campaign techniques used to persuade voters.

THE CALIFORNIA VOTER

Any 18-year-old citizen of the United States who has resided in the state for at least 15 days may vote in California elections. (Persons with fewer than 15 days' residency in

California may vote for president and vice president of the United States but not for state or local offices.) In addition to these general qualifications, neither felons in prison or on probation nor persons legally designated as mentally incompetent may vote. (See Box 9.1 for a discussion of the citizenship requirement for voting.)

During the first 70 years of the twentieth century, a person had to be literate in the English language to be eligible to vote in California. In 1970, the California Supreme Court struck down this limitation on voting rights. In conformity with the U.S. Voting Rights Act, state law now also stipulates that non–English-speaking citizens shall be encouraged to vote. To implement this provision of the law, ballots and other election materials are to be available on request in Spanish and Chinese as well as English.

 BOX 9.1

Noncitizens as Voters: A Revolutionary Idea?

As explained above, only American citizenship, not mere residency, bestows eligibility to vote in California. That's the law in the 49 other states as well, though this was not the case in certain eastern states at the end of the nineteenth and beginning of the twentieth centuries. In a state with as many immigrant resident noncitizens as California, extending the vote to anyone who has been a constant state resident for, say, five years, would dramatically increase the state's eligible electorate. It might also, depending on the actual electoral behavior of these new voters, shift the partisan and ideological balance.

Those in favor of such a change argue that permanent residents, regardless of their citizenship, pay taxes, rely on state services, and must obey state laws just as much as citizens. Why, then, ought they not have an electoral voice in the way these policies and laws are made and implemented? Members of the opposition, of course, see the issue differently. They see the act of gaining citizenship through naturalization as the only appropriate means by which immigrants can gain the vote, since such an act evidences a level of loyalty to their "Americanism" that all voters should possess. As well, the argument goes, requiring citizen status is an effective way to encourage eligible immigrants to become full-fledged citizens; doing away with the requirement would result in fewer immigrants ever becoming American citizens.

In 2004, San Francisco voters very nearly passed a proposal allowing resident noncitizens with children who attend public K–12 schools in the city to vote in local school board elections. Advocates of this move argued that these parents have vital interests in, and need to be vitally engaged with, the education of their children. Opponents, in addition to their general opposition to noncitizen voting, cited the California Constitution, which limits voting to citizens and which, in their view, preempts local attempts to change the definition of legal voter, even for local elections in charter cities such as San Francisco, which have some powers to craft their own electoral processes. Because the measure did not pass, the constitutional questions it raised have yet to be settled. But the question of noncitizen voting is not likely to disappear.

Beyond the legal issues, and the general pro/con statements about noncitizen voting, the question touches on core disagreements over immigrants and their role and place in California. How do you feel about this issue?

Beyond meeting the age, citizenship, and residency qualifications, persons must register to vote to be eligible to receive and mark a ballot on election days. They must fill out a registration form and get it to the county clerk before the close of registration, 15 days prior to elections. They may return the completed form by mail or leave it with a deputy registrar of voters—any registered voter may serve as a deputy registrar—for delivery to the county clerk. Getting on the voter rolls is one thing; getting off is another. Prior to 1974, election officials were empowered to remove individuals from the voter registration list for habitual nonvoting. This system, called an *active purge*, keeps the registration lists relatively accurate and up to date. However, since 1974, federal and state election laws no longer allow for the removal of names merely for nonvoting. Instead, those charged with maintaining the voter lists, county clerks or recorders at the county level and the secretary of state at the state level, must obtain positive evidence, such as a death notice or change of address form, that a citizen is improperly registered before removing that name from the voting rolls. In his eight-year (1995–2003) tenure as secretary of state, Bill Jones aggressively pursued the "deadwood problem," utilizing new technology and information sources to identify, for instance, voters who were double-registered under two separate addresses. His office estimated that between 1 and 2 million faulty registrations were identified and removed. How many still remain? No one knows for sure, since a full and complete canvass has not been conducted, but 1 million might be a reasonable estimate.

Political parties periodically conduct voter registration drives, often paying workers for each new registrant. (These so-called bounty hunters are another source of invalid voter registrations.) However, getting an individual to register to vote is often much easier than actually getting that person to the polls. As discussed in Chapter 8, of the approximately 22.8 million Californians eligible to register, only about 69% actually have done so. And the approximately 1 million of those registrants that are deadwood reduce the "live" registration figures even further. Another sharp decline is evident between the number who register and the number who vote. The registered voter turnout percentage is highest for presidential elections and shrinks for gubernatorial elections. In the 2004 presidential election, approximately 76 percent of registered voters and just over 57 percent of eligible Californians turned out. Those figures, as unimpressive as they might be, were considerably higher than the 2006 governor's election, where only about 56.2 percent of registered voters and 39.3 percent of eligible citizens cast ballots. Voting turnout for the recall election of 2003 was actually higher than for the regularly scheduled 2002 and 2006 gubernatorial election, totaling 61.2 and 43.1 percent of registered voters and those eligible to vote, respectively (California Secretary of State, 2004, 2005, 2006). Further, as pathetic as these numbers may appear, they dwarf the percentages of Californians who bother to vote in statewide partisan primary elections and local nonpartisan elections.

Such low election participation rates would be troublesome even if those who voted were representative of the entire population. But, in fact, they are not. As Table 9.1 indicates, voters differ from nonvoters along characteristic lines that can be politically relevant. In this table, a group's voting/nonvoting score of 1.0 would be neutral meaning that this group's percentage of the population that votes is the same as its percentage of all Californians that are eligible to vote. A score higher than 1.0 indicates that the group is "overrepresented" in the electorate compared to its percentage of eligible voters, and a score of less than 1.0 indicates that it is "underrepresented."

TABLE 9.1 Eligibility Rates Versus Actual Voting Participation Rates	Voting/Nonvoting Ratio
Region	
Los Angeles County	0.90
Other Large Southern California Counties	0.95
San Francisco Bay Area	1.13
Education	
High school diploma or less	0.57
Some college	1.13
College graduate or more	1.50
Age	
18–29	0.54
30–49	0.69
50–59	1.73
60 and older	1.68
Household Income	
Less than $30,000	0.66
$30,000–$75,000	0.98
Over $75,000	1.78
Race/Ethnicity	
Anglo	1.10
Latino	0.78
African American	1.0
Children in Household	
Eligible voters with children in household	0.78
Eligible voters without children in household	1.18

Source: Adapted from Field Research Corporation, California Field Poll *(San Francisco: November 2004 and February 2006), and California Secretary of State,* Statement of the Vote *(Sacramento: 2006).*

What Table 9.1 indicates is that generally Anglo, more educated, wealthier, and older Californians are more likely to vote than are eligible non-Anglo, less educated, poorer, and younger citizens. These discrepancies between the eligible voter pool and the voting pool would seem to clearly favor Republican candidates, but the electoral reality is more complex. For one thing, eligible voters in the San Francisco Bay Area, the heart of Democratic support in the state, turn out to vote at higher rates than do potential voters from Southern California. Moreover, the turnout rates for any particular group fluctuate with each election, depending on the issues and candidates. Recent general elections, for example, saw modest upswings in non-Anglo voting rates and corresponding decreases in Anglo turnout.

Still, in some issues, the composition of voters clearly skews the outcome. For example, health care and education are two areas that demand, and compete for, public resources. With an electorate that overrepresents older citizens who do not have children in school, proponents of educational spending may be at a clear disadvantage. Similarly, because homeowners are much more likely to vote than renters, those who favor policies such as rent control face steep electoral odds.

Plenty of theories attempt to explain why so many eligible citizens do not vote, and all are probably correct to a certain degree. Nationally, lack of facility in English is certainly one reason why some don't vote and may be especially relevant for California, where so many citizens are immigrants from non–English-speaking countries. California's long and confusing ballot may deter potential voters, as might the increasing reliance on negative advertising by political campaigns. The prevalent sense that the political system does not engage the needs and concerns of average citizens may be still another factor. Less often cited, but perhaps crucial in understanding California's low voting rates, are modern, high-tech campaign techniques. Because these techniques are so expensive, campaign messages must, for cost efficiency, be "targeted" at the most likely voters—for example, members of politically relevant organizations whose mailing lists are purchased by campaign consultants. As a result, those citizens who are not already "networked in" organizationally are not likely to be a focus of campaign efforts. Put another way, modern campaigns are geared toward reaching the existing pool of likely voters rather than toward mobilizing new voters. Mobilizing new groups of voters (such as the immigrants to America that arrived in the late nineteenth and early twentieth centuries) traditionally has been an activity of political parties. In weak party states such as California, less organizational support is available for such mass grassroots mobilizations.

The voter registration law is a legal impediment to fuller voting participation. As mentioned, a citizen must register to vote in California at least 15 days prior to the election. Because many potential voters don't get interested in elections until the end of the election season, some who would vote find they cannot because they neglected to take the earlier step of registering. The federal "motor voter" law seeks to remedy this lack of timely registration by mandating that state agencies dealing with the public, such as the Department of Motor Vehicles, make voter registration materials available to citizens who enter their offices. The secretary of state estimated that more than 8 million individuals registered or reregistered to vote under the auspices of "motor voter" during the first six years of the act's implementation. How many of these individuals would have registered even without "motor voter" is impossible to say. Even more problematic is any estimate of how many of these newly registered Californians vote.

Absentee, Early, and All Mail Voting

Prior to 1978, voting by mail was limited to housebound persons and to persons physically absent from the precinct on election day (e.g., soldiers and travelers). However, these rules were relaxed in 1978 to allow any registered voter who so desired to vote by mail. That change produced a minirevolution in voting habits. Absentee voting, languishing at around 4 percent at the time of the relaxation of the rules, currently accounts for slightly more than 40 percent of all votes cast, and this number is still rising. Given these figures, candidates, political consultants, and the political parties adopted new strategies to "lock up" early voters rather than assuming that undecided voters would wait until the final days of the campaign to make up their minds. And having identified supportive voters, these organizations attempt to assure that "friendly" voters actually mail in their ballots by utilizing ballot receipt records provided by county election offices.

There is some evidence that the greater use of mail ballots has increased voter turnout (Field, Feb 2006). Given the time pressures on the lives of all of us, the connection between absentee voting and greater turnout makes sense. Absentee voting provides voters with more time to consider all issues on the ballot and to utilize any information and cues in their possession. It also avoids the problems caused when voters must somehow get themselves to the polls and vote during a single election day, sometimes after waiting in a long line of voters. As well, local election officials now actively encourage absentee voting as way of reducing election costs. One area of concern is that this "new, improved" way to vote is not being utilized at the same rates by all parts of the electorates. Latino voters, in particular, utilize this method at lower percentages than do Anglo voters.

Given the growing popularity of absentee/at-home voting, some reformers have urged elimination of the traditional voting polling place and its replacement with all-mail elections. Under an all-mail system, registered voters would automatically be sent their ballots through the mail and given a specified time, about three weeks, in which to fill them out and return them by mail to their local election office. The all-mail approach has been utilized for statewide elections in Oregon as well as in Sierra and Alpine, two small rural counties in California. Its supporters point out that these early experiments indicate voter participation is higher than for traditional polling-place elections and that the costs of election administration are reduced.

On the other hand, it is the unsupervised nature of at-home voting that concerns some critics. They contend that the system is vulnerable to manipulation by party and candidate activists more than willing to "coach" voters, such as those living in convalescent hospitals, while they fill out their ballots. In addition, voters who mail in their ballots early, and then change their mind due to late-breaking campaign developments, will find that their vote for the "wrong" candidate is irreversible. Finally, some concern surrounds a weeks-long voting option, as compared to the traditional single voting day, and the possibility that it may further drive up campaign costs for candidates who feel compelled to maintain a high-intensity barrage of media and mailer advertising over the entire length of the voting period.

Nonetheless, it's safe to say that the increasing use of absentee ballots has set the stage for a strong push toward mail-only elections. After all, we live in an era where citizens increasingly work, pay their bills, order purchases, do their banking, and even file their taxes in the comfort of their homes. Are universal mail ballots the next logical step?

CALIFORNIA AND DIRECT DEMOCRACY

Time and time again we refer to the California progressives and their legacies to modern California politics. None of these legacies is more important than the "direct democracy" provisions they adopted. Most observers would argue that none of these currently works the way their creators had envisioned; nonetheless, the recall, referendum, and initiative are hardly less important than "regular" political institutions, such as the governorship or the state legislature. In fact, the initiative process arguably has eclipsed both these in terms of its policy and political significance.

The Recall

In the vast majority of cases, a person's name appears on the ballot as a result of his or her own actions. Would-be officeholders get on the ballot by taking out nomination papers, obtaining signatures of 20 to 100 registered voters (the number varies with the office being sought), and filing them with a county clerk or the secretary of state. In some instances, however, an individual faces the voters without having personally filed papers of candidacy. For example, state law requires that the secretary of state place the names of all persons generally recognized to be candidates for the U.S. presidency on the presidential primary ballots of the major parties. A person not wishing to appear on the ballot may withdraw his or her name by notifying the secretary of state; thus, the "candidate" is not forced to remain on the ballot. But by using a device instituted in California in 1911 by the progressives, registered voters are able to put state and local officeholders' names on the ballot whether they like it or not, preventing such officials from avoiding a day of reckoning with the electorate.

Elective officials, including judges, at all levels of government in California are subject to being recalled (removed by popular vote) during their terms of office. Recall has two major phases, with several steps in each. The *qualifying phase* entails notifying a county clerk or the secretary of state that an effort will be made to unseat an official. The proponents of a recall must submit a brief statement of reasons for the removal attempt, although any reason is legally acceptable. Petitions are then circulated to obtain a legally specified number of signatures within a legally fixed time period. The larger the size of the district in which a recall is attempted, as may be seen in Table 9.2, the lower the percentage of signatures required and the longer the period to obtain them.

Should sufficient signatures be collected within the prescribed number of days, the *election phase* of recall then commences. Voters are asked: "Shall [name of official] be retained in the office of [title]?" If the negative votes are in the majority, which is about half the time, the individual is removed from office. The vacancy is then filled by appointment on the part of other officeholders or by election. If replacement is by election, and in order to avoid the expense of holding a second election in the event removal is successful, it is common to hold the election to fill the possible vacancy at the same time the recall vote is being conducted. If the public official in question survives the recall effort, the outcome of the race to fill his or her post is immaterial. But a recalled official may not run to replace himself or herself. This fact leads to a somewhat awkward possibility. The "yes" or "no" vote on recall is a *majority* decision, whereas the contest to replace a recalled official may have a *plurality* winner if more than two candidates file for the race. A recalled person may have received the support of 49 percent of the electorate and still have to surrender office to someone who received only 30 percent of the vote in a crowded replacement field.

Also, under current law, an official who is retained after a recall vote is eligible for reimbursement from the state government for expenses accrued in the successful defense. Two problems arise here: Is it fair to burden government for such expense when it was private citizens who forced the election in the first place? And what do we

TABLE 9.2	Recall Requirements in California		
	State Officeholders		
Allowed	**Percentage of Last Vote for the Office Required to Sign Petition**		**Number of Days to Obtain Signatures**
Executive	12%		160
Legislative	20		160
Judicial	20		160
	Local Officeholders		
Number of Registered Voters in Local Unit	**Percentage of Registered Voters in Local Unit Required to Sign Petition**		**Number of Days to Obtain Signatures**
Fewer than 1,000	30%		40
1,000 to 10,000	25		6–90
10,001 to 50,000	20		120
More than 50,000	10–15		160

mean by expenses incurred by the officeholder? Probably, the original idea was that out-of-pocket personal expenses should be reimbursed. But in a modern setting, a recall defense could run into the millions of dollars. Should government be responsible for replenishing the official's campaign war chest?

Until recently, the real potential for successful recalls was limited to local governments, and usually those in smaller and more rural jurisdictions. In keeping with the sparsely settled locales within which much recall activity takes place, the motivation behind recall drives can be quite personal or the rationale, at least by "big-city standards," quite trivial. For example, a 1997 Nevada County recall movement against the sheriff, district attorney, and two judges was based on their role in a homicide case. The leader of the recall? The mother of the defendant who was convicted of the murder (Cooper, 1997). In Lassen County, during that same year, two county supervisors incurred a recall attempt based on their vote to remove the county courtroom from the old courthouse to a newer building (Litle, 1997).

More prominent local officials, such as big city mayors, have from time to time been the subject of recall attempts, but these attempts have not been as successful. In 1983, Mayor Dianne Feinstein of San Francisco was targeted by a recall effort that she defeated by a four-to-one margin. And until 1995, attempts to recall officials above the local level were exercises in futility. For example, California Supreme Court Chief Justice Rose Bird was highly unpopular; however, several recall attempts fell short of the needed number of signatures. A 1994 recall attempt, spearheaded by anti–gun-control interests, was aimed at state senator David Roberti, a former senate president pro tem and a strong gun-control advocate. The recall attempt qualified for the ballot but was rejected by the voters.

But state officeholder immunity from recall evaporated in 1995 when the Republican assembly caucus, and local Republican activists successfully recalled two Republican members of the assembly who sided with the Democrats in a prolonged partisan fight over who was to control the lower house. A third 1995 recall attempt, this one against a Democratic assembly member, qualified for the ballot but lost badly on recall election day.

Despite the 1990s expansion of recall politics into the state legislative realm, few observers believed the device could be successfully employed against a statewide elected official. The signature requirement, 12 percent of the last vote for a statewide executive office, or nearly 1 million, seemed too high a hurdle. And the complete failure of earlier statewide attempts was taken to indicate that such exercises were futile. As in many instances, however, events proved the "experts" wrong. The combination of a personally unpopular governor, a budget crisis of unprecedented proportions, a timely infusion of cash into the signature drive, and a recall candidate with name recognition and glamour that eclipsed practically any politician in the land, created the "perfect storm" for Governor Davis's recall.

The recent expanded use of recalls raises broader questions about the uses and misuses of the recall options. Some argue that the object of a recall should be able to run against the other candidates who seek to fill the vacated office. The fact that recall elections, which are usually not a part of broader elections such as those for president or governor, are lightly attended leads some to argue that their use should be limited to specific charges of misconduct rather than being employed for partisan or other political advantage. Finally, in the case of failed recall election attempts, the questions of who is responsible for reimbursing the officeholder and what costs are reimbursable need to be more clearly answered. These concerns aside, however, the 2003 Davis recall election was, at least in most voters' eyes, a resounding success that lived up to the original intent behind and proved the ultimate worth of the recall process. (See Box 9.2 for a discussion of this issue.)

Initiative and Referendum

In addition to electing candidates, Californians have the opportunity to vote on several types of propositions. Ballot measures at the state level are identified by number (e.g., Proposition 13), whereas issues on local ballots are referred to by letter (e.g., Measure A). Issues are placed on the ballot due to either legislative action or successful signature-gathering drives. Although some 23 states possess the initiative process, California, perhaps along with Oregon, is considered the prime user of ballot measures originating from the circulation of petitions. These initiative propositions bypass the legislative and executive branches of state government, but the judiciary may review the legality of ballot measures.

However, not all ballot propositions begin with a voter initiative drive; three types of propositions originate with legislative action. The first of these is bond issues approved by the legislature but requiring voter ratification. Second, whenever amendments to the state constitution or to local charters are proposed by legislators, such items go directly on the ballot without any need to collect signatures. Third, legislative amendments to laws initially passed as ballot measures go on the ballot automatically. This requirement is intended to guard against legislative tinkering with statutes created by the voters. Because it is mandatory that the public be given the opportunity to review

B O X
9.2

The Great Recall Election of 2003:
Vindication of the Process?

As the recall movement against Gray Davis was first starting to take shape, many skeptics voiced the problems inherent in the recall, especially when directed at statewide office-holders: The signature requirement was so high that only big-money players could afford to play this game; a crowded replacement ballot would only confuse voters, and fewer persons would vote for the winner than would vote to keep the incumbent in power; and low turnout at the election would dilute the representative validity of the election results.

What actually occurred was something different. It did take $2 million to put the signature drive over the top, but by California standards, this is not a huge amount for a statewide electoral effort. There was a small army of replacement candidates on the ballot, ranging from fairly prominent political figures to a porn queen, a bail bondsman, and the publisher of *Hustler* magazine—in all, over 130 names appeared on the ballot. But voter interest and support quickly focused on a very few candidacies, and especially on that of Arnold Schwarzenegger. As a result, he received a near majority of all replacement votes cast and, in fact, outpolled the number of votes for retaining incumbent Gray Davis. Finally, the recall election, which generated a tremendous amount of interest, drew 1.7 million more voters to the polls than did the regularly scheduled gubernatorial election in 2002.

None of these facts will sway opponents of the recall concept. They argue that when recall movements are not required to demonstrate specific malfeasance of officeholders, they undercut the legitimacy of the regular election process; after all, Davis had been reelected just months previous to the recall. They might also argue that without the "Arnold factor," the whole recall effort would have been accurately perceived as a Republican-financed effort to undo the results of yet another losing statewide election. Nor have the state's periodic budget crises, the main cause for Davis's demise, been resolved by a change of faces in the governor's office. And what if Davis had prevailed? How would voters have reacted to the $20-million-plus bill that Davis, as the successful survivor of the recall, could have presented to the state to cover the costs of his campaign to save his job?

the ballot measures stemming from these three legislative actions, they are called *compulsory referenda*. If a local jurisdiction wishes to gauge public sentiment (i.e., conduct a straw poll) on a controversial issue, an *advisory referendum* may also be placed on the ballot.

In most election years, it is more common for ballot measures to originate in the legislature than to begin through petition drives. However, petition-based propositions receive more attention than compulsory referenda, usually because these propositions are more controversial (e.g., affirmative action, bilingual education, school vouchers, or gay marriage), involve heavier campaign spending (e.g., Native American gaming casinos), and result in more far-reaching consequences (e.g., coastal zone management, property tax limitation, or abolition of partisan primary elections) than ballot measures prompted by legislative action. In short, hot issues avoided by the California legislature become initiatives.

Three devices are available by which registered voters may place issues on the ballot. These methods of enacting or nullifying laws are known, along with the recall process, as *direct democracy* because legislators and executives are bypassed. With the exception of possible review by the judiciary, laws adopted directly by the electorate do not require approval by elected representatives. If a change is desired in the state constitution, proponents of the alteration may sponsor an *initiative constitutional amendment.* Advocates of an addition to the state's statutory code may author and attempt to pass an *initiative statute.* If any state or local legislative body enacts a statute that provokes strong disagreement, opponents of the legislation may carry out a *protest referendum* to give voters the opportunity to nullify the legislative enactment. A statewide protest referendum had not been held in California for 35 years until four referenda qualified for the ballot in June 1982. The legislation authorizing the peripheral canal (SB 200) and three enactments that redrew the boundaries of congressional districts, state senate districts, and state assembly districts were placed on the ballot due to strong reservations concerning the legislature's action. The electorate nullified the work of the legislature in all four instances. Then the protest referendum disappeared again for almost two decades, only to resurface beginning in 2000, although its latter use differed sharply from the earlier examples.

The peripheral canal, involving the always controversial shipment of northern water to the south, and redistricting, affecting partisan balance over the next decade, are high-level issues that drew wide public interest and involvement. But the three referenda presented to voters on the March 2000 ballot concerned not so much public policy questions of concern to the general population as they did more narrow questions of concern to the affected interest groups. In particular, two of them, Propositions 30 and 31, were attempts by insurance interests to overturn recently passed legislation that eased restrictions on civil lawsuits. That legislation and the ensuing referenda were a continuation of a perpetual struggle between insurance companies and trial lawyers but not the type of question normally associated with protest referenda. The success of Propositions 30 and 31 has encouraged other interest groups who lose in the legislative arena, such as businesses who opposed a successful legislative bill to require employers to provide health care or to pay into a compensation fund, to bring their case to the public via the referendum route (see Box 9.3).

The state constitution prohibits use of the referendum on money bills such as the budget and on urgency legislation. Urgency legislation takes effect immediately (instead of January 1 of the year following passage) and requires a two-thirds vote in the legislature. After their redistricting laws were rejected by the electorate in June 1982, legislators passed another set of redistricting laws for the senate and assembly in December 1982, which they designated as urgency statutes in order to forestall the possibility of more protest referenda. Taking a page from that same playbook, the Democratic majority lined up enough Republican support for its 2000 remapping plans to pass them as urgency measures and thus foreclose the possibility of a referendum attack. (The 2000 redistricting episode is discussed in Chapter 3.)

All three of the direct democracy devices originate with proponents drafting a ballot measure and giving notice of intent to gather signatures. At the state level, the attorney general gives a title to the measure and prepares a brief summary of it for use at the top of each signature petition. Each of the three devices is subject to slightly

BOX
9.3

New Uses (or Misuses) of the Referendum

Protest referenda historically were limited to issues with wide public impact. The fact that the signature-gathering period is just 90 days, rather than the 150 days allowed for initiative signature gathering, makes it much harder to qualify a referendum. Also, sponsors of an initiative are the ones who begin the official process; thus, they can complete organizational formation and strategies before beginning the 150-day period. But a referendum's clock begins to tick as soon as the legislation in question is enacted, not leaving much time for pre–signature-gathering arrangements to be made.

The success of recent special interest referendum campaigns, however, indicates that, with the help of cutting-edge technology and lots of money, referendums may now be a more viable option. Recent victorious referenda, such as the 2004 referendum that killed a pending worker health care guarantee law, are likely to spur yet more serious attempts among interest groups who fail to stop legislative enactment of bills they oppose. The most likely scenario for these to occur is in reaction to enactment of policy that economic interests consider "antibusiness," probably during a period when Democrats control both the legislature and the governorship. And even then, use of this strategy will be limited to those very rich interests who can afford the cost of a speeded-up signature-gathering program and the follow-up advertising campaign on behalf of the referendum.

different requirements regarding the number of signatures to be gathered and the time allowed to circulate the petitions. The total gubernatorial vote in the most recent general election is the basis for calculating the required number of signatures. In 2006, approximately 8.6 million votes were cast in the governor's election. As a result, the 5 percent signature requirement to qualify a statewide statutory initiative is about 434,00. The 8 percent threshold for state constitutional initiatives results in a requirement of just under 695,000 signatures. Initiative sponsors are allowed 150 days to obtain signatures for statutory or constitutional initiatives. Under the direction of the secretary of state, who is the chief elections official in California, city and county clerks verify that persons who have signed petitions are indeed registered voters. If the petition drive secures sufficient valid signatures within the proper time frame, the measure is placed on the next statewide election ballot. Protest referenda also have a 5 percent signature requirement but are allowed only the first 90 days immediately following the bill's enactment for circulation of the petition.

GOVERNMENT BY INITIATIVE

In terms of the most emotional hot-button issues, as well as policy questions over which major interests deadlock, it is no exaggeration to say that the initiative process has supplanted the state legislature as California's lawmaking institution. Beginning with the massive property tax cuts mandated by Proposition 13 in 1978, major portions of state and local fiscal and budgetary options are now limited and defined by a series of successful petition initiatives. Similarly, many of the state's current tough law-and-order policies have been the creation of ballot propositions, as have decisions on a variety of political, social, ethnic, and educational issues such as term limits, illegal immigration, affirmative action, bilingual education, Native American gaming, and same-sex marriage.

Many other major policy proposals ultimately defeated by the voters, such as private school vouchers, limitations on labor union political activity, changes in the way legislative districts would be drawn, and requirements for parental notification prior to teenage abortions, have also been addressed at the ballot box rather than through regular legislative action. None of this activity implies that the legislature has stopped legislating; in fact, thousands of new laws come out of it each session. But, increasingly, the big-ticket items on the political agenda, those questions that engage the strongest feelings among citizens or that are the top priority of organized interest groups, find expression as signature-initiated ballot propositions.

As indicated in Table 9.3, the use of the initiative was widespread immediately after this option was "invented" early in the twentieth century but then declined during the 40-year period between 1940 and 1980. Even though the initiative has existed for over 90 years, almost half of all ideas qualifying for the ballot were generated in the last 26 years, and more than half of all those ideas ultimately accepted by voters have been passed during this same span. Peter Schrag, former editorial page editor of the *Sacramento Bee* and a longtime observer of California politics, characterizes the current reliance on initiatives as nothing less than a fundamental change in the nature of the state's governmental and political process.

> Some twenty years have passed since the passage of California's Proposition 13, which set in motion not merely the holy crusade against taxes in which most of the country now seems irretrievably stuck, but a condition of permanent neo-populism in California, and to some extent elsewhere, for which there is no real precedent, even in the Progressive

TABLE 9.3	Historical Overview of Initiative Petitions' Frequency and Success		
	Qualified Petitions	**Voter Approved**	**Approval Rate**
1910s	30	8	27%
1920s	35	9	26%
1930s	37	11	30%
1940s	20	6	30%
1950s	12	2	17%
1960s	9	3	33%
1970s	22	6	27%
1980s	46	22	48%
1990s	61	24	39%
2000–2006	41	12	29%
Totals	313	103	33%

Source: Adapted and updated from California Secretary of State, A History of the California Initiative Process (Sacramento: 1998).

Era of the early years of the twentieth century. During the two decades since the passage of 13, California has been in a nearly constant revolt against representative government. (Schrag, 1998, pp. 9–10)

Interestingly, very few initiatives reached the ballot for the 2002 and 2003 elections or for the 2004 primary election. But that was most likely an abnormal blip on the screen rather than the beginning of a downward trend in the use of the initiative process. Beginning with the November 2004 general election, and continuing through the 2005 special election and the 2006 primary and general elections, voters were asked to decide the fate of 28 ballot initiatives. And with three separate 2008 elections (presidential primary, non–presidential primary, and general), the number of ballot eligible initiatives is likely to swell even further.

What contributed to the increased use of the initiative in California? The inability of the California legislature to fashion policies in areas such as property tax reduction, car insurance reform, and political campaign finance prompted some people to turn to the initiative process. However, much more than legislative inactivity fueled the initiative binge. The initiative presents an attractive option that interest groups and politicians find difficult to resist. An initiative contains precisely the content its sponsors desire with none of the concessions nor compromises demanded by opposing lobbyists and skeptical legislators as part of the normal legislative process. Sophisticated technology now enables initiative users to identify their financial supporters, likely petition signers, and potential voters during elections. Many profitable businesses exist to supply services (e.g., signature gathering, media buying, and direct mail) to those advancing initiatives.

Although the progressives who gave California the initiative in 1911 probably intended it for the use of ordinary citizens, the results of a blockbuster proposition can be so stunning that candidates and officeholders sponsor quite a few initiatives as well. Legislators have qualified initiatives in areas such as campaign regulation and tax increases on cigarettes and liquor. Governor Pete Wilson was the unrivaled champion of the politician's use of the initiative process. He sponsored a whole score of them, including initiatives dealing with affirmative action, illegal immigration, political use of union dues, and governors' budget powers, among others. In fact, the initiative process became the main vehicle for Wilson's policy and political agenda. One student of the state's initiative process, in assessing the connection between initiative politics and Governor Wilson's electoral success in 1994, argued that "it is probably not an exaggeration to say that Proposition 187 was Wilson's guarantee of reelection" (Young, 1998, p. 53).

Early in his administration, Arnold Schwarzenegger eagerly adopted the Wilson strategy. (It may not be coincidence that many of the new governor's early advisors were also part of the Wilson administration.) A central piece of his initial budget strategy was his success in getting voters to approve a deficit reduction bond issue. He later sponsored a series of initiatives aimed at achieving several of his policy, budget and political goals, which were placed on a 2005 special election ballot. But that tactic, leading to voter rejection of all four of his proposals, marked the low point of his gubernatorial career. (See Chapter 4 for a fuller discussion of this episode.)

Clearly, California politicians, interest groups, and concerned citizens no longer view the initiative as a safety valve to be used only in emergencies when representative institutions fail; now their common practice is to use it as a conventional approach to making law. In short, the initiative became a first resort, not a last resort. When this reality could no longer be denied, the era of the counter-initiative descended on California. Concerned that voters might adopt a particular initiative, opponents of that idea qualify rival measures for the ballot as the best way to stop the original proposition from passing. In essence, initiatives beget still more initiatives. Examples of counter-initiatives abound. In June 1988, a proposition, authorizing public financing of campaigns in California, was countered by yet another proposition, which explicitly forbade the practice of public financing in candidate races. In November 1988, five separate initiatives dealing with car insurance reform all qualified for the ballot. Some of these measures were proconsumer, whereas the remainder were viewed as measures advanced by the insurance industry. In 1990, voters were asked to choose between rival term-limitation initiatives. In 1996, attempts to qualify a ballot proposition banning affirmative action were answered by an unsuccessful attempt to also qualify an initiative expressly protecting affirmative action. That same year also saw the qualification of two rival campaign reform measures. In 2007, Republicans launched an initiative campaign that would change the allocation of California's electoral college votes in a manner that would advantage the Republican presidential candidate. Democrats immediately responded with an initiative of their own that would effectively void the Republican change.

Given the centrality of the initiative process in California's politics, it is important that we develop a clear understanding of its workings. We begin with a description and analysis of the initiative's various stages of development and adoption.

Drafting Stage

Despite the use of the term *direct democracy* to refer to the initiative process, the drafting of ballot measures requires almost no involvement of the people. Self-appointed individuals or small committees decide on the wording of measures. Initiative writers are not required to consider objections that may be raised by anyone who is not involved in the drafting process. There are lawyers and law firms specializing in crafting initiative language, but no requirement that sponsors use these expert services. Although the attorney general must prepare an abbreviated summary of each initiative and give each proposal a title, drafters are not required to negotiate the content of their measures with this official. Once the signature-gathering process begins, no changes whatsoever may be made in the proposal. Under these rules, it is not surprising that drafting errors are found in initiatives. Proposition 140, for example, which limited the number of terms state legislative and executive officials are allowed to serve, left out one statewide executive post (insurance commissioner) under the provisions of the act. One lawyer offered this assessment of the drafting of the landmark initiative lowering property taxes in 1978:

> I like to call Proposition 13 "The Lawyers' Relief Act of 1978." Never in the history of California electoral politics has an initiative been so sloppily drafted. And that is saying a mouthful, given how many ballot measures appear to have been written by one person over the course of a weekend he or she spent in a closet. (Ulrich, 1990)

Even if a ballot measure is not legally or technically flawed, it may be so broad and complex as to defeat the attempts of the best-motivated voter to understand it. Proposition 34 in 2000, which dealt with campaign finance law, was nearly 10 pages long with small type and referenced terms and issues that few voters could be expected to comprehend. Nor can voters hope to learn much from the pro and con advertising over the propositions because those ads rely on simplified tag lines rather than systematically presenting the propositions' strengths and weaknesses.

Qualifying Stage

Petition circulators must be registered voters in California. Of the three methods now in use to obtain signatures on petitions, one would please progressives and the other two would not. Having citizens volunteer their time to circulate petitions is what progressives would endorse. Beyond this method, groups with ample financial resources may hire signature-gathering firms or employ direct-mail houses to solicit signatures. Hired crews, usually paid per signature, circulate petitions at malls, at sporting events, in unemployment lines, and outside polling places. (The more difficult signatures are to obtain on a petition, the higher the price charged by firms.) The direct-mail approach consists of sending minipetitions to selected addresses with a request that signatures and a campaign donation be returned in the envelope provided. Signature-gathering firms, like all the businesses who profit from initiative campaigns, have every reason to encourage their proliferation.

Campaigning Stage

Two aspects of initiative campaigns continue to draw critical attention: deceptive campaign advertisements and wide disparities in the amounts of money spent on the pro and con sides of these races. Given the complexity of the issues facing the voters, initiative sponsors feel the incentive to simplify choices with catchy slogans. In 1998, supporters of Proposition 5, the initiative that opened up the state to casino-style gambling on Native American properties, managed to spend a megafortune on television advertising without actually mentioning "gambling" or "casinos." Two years later proponents of a plan to reduce the voting threshold for passage of local school bonds from two-thirds to 55 percent (Proposition 39) talked about everything but the proposed reduction. In fact, it may be no easy matter to know just who is behind all those "yes" and "no" ads. Initiative sponsors (as well as opponents) are free to form themselves into organizations to which they can append any name, thus often disguising the policy thrust and special interest angle of their efforts.

No limits or "truth tests" are applied to what proposition proponents and opponents can claim in their advertising, which, of course, is also true of all political campaigns. In regular elections, however, voters have some knowledge about the candidates, such as their party affiliation or their previous record, to help them decide. Moreover, politicians do not like to be caught in bald-faced campaign lies. Groups that back or oppose ballot propositions are not so constrained. They do not themselves run for political office, nor can they be held accountable for misstatements. Few, if any, negative ramifications arise from statements about a proposition's impacts that turn out to be groundless distortions. The groups that bankroll initiative campaigns, both pro and con, disappear into the woodwork once the election is over. Later they can reconstitute themselves, complete with a new name, to once again do battle in the next round of initiative wars.

Campaigns on behalf of and against initiatives involve heavy, though often quite uneven, spending. How much money does it cost to pass or defeat a ballot measure? The answer to that question depends on the nature of the issue and the amount of money the initiative's opponents can spend. Some issues that resonate with strong existing voter support can be passed without huge expenditures on their behalf. In recent years, propositions dealing with immigration, prison sentences, and affirmative action all passed easily despite the lack of a huge "yes" campaign on their behalf. In other instances, where the public is less aware of or more ambivalent about the issue, a big spending edge on the pro or con side can spell the difference because the issue can be defined by the dominant—that is, the most expansive and expensive—campaign. (See Boxes 9.4 and 9.5 for further discussion of the money issue as well as proposed general reforms of the initiative process.)

If the issue is not well understood and both sides spend a great deal, the usual result is defeat for the initiative. Presumably, voters who lack a firm grasp of the issue, when bombarded by noisy "yes" and "no" campaigns, will ultimately deal with their confusion by casting a "no" vote to maintain the status quo rather than voting "yes" to a change whose consequences have been obscured rather than illuminated by the barrage of conflicting 30-second television spots.

The Voters' Choice

No one could blame a voter for feeling a little overwhelmed by the volume and complexity of choices thrust upon him by the bundle of initiatives that appear on each statewide ballot. Not only must a voter try to make sense out of the complex issues and arguments surrounding any individual proposition, but also she may be called on to grasp interconnections and comparisons between different propositions, which often aren't even numbered consecutively on the ballot. (Ballot placement for initiatives is determined by the date they are officially qualified, not by subject matter.)

Voters, trying to wade through this ballot-proposition forest of complicated, often interrelated proposals, may come to rely on the official voter's pamphlet, compiled by the secretary of state. The pamphlet contains a description of the main policy changes contained in each proposition and a series of pro/con arguments about each proposition. The full text of each ballot measure is also printed in the back of the booklet. For the voter who is diligent, an excellent reader, and possessed of ample free time, the pamphlet, and particularly its descriptions of the main elements of each proposition, can be quite illuminating. But because the initiatives are often complicated, even unbiased descriptions can be difficult to decipher. The actual language of the propositions is understandable only to attorneys and legislative analysts. As for the pro/con arguments, the pamphlet itself contains the following warning: "Arguments printed on this page are the opinions of the authors and have not been checked for accuracy by any official agency."

Remember, too, that any statewide ballot also contains statewide races, congressional and legislative elections, and often local contests and ballot propositions. All told, voters are asked to make dozens of decisions each time they step into the voting booth or fill out their absentee ballot at home. Given that even the most diligent voter is subject to "voter fatigue," low turnout among marginal voters may not be so surprising. Finally, most voters realize that even when they sort through all the advertising and

BOX 9.4

Initiatives as Direct Democracy: The Million Dollar Question

When the progressives introduced the ballot initiative to California politics almost 100 years ago, they presumably intended it to be used by citizens as a counterforce against unresponsive politicians and selfish special interests. What would they think now if they could see their handiwork in use?

The fact that initiatives are now often sponsored and backed by elected officials as part of their own political agenda would not likely please Hiram Johnson and his progressive allies. Perhaps even more troublesome is the initiative's capture by interest groups. The cost of gathering enough signatures to qualify an initiative, which rises along with the state's population, is one factor behind the intrusion of big money into citizens' initiatives. Costs of campaigning on behalf of and against ballot propositions put the whole enterprise even further out of the reach of average citizens.

In fact, before most groups can even engage the services of those specializing in initiative politics, they must bring a bag of money to the table. One initiative campaign professional put it this way:

> When somebody walks in [with an initiative proposal], I always ask the million-dollar question, which is, "Where's your million dollars?" (Broder, 2000, p. 84)

What can be stated with certainty is that initiative campaigning costs continue to climb. Practically each election sets a new record for total and individual campaign expenditures. But even in this era of sky-high expenditures, the 1998 battle over Native American gaming, Proposition 5, raised eyebrows. Ironically, gaming interests bankrolled both the "yes" and the "no" campaigns. Money against the proposition came from Nevada gambling interests, obviously fearful of losing California customers to the more alluring and widespread gambling opportunities that Proposition 5 sought to make available on Indian lands. The bulk of "yes" campaign money also came from gambling interests, most of it from two California Native American tribes possessing a huge political war chest generated by their existing gaming operations.

The "no" campaign attempted to frame the question in terms of public security and safety, hinting that Proposition 5 would allow gambling casinos anywhere, including residential neighborhoods, and that these casinos would be exempt from environmental, worker protection, and health and safety regulations. The "yes" side's campaign spun the question around the issue of Native American "self-sufficiency" and the opportunity to break the poverty-welfare cycle that has plagued Native Americans. Both sides were careful to employ real Indians in their television spots. When the dust finally cleared from this two-way media blitz, the "yes" forces prevailed by a comfortable margin. Perhaps they won just because a lot of Californians like to gamble and, in this age of state-run and state-advertised lotteries, the moral argument against gambling has been eroded. Or perhaps it was because the opposition spent "only" about $30 million, just about a third of the amount spent by the proponents of Proposition 5. At any rate, the contest ushered in the era of the $100 million ballot proposition campaign. How far into the twenty-first century will we reach the $200 million mark?

BOX 9.5	**Reforming the Initiative Process**

As concern with the uses and misuses of the initiative process grows, reform proposals proliferate, ranging from minor tinkering to outright abolition. The California Constitutional Revision Commission suggested a few of the tinkering variety:

- Require that proposed constitutional (as opposed to mere statutory) initiatives be placed only on the November general election ballot and not on the primary election ballot, where voter turnout is much smaller;
- Involve the legislature in the initiative drafting process; and
- Allow laws passed through the initiative to be amended by the legislature after a certain time has passed (California Constitutional Revision Commission, 1996).

Although these proposals were considered too radical for serious legislative consideration, many harsher critics of the initiative process think they failed to go far enough. Some even question the validity of the process: how can we expect voters to play the role of making specific policy decisions, as opposed to their traditional role of providing general policy guidelines through their selection of elected officials?

Nonetheless, the idea, if not the current practice, of initiatives remains popular with California voters. Attempts to abolish it altogether hold no political viability.

Short of abolition, what could be done to conform the modern use of the initiative to the goals and expectations of its inventors? Or should this form of direct democracy be left alone?

information and eventually pass an initiative, more likely than not the courts will have the final say.

Judicial Review

Although initiatives bypass the legislative and executive branches, the judiciary reviews propositions when lawsuits are filed. For the most part, courts do not intervene in the initiative process prior to the popular vote, though on occasion they have ordered the removal of propositions from the ballot before election day. Most judicial review occurs after the popular vote has been tallied and results from lawsuits filed by those very groups that urged a "no" vote but lost on election day. Proposition 103, a successful 1988 initiative that, among other things, sought to provide a customer rebate on auto insurance premiums and impose tight fee regulations on the industry, was litigated in the courts by the insurance industry for nearly a decade following its passage. More recently, the opponents of initiatives that imposed term limits and campaign reforms and that ended affirmative action and bilingual education sought to have those propositions voided by the courts. On Tuesday, November 3, 1998, the previously discussed gaming initiative, Proposition 5, passed handily. On Wednesday, November 4, 1998, opponents of the proposition announced the commencement of legal action against its implementation.

Traditionally, courts are asked to set aside a successful proposition on the grounds that the new law violates the federal constitution or federal law or that it violates the state constitution. This last remedy is not available if the proposition called for a change in the state constitution itself. Proposition 198, which created the state's short-lived blanket primary, is an example of an initiative that was judicially voided on the grounds that it violated the federal constitution. Of course, not all legal challenges are upheld. Term limits and the end of affirmative action are just two controversial ballot measures that overcame challenges to their legal validity.

The California Constitution limits initiatives to a single subject, and state courts are empowered to remove a proposition from the ballot if it violates this single-subject rule. (Or, as the court did in dealing with a 2004 legislature-approved enactment dealing with two subjects, it can require the secretary of state to break up the proposal into its constituent parts and list them as separate ballot questions.) Unfortunately, no legal definition outlines what constitutes a violation of the rule, and thus, traditionally, courts were reluctant to apply it. However, over the last few years, courts have been somewhat more willing to utilize the single-subject rule. But the burden of proof is borne by those seeking to invalidate the proposition, and, for the most part, judges are mostly willing to grant ballot propositions the benefit of the doubt when applying the single-subject rule.

Generally, initiatives are more vulnerable to challenges based on the U.S. Constitution or federal law. These suits are heard in federal courts, whose judges, nominated by the president and approved by the U.S. Senate, serve for life. Cases involving the single-subject rule or other California constitutional issues are heard in the state's court system. State judges, appointed by the governor and subject to periodic election or retention votes, may be more leery about setting aside voter-approved initiatives than are federal judges, who are far removed from state politics and state voters.

At any rate, a successful, though controversial, initiative is now almost certain to face legal challenges mounted by the campaign's losers; major initiative battles now seldom end when the votes are counted. Courts and judges have become regular players in California's politics-by-initiative system.

ELECTIONEERING, CALIFORNIA STYLE

In the 1930s, California introduced to American politics the concept of professional campaign management. The subsequent growth of campaign management businesses in California was hardly surprising. The legal restrictions on political parties during partisan primaries and the nonpartisan nature of local elections created the need in such contests for organizations possessing electioneering skills. The more recent proliferation of ballot initiatives provided another set of needs for professional campaign assistance.

As the campaign industry grows in size and complexity, more and more job titles come into use: media buyers, media producers, media coaches, pollsters, direct-mail houses, and focus groups, not to mention the traditional speechwriters, schedulers, and advance teams that handle preparations for candidate appearances. Web site design and maintenance is the newest technology required by all serious campaigns.

This discussion first requires clarification of commonly used terms such as *campaign manager* and *campaign consultant*. The first of these titles usually refers to an individual who actually runs the day-to-day operations of *one* campaign. This person ordinarily is responsible for the detailed implementation of campaign tactics, and he or she generally hires and supervises the campaign staff. On the other hand, campaign consultants usually work with *several* candidates and ballot measures at the same time. Consultants provide advice on major themes to be followed but generally try not to become bogged down in the particularities of campaign administration. Confusion occurs, however, because some consultants occasionally consent to take on the direct management of campaigns.

The rise of consultants adds an important set of players to the electoral process. In the precampaign period before massive efforts are undertaken to reach voters, a candidate's ability (or inability) to place a well-known consultant under contract for an upcoming campaign confers instant credibility (or the lack thereof) on a candidacy. Campaign donors and journalists take a candidate much more seriously if he or she has signed with a well-known consultant. The most prominent consultants are in a position to pick and choose among candidates they believe have the best chance of winning, and thus further enhance their reputation as campaign miracle workers. Prominent consultants can parlay past successes into candidate contracts that enhance their electoral records and their reputations going into future election seasons.

Campaign consultants prepare a strategy (or plan) to be used by a candidate or by one side of a ballot-measure contest. Ideas are developed on the overall theme or message of the campaign and the timing of media saturation. Should a candidate commit a blunder during a campaign, consultants provide advice on methods of damage control. If a consulting firm offers a broad range of services, it may manage almost all areas of a campaign. More commonly, specialized firms are retained to handle specific parts of a campaign. The new, high-tech world of political campaigning involves many technical specialties, including polling, direct mailing, media production and purchases, and voter targeting.

With the growing expense of campaigns, it is important that consultants and managers not waste money on fruitless endeavors. Many people will not vote on election day and others are unlikely to change strongly held views. In short, targets must be selected. Skillful campaigns identify persuadable voters as well as the issues that will help secure their support. Survey research is instrumental in establishing the target groups and the target issues.

Polling

Most political polls today are conducted over the telephone by part-time interviewers under the direction of professional supervisors. Firms maintain lists of competent interviewers to assist in the collection of reliable information from the public. Initial polls are used to determine the strengths and weaknesses of a candidate's image and to learn the voters' views on various issues. This information helps consultants tentatively settle on a campaign theme. Well-funded campaigns for major offices never stop polling throughout the course of a race so that immediate adjustments may be made, should slippage be detected. Pollsters gauge public reaction to televised commercials and to mass mailings, hoping to find the key idea that can be used to harvest a particular cluster of votes. Most contemporary practitioners would agree with consultant David Townsend: "You would not run for dog-catcher without a poll" (Kushman, 1990).

The results of some polls are disseminated in the mass media, whereas other surveys are kept private and used strictly within a campaign. The California Poll, founded by Mervin Field in 1947, is syndicated to newspapers throughout the state. Several metropolitan dailies, including the *Los Angeles Times* and the *Sacramento Bee*, also conduct voter studies and publish the outcomes. The release of polling data presumably fascinates viewers and readers. The public, similar to spectators at a horse race, likes to see who is gaining and who is dropping back. Upward momentum in the polls produces an influx of campaign donations, whereas stable or declining ratings tend to reduce contributions.

Campaign Media

Although the cost of polls, travel, and telephones is not to be dismissed lightly, the great bulk of campaign money is expended on media. Most statewide campaigns allocate 60 to 80 percent of available funds to the purchase of media of all kinds. The production and airing of television advertisements used to receive the lion's share of this allocation, but increasingly money is being directed to printing and mailing campaign materials directly to voters. Internet campaigning is the latest strategy for establishing direct contact with voters.

Direct Mail

Computers provide numerous applications in campaigning. Aside from tabulating voter survey results with dispatch, computers enable campaign professionals to segment the electorate and then direct highly refined messages to each component of the voting public. With the large memory capacity now available, computers can store information on voters' age, gender, income level, occupation, party affiliation, race, magazine subscriptions, and sexual preference. Much of this information is readily available through published sources such as the census, voter rolls, and employee listings. Ethnic and gay databases (known as dictionaries) must be painstakingly derived from phone books, precinct visits, and expert judgment. As firms acquire more and more knowledge of the electorate over the years, their ability to help candidates increases. When recent polling data and election results are analyzed together with the socioeconomic information already on file, campaign consultants are able to say with some assurance what attitudes are held by certain categories of voters. To put it succinctly, targeting has improved immensely in recent years.

Direct mail is particularly cost-effective in legislative district races. First, direct mail does not waste money outside the legislative district, as television advertising frequently does. Second, mail targets persuadable voters (not others) precisely inside the district. In the past, it was common to send out the same campaign brochure to a districtwide audience. This practice may have done more harm than good if broadly worded mailers contained positions that offended almost every recipient. The direct mail of today targets narrow groups and highlights carefully selected issues. Mailers are designed to work on voters' partisan, religious, ethnic, and occupational predispositions. In addition, the letterhead printed at the top of a campaign letter can be adjusted to appeal to the targeted audience. For instance, influential Latinos are shown as campaign committee members on letters going to Spanish-speaking neighborhoods, whereas prominent persons in business are shown as sponsors of mailings to affluent communities. Great effort is even expended on the design of envelopes to keep recipients from throwing mailers into the wastebasket unopened.

There is considerable support for the claim that targeted mail facilitates the use of highly negative brochures called "hit pieces." By carefully planning when a piece is to be mailed, it is possible to blast an opponent in the last days of a campaign and to deny that person sufficient time to design, print, and mail a response. Knowing that a piece is being sent primarily to a sympathetic audience (i.e., is not for mass consumption) may incline direct-mail operatives to use stronger language and graphics. One of the reasons so much effort is being put into encouraging absentee voting is to minimize the damage from hit pieces late in the campaign.

The precise targeting now possible with computers may be connected to other delivery methods besides mail. Some campaigns experimented with sending videocassette recordings to selected voters. With detailed knowledge of particular residents, personal contact can be made through phone banks and precinct walkers. The cyberspace "information highway" creates a whole new frontier of targeted campaigning. Full political use of "the highway" is the current great advance in high-tech electioneering.

Television Commercials

One 30-second political advertisement in a metropolitan area will reach more Californians than a candidate could meet by walking precincts for a year. It should be added that the huge audience provided by television comes with a huge price tag as well. The price of air time is related to the number and type of viewers tuning in to a given channel. The time of day or night, the size of the media market, and the popularity of the program during which an ad is run all influence cost. Though more difficult to target than direct mail, it is possible to some degree to focus televised commercials. Specialists in buying media like to obtain slots near news broadcasts and public affairs programs because people watching these shows are more likely to vote. Further, conservative voters are thought to be viewers of police dramas, whereas young and liberal members of the electorate presumably are the audience of shows such as *Grey's Anatomy*. In the radio market, various types of listeners can be reached by placing ads on Spanish-language broadcasts, all-news shows, and sports coverage—not to mention the different audiences available on rock, country, and classical stations. It is not uncommon for statewide candidates to spend half of their media budgets at television stations in Los Angeles. The signals from these channels carry to San Diego, San Bernardino, Riverside, Orange, Ventura, Santa Barbara, and Kern Counties. Media buyers now also place ads on cable channels because the cost is low and the ability to target a specific audience is superior to that available over the major networks.

The typical campaign advertisement on television is a 30-second spot. After careful review of polling data, a concept for the piece and a closing tag line are developed. Tag lines are what consultants hope the voters will remember. In the 1998 Democratic gubernatorial primary election, Gray Davis was the underdog against two very rich, though not very seasoned, opponents who could greatly outspend him. His tag line, "experience money can't buy," got just the right message across: Davis was the candidate with a proven track record, while his opponents had only money and were, in effect, trying to buy the election. Unless the campaign is hit with a catastrophe, the fundamental theme is not altered in midcampaign.

Next, an eye-catching video is shot, sound is recorded, and charts or other graphics are prepared. When all the ingredients have been mixed and edited, the results are shown to focus groups to determine their reaction. Test audiences made up of a cross-section of the electorate view a number of commercials and comment on what they like and dislike about each. Actors, dialogue, and tag lines are all evaluated for their ability to put across the desired message. Given the brevity of spots, it is common for these ads to oversimplify complex propositions and to focus more on candidates' images than their issue positions. Whereas television advertisements usually present a grand theme for a campaign, many subthemes tailored to fit specific segments of the electorate are typical of direct mail.

Rather than being positive and accurate, some television spots are negative and deceptive. Of many examples that might be cited here, one will have to suffice. The redistricting commission proposed by Proposition 39 in 1984 was to be composed of retired appellate justices. The television ads used to defeat this initiative showed judges (with party bosses peering over their shoulders) taking their oath of office, saying "I swear to uphold my-my-my political party." These commercials conjured up judicial corruption and entirely avoided the issue of unfair lines for legislative districts. Then Assembly Speaker Willie Brown (D, San Francisco), an opponent of Proposition 39, later admitted that the negative commercials were created mainly to mislead and confuse. In recent elections, newspapers have critiqued television campaign ads, judging their honesty and germaneness. Whether this type of evaluation forces a higher standard of advertising remains to be seen.

PHOTO 9.1   Big-time free media: Arnold and his "friend" on one of the nation's most-watched TV shows. *(Monica Almeda/The New York Times)*

Free Media

Not all media exposure is by means of paid advertisements. Campaign managers endeavor to have their candidates appear as often as possible on news broadcasts, on talk shows, and in newspapers. In addition to press conferences to attract media coverage, staged or pseudo-events are carefully organized for the same purpose. Candidates visit elementary schools, watch space shuttle landings in person, engage in long hikes along the state's highways, and take rafting trips to provide interesting visual situations that news editors would be likely to use. Though considerably less expensive than paid media, expenditures for advance work by staff, telephoning, and travel can make media events anything but free. Then again, for a very few lucky politicians, free media attention is guaranteed. And in California's history, no one rivals Arnold Schwarzenegger in this regard. In analyzing this phenomena one communications scholar said, "Arnold is getting more free media than God" (O'Connor, 2003).

So-called free, or "earned," media coverage has its drawbacks, however. Candidates and ballot-measure advocates need the cooperation of news organizations. An international crisis, a strike, or a sensational crime may push a staged event off the news. Publishers and editors opposed to the point of view of those seeking free exposure can deny coverage of particular media events. Candidates with money to buy media improve their standing in voter surveys and thereafter receive more coverage by the news media. Lately, candidates hold press conferences to screen their television spots for reporters, a clear example of paid media begetting free media. But because newsworthiness is related to standings in voter surveys, it is difficult for someone trailing badly in the polls to use free media to improve his or her position.

Ordinarily, the message projected at a media event cannot be as easily controlled by a candidate as the language in a paid commercial. Recently, however, candidates have achieved a measure of control of their free media by tightly scripting the event and refusing to take questions from the press. When news organizations become frustrated with such canned performances, they can force spontaneity out of candidates by refusing to air their highly planned events.

Candidate debates are a variation of free media. These events are staged for media coverage, but the power of news organizations to edit is lessened, provided debates are shown in their entirety. (Later newscasts, of course, show selected excerpts from debates.) The conventional wisdom about debates is that they represent a chance for the candidate who is trailing to make up ground; the leader has nothing to gain but potentially plenty to lose by debating. On the other hand, a certain pressure is exerted on both candidates to debate, and no candidate wants to be pictured as fearing a face-to-face confrontation. The audience for debates is a product of how interested the public is in the election contest. The 2002 two-person governor's election debate between Gray Davis and Bill Simon did not attract much of an audience; the following year, a recall election roundtable debate among five of the leading candidates, most notably including Arnold Schwarzenegger, drew a prime-time network-sized audience. This debate was also noteworthy in that it featured five, not just two candidates, including two Republicans, a Democrat, a Green Party hopeful, and an independent. Also, unlike earlier election debates, the candidates were given the questions in advance. The debate's "winner" was likely Schwarzenegger, who demonstrated that he could hold his own with the other, often more experienced, high-profile candidates on the podium.

PHOTO 9.2 2006 Schwarzenegger/Angelides gubernatorial election debate. (*Associated Press*)

THE HIGH COSTS OF ELECTIONS: CAN ANYTHING BE DONE?

Democrats and Republicans, liberals and conservatives, and just about anybody else who follows state politics agree on one thing: California campaigning is obscenely expensive. By the end of the twentieth century, statewide campaign expenditures of $30 million or more no longer were surprising. In fact, in 1998, Al Checchi spent about that much of his own money on his unsuccessful primary election campaign for the Democratic gubernatorial nomination. Spending on a single ballot initiative reached the $100 million mark during that same year. Legislative races costing more than $1 million are no longer uncommon.

Agreement that campaigns are too expensive has not translated into any agreement about how to regulate campaign finance. Reform attempts are limited by the 1976 U.S. Supreme Court ruling in *Buckley v. Valeo* that, while *contributions* to candidates could be limited, *expenditures* by candidates could not, except in those cases where the candidate voluntarily accepts public financing. Nor can the amount of personal money a candidate spends on behalf of his or her own campaign be limited.

Finally, interest groups can get around limitations on candidate contributions by operating campaigns in favor of a candidate (or in opposition to her opponent) that are not organized or directed by the candidate's official campaign. These "independent expenditures," as well as policy advocacy media purchases related to the campaign contests, which are clearly pitched toward helping one of the candidates, do not count as candidate campaign contributions and are thus cannot be constrained by contribution limits. Moreover, the U.S. Supreme Court has taken the position that spending money to influence election outcomes is a form of political speech protected by the First Amendment. This logic has led the court to take a very restrictive view of attempts to reduce the role and extent of interest group money in the campaign process. In California, court-imposed limitations on attempts to limit political money and the lack of legislative enthusiasm for campaign donation and expenditure limitations have been effective roadblocks to campaign finance reform. Nonetheless, on several occasions voters have demonstrated their desire to reform the system through support of various campaign finance ballot initiatives.

The Political Reform Act (approved by the voters in 1974 as Proposition 9) addressed the role of money in California politics on several fronts. It established a comprehensive reporting system for donations to candidates and for campaign expenditures. The disclosure requirements, as well as other provisions aimed at regulating conflict of interest and lobbying activity, are administered by the Fair Political Practices Commission, which was created by Proposition 9. Those disclosure laws were recently expanded to mandate that the reports be available to the public on a Web site maintained by the secretary of state. (See Box 9.6.)

Campaign Disclosure

All campaigns at the state and local levels in California—whether they be candidate or proposition contests—must file detailed reports on campaign contributions and expenditures. The theory behind disclosure, or so-called sunshine laws such as these, is that the public needs to know the sources of money spent by candidate and ballot initiative groups. This information might provide a clearer picture of candidates' and ballot initiatives actual policy inclinations and goals. For this to work, however, journalists need to publicize the contents of disclosure reports, and voters need to pay attention to their stories. And there is no indication that disclosure laws have diminished the willingness of big campaign contributors to give money nor the willingness of campaigns to spend that money.

BOX 9.6	**Surfing the Net for Campaign Finance Scoops**

One complaint about campaign finance information has been that it is not readily available to voters and often is made public only after the election. But beginning with the 2000 elections, all state candidates are required to post their campaign contribution and expenditure reports on the secretary of state's Web site. Will many voters who are not political junkies actually seek out this information before voting? The answer remains to be seen, but the potential audience for timely campaign finance reporting is at least theoretically much larger now.

Campaign Contribution Limits

Disclosure and conflict of interest laws certainly possess political reform value. The biggest problems, however, in terms of the integrity of the electoral system and the perceived and real corruption of the process involve the financing of and spending for election campaigns. In no state is the problem more acute than in California, where, as already discussed, the costs of running for office are high. California voters demonstrated their willingness to attack these problems by passing several campaign finance initiatives; but none has survived legal challenge long enough to have any prolonged effect.

Two separate campaign finance reform initiatives in 1988 (Propositions 68 and 73) received voter approval, thereby creating a huge legal snarl. Ultimately, neither survived subsequent legal challenges, and the mostly unregulated system was restored. In 1996, voters were given another chance in the form of Propositions 208 and 212. This time voters accepted 208 and rejected 212. Proposition 208 was a comprehensive attempt to limit both campaign donations and expenditures within the regulatory limits imposed by the *Buckley v. Valeo* decision. It set low contribution limits for donors: $250 for legislative candidates and $500 for statewide candidates. It also stipulated "voluntary" expenditure limits on candidates' campaign expenditures. In order to entice candidates to accept the expenditure limits, 208 doubled the contribution limits for those office seekers accepting the expenditure caps. An additional provision raised the voluntarily accepted spending caps when the volunteer candidate's opponent (who did not accept the voluntary limits) made expenditures in excess of the limit.

Proposition 208 also banned the transfer of funds from candidate to candidate (see Chapters 3 and 8 for a discussion of this practice in legislative elections) and limited fund-raising by candidates to specified periods (nearer the upcoming election) in order to eliminate the current practice of nonstop fund-raising by elected officials. Under Proposition 208, money left in a campaign treasury at the end of an election was to be turned over to the state in order to prevent politicians from building huge campaign war chests in order to scare off potential future challengers. Proposition 208 even attempted to limit how much could be contributed by individuals to interest group organizations who, in turn, contribute to candidates, and it sought to limit the percentage of total campaign funds that a candidate could accept from interest groups, as opposed to funds accepted from individual donors.

Proposition 208 was clearly an ambitious, wide-ranging attempt to deal with the most troublesome aspects of campaign finance. It sought to weaken candidates' reliance on large-scale interest group donors and shift the fund-raising emphasis to individual small donations. It also aimed at limiting the ever-increasing costs of campaigning in California and at reducing the fund-raising and campaign-spending advantages enjoyed by incumbents over challengers. Like its predecessor reforms, however, Proposition 208 faced legal challenge and was initially struck down at the federal district court level on the grounds that its contribution limits were unreasonably low. Implementation of the act's other provisions was enjoined pending appeal to a higher court. Then, while this litigation was going forward, the state legislature moved into the area of campaign finance regulation by passing its own reform version, which was subsequently approved by the voters as Proposition 34 in the November 2000 election.

Proposition 34, on the surface, looked a lot like Proposition 208, but in fact its provisions provided a much milder set of changes. For example, its campaign contribution limits were much higher than those of 208, as were its voluntary campaign expenditure ceilings. Proposition 34, unlike 208, does not limit campaign fund-raising to specific time periods, thus preserving the very important fund-raising advantages enjoyed by incumbent officeholders.

Political reformers called "foul" when Proposition 34 was presented to the voters, seeing it as a product of legislators' fears that the courts were about to revive Proposition 208 rather than a "real" reform attempt. Because 34 repealed the provisions of 208, it rendered the court battle moot. Certainly 34's provisions were much less stringent than those of its predecessor. It was, after all, the product of politicians whose political careers had thrived in a weak regulatory era; expecting winners in any game to suddenly want to change the rules is something of a stretch.

Another school of thought argues that even the best-intentioned reform attempts, such as Proposition 208, will not make things better. For one thing, "independent expenditures," meaning money spent by individuals or interest groups on behalf of a campaign but not as an official part of the campaign, may not, according to *Buckley v. Valeo*, be limited. Thus, lowering the limit on campaign donations may not reduce the role of interest groups in campaign finance but instead just encourage more independent expenditures by these same groups. Also, any reform that makes it harder for candidates to raise money only increases the advantages enjoyed by the very wealthy, who are able to finance their own election bids, and the advantages of incumbents, who typically begin their campaign with more name recognition than their challengers. (See Box 9.7 for an alternative approach to campaign finance regulation.)

California Voting Turnout in National and Western State Perspective

Percent of Those Eligible to Vote Who Actually Voted in the 2004 Presidential Election

California: 59.8% (Rank: #30)

National Average: 60.7%

Highest: Minnesota, 77.3%

Lowest: Arkansas, 51.2%

National Rankings of Other Western States

Oregon #5	Idaho #28
Washington #13	Utah #33
Colorado #14	New Mexico #37
Wyoming #18	Nevada #42
Montana #20	Arizona #45

Source: Center for the Study of the American Electorate, American University, Washington, DC.

<table>
<tr><td>BOX
9.7</td><td>Reforming the "Demand" or the "Supply" Side of
Campaign Finance?</td></tr>
</table>

Given the interrelated but contradictory goals of reducing the electoral influence of interest groups, reducing the electoral advantage of incumbents, and ensuring that candidates other than the super-rich have a chance of winning, Californians need to reevaluate previously attempted methods of campaign finance reform. Standard reforms attack the "supply" side of the election money equation by limiting when contributions may be made and how much may be contributed to candidates or how much candidates may spend. But, as discussed, these solutions may create their own set of new problems. Nor are the courts likely to approve any serious reduction in the amount of money that a political campaign can raise and spend.

Maybe it's time to look at the "demand" side of the picture. Because California elections are so expensive, candidates need a lot of money to win. It is this basic fact that creates the problems caused by big-donors' influence, incumbents' advantage over challengers, and electoral domination by the super-rich. If candidates could run an effective campaign on a low budget, these problems would be greatly alleviated. But in California, elections are high-tech, and hence expensive; so what can be done?

Public financing of candidates is one solution. Right now, though, given the public's distrust of and distaste for politicians, convincing voters that a few of their tax dollars should go toward financing political campaigns is a hard sell. But what about the provision of free campaign services to candidates? For instance, because the airwaves are publicly owned (networks and local stations obtain a license, not ownership, to operate), free electronic media for candidates could be mandated. Similarly, the mail service is public. Why not allow all candidates for office a certain amount of free mailings during the campaign season?

A perfect system? No. For example, a complex set of rules would be needed to govern candidates' free television advertising. Who should be in charge of making sure that all qualified candidates received their fair share of prime-time spots? How do we define a "qualified candidate"?

Nonetheless, if we are really interested in reducing the role of political money in the electoral process, making money less important to candidates seems to be worth some serious consideration. California might take a cue from states such as Arizona and Maine, who have enacted broad-based campaign finance reforms that attack the demand side of the political money equation.

SUMMARY

California's electoral system is not working well. Out of the total pool of eligible voters, citizens 18 years and over, only about two-thirds register, and many of these fail to vote. Those who do show up at the polls are not particularly reflective of the state as a whole. California's high-tech campaign styles are, in addition to their technical complexity, very expensive. Expensive campaigns raise serious questions about the role of big money in buying candidates and elections, the advent of super-rich candidates funding their own campaigns, and the integrity of the electoral system. Unfortunately, attempts to reform campaign finance tend to run afoul of the courts or, if allowed to stand, create new problems for every one they solve.

Meantime, one of California's direct democracy institutions—the initiative—is now the state's authoritative source of major policy change. Unfortunately, the device is subject to interest group manipulation and is a source of voter confusion rather than voter input into the political system. The progressives created the initiative, referendum, and recall assuming they would reduce the influence of special interests and enhance the power of the people. How pleased would they be with the results of their invention a century later?

REFERENCES

Broder, David S. *Democracy Derailed.* New York: Harcourt, 2000.

California Constitutional Revision Commission. *Final Report and Recommendations to the Governor and the Legislature.* Sacramento: 1996.

California Secretary of State. *A History of the California Initiative Process.* Sacramento: 1998.

California Secretary of State. *Statement of the Vote.* Sacramento: 2004, 2005, 2006, 2007.

California Secretary of State. *Report of Registration.* Sacramento: 2007.

Cooper, Claire. "Nevada County Hit with Four Recall Petitions." *Sacramento Bee* (October 7, 1997).

Field Research Corporation. *California Field Poll.* San Francisco: November 2004.

Kushman, Rick. "Candidates Today Trust Polls." *Sacramento Bee* (April 1, 1990).

Litle, James Baxton. "Five File to Replace Supervisors Targeted for Recall." *Sacramento Bee* (September 12, 1997).

O'Connor, Barbara, as quoted on National Public Radio's *All Things Considered* (August 15, 2003).

Schrag, Peter. *Paradise Lost.* New York: New Press, 1998.

Ulrich, Roy. "Proposition 13: Taxing Courts, Rolling Back Logic." *Sacramento Bee* (March 30, 1990).

Young, E. Morgan. "Government by the People: The Evolving Impact of Citizen Initiatives on Public Policy and Government Advocacy in California." Master's thesis, George Washington University, 1998.

CHAPTER ten

BUDGETARY POLITICS IN CALIFORNIA: TRYING TO MAKE ENDS MEET

The capital's almost annual protracted budget impasse is an object of politicians' embarrassment and citizen disgust. Perhaps more than any other news story, reports of the wrangling and delays in producing the budget, and the faulty assumptions and accounting tricks on which the finished "balanced budget" is based, have crystallized citizen disgust with their political system. Budget delays past the constitutionally mandated date of July 1 are nothing new, but their predictability and length have increased over the last 20 years. As the new governor, Arnold Schwarzenegger heavily stressed the importance of an on-time budget as part of his results-oriented approach to policy making. But in the end, despite his popularity and the prestige he put on the line, his first budget was fully four weeks late. His budget for fiscal year 2007–2008 was seven weeks late. Probably even more serious, however, is the fact that these budgets have often been not honest and accurate projections of the next year's revenues and expenditures but instead the product of "smoke and mirrors" accounting tricks and inflated revenue estimates that have rendered the budget out of balance almost as soon as its ink has dried. For example, just three months after passage of the "balanced" fiscal year 2007–2008 budget, the legislature's budget was already nearly $6 billion in deficit (Walters, 2007).

As annual budgets establish spending priorities for all of state government, it is a serious indictment when this process is flawed. The state's financial plan literally contains life-or-death decisions. Failure to spend public funds to reinforce an elevated freeway in Oakland cost 42 people their lives when the Loma Prieta earthquake collapsed the upper roadway onto the lower lanes in 1989. The seemingly endless delays in funding and completing earthquake retrofitting of the San Francisco Bay Bridge could have yielded far more devastating results. Even when the results are less dire, budget decisions constitute the state government's real commitments and priorities. Should more money go to training schoolteachers, immunizing children against infectious diseases, enhancing law enforcement, and providing more college scholarships? In a perfect world, the answer to all these options would be "yes," but there is never enough money to fund all the desirable programs and goals at an optimum level. The budget represents those hard choices in prioritizing options and deciding what and who gets more, less, or nothing at all. And underlying the bickering and bitterness that attend each year's budget debate is a core philosophical, partisan, and fiscal question: what is the best balance point between our desire for more and better government programs and our desire to keep taxes as low as possible?

The formal progression of events leading up to the adoption of a state budget each year can be set forth with a fair degree of certainty. Conversely, the informal negotiations that accompany the passage of the budget are fresh and unique each and every year. Unlike at the national level, deficit budgets may not be enacted into law in California. That is, decision makers are not, at least legally, supposed to approve budgets in which projected spending exceeds anticipated revenue. But in fact many budgets are "balanced" on paper (rather than in reality) by accepting overly optimistic revenue estimates or depressed expenditure forecasts. As well, after a state or local budget has been adopted, it may fall out of balance during its period of operation due to economic developments that generate less revenue than expected and/or expenditures in excess of original projections.

The annual budget for the State of California is adopted as a legislative measure and signed by the governor. The budget bill, however, differs in significant respects from regular policy bills that typically amend the state's statutory codes. Most important, the budget act is law for only 365 days. In contrast, policy acts usually remain in statute books for many years—until they are repealed or amended. The one-year duration of a spending plan means that its replacement must be approved each and every year; thus, each year's budget bill cannot be allowed to die. (Without a lawfully approved budget in place, the state controller is, technically, not authorized to pay the state's bills.) Also, deliberations over the budget are subject to greater time pressures than are those over regular legislation. A normal bill introduced in the first year of a legislative session has almost two years before it must be passed. By contrast, the legislature has only about four months to deliberate and pass each year's budget.

The budgetary or fiscal year (FY) in California begins on July 1 and ends June 30. To keep budgets in various stages of development from being confused with one another, it is necessary to always identify which fiscal year (e.g., FY 2007–2008) is being discussed. State government deals with three different budgets each spring. Using January 1, 2008, as a starting point, the *current year* spending plan (FY 2007–2008) refers to an approved budget that is presently being spent by executive departments. The *budget year* spending plan (FY 2008–2009) is a proposed budget for the next fiscal year that will be undergoing review by the legislature between late February and July of 2008. The *planning year* spending plan (FY 2009–2010) is the compilation of budget figures within the executive branch that has yet to be submitted to the legislature. Therefore, departments simultaneously administer (i.e., spend) one budget, seek legislative approval of a second budget, and plan the contents of a third budget to be sent to the legislature the next year. To the extent that any rhythm can be found in state government, these budget-making cycles provide the beat.

The governor and key legislators are the central and most publicly visible players in shaping the state budget, but other actors also influence budgetary outcomes. By ruling on legal claims filed against the state and by interpreting the constitutionality of various revenues and expenditures, courts affect the character of budgets. Likewise, activists who qualify ballot measures to increase or decrease taxes and appropriations or to allocate specific sums to certain programs play a major role in California's budgetary decisions. Those responsible for making federal budgets also impact the state's budgetary outlook. In addition, private businesses and consumers in California and throughout the nation and the world make millions of individual decisions about investing, saving, or consuming that collectively determine the condition of California's economy.

The state's economic health is the most crucial factor in shaping state budget options and limitations. Thus, although the formal budget cycle is essentially the same from year to year, each year's budget process is also unique due to ever-changing economic and political circumstances. For example, the national economic downturn of 2001 and the state's dot-com bust, events well beyond the control of the legislature or governor, completely reshaped this state's budgetary outlook and options. More recently, weaknesses in the lending industry, leading to a faltering housing market and ensuing broader economic turndown, has had the same effect.

THE BUDGET CYCLE

From origination to final approval, the state budget takes 18 months to prepare (see Figure 10.1). The first 12 months of the process take place at the various levels of the executive branch. The yearlong process by which the administration arrives at requested budgetary amounts is not open to public view. After the governor's budget is made public and sent to the legislature in January, the proposed figures are reviewed in open legislative hearings during the next four to five months. After legislative passage of the budget bill, the action once again returns to the governor's office, where line-item veto decisions are made in private.

Executive Preparation

Even as the governor submits a spending proposal to the legislature on or before January 10 each year, civil servants throughout state government are considering what to ask the governor and the legislature for one year hence. Each bureau or division within the various executive departments calculates what spending levels will be needed to maintain current services. Because roughly 80 percent of the state budget consists of employee salaries and related benefits, close attention is paid to the number of positions authorized in each department. Any new position or personnel year (PY) must be fully justified both within the department and within the administration as a whole.

After some six months of discussion between division chiefs and departmental budget officers, determinations are made concerning the need to request new positions. Budget change proposals (BCPs) are drafted to justify any new PYs. After considerable negotiation among the various divisions within a department, a priority listing of BCPs is forwarded to the departmental director for approval or disapproval. The development of BCPs inside departments is well advanced by the end of June, about the same time the new state budget is enacted to fund state government for the next fiscal

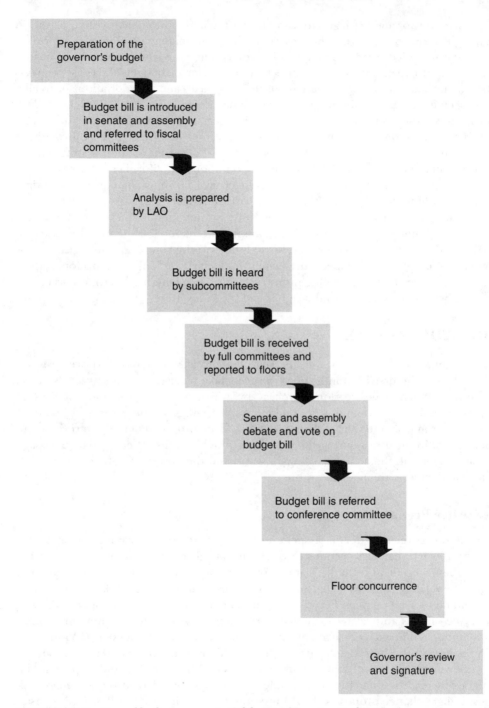

FIGURE 10.1   Formal budget process in California. *(Department of Finance)*

year. With a recently approved budget as well as BCPs in hand, departments are ready to take their financial requests up the hierarchy within the executive branch.

Before continuing with the next steps in the budget cycle, it is necessary to provide a short description of the role of the Department of Finance (DOF). In addition to compiling demographic and population figures and making economic projections, the main responsibility of DOF is to assist the governor in preparing and managing the annual budget for the State of California. DOF analysts are assigned to every department in state government. Depending on how close a DOF analyst is to his or her assigned department, it is possible that the analyst will be invited to participate in budgetary discussions inside the department. Because all BCPs and requests for new PYs ultimately are reviewed by DOF, it is advantageous for departments to provide full background information as soon as possible to the governor's fiscal watchdogs.

Returning to the budgetary cycle, the most recently enacted budget for each department is referred to as the current services (or baseline) budget. In the usual course of events, departments are not required to justify their baseline budgets each year. However, DOF, in its role as agent for the governor's budget and policy priorities, may prepare BCPs of its own to cut certain services in a department. Should this happen, a department then must defend the base for the affected program. Careful scrutiny is given to all proposed changes in the baseline budget. Shortly after the beginning of the fiscal year on July 1, DOF sends what are known as price letters or budget letters to all departments. These letters establish the allowable size of inflationary adjustments for items commonly purchased by departments and for changes in salary and benefit levels. Using this information from DOF, departments adjust their baseline budgets.

Most departments in state government report to the governor through an intermediate (or agency) level. Groups of 5 to 12 departments are organized under such agencies as Business, Transportation, and Housing; Corrections; Resources; Health and Welfare; and State and Consumer Services. (Departments that are not located under an agency report directly to DOF.) After preparation within departments, BCPs and adjusted baseline budgets are sent to the appropriate agency for review during July and August. BCPs may pass through the agency unchanged, be reduced in amount, or be rejected entirely.

Budget requests from departments throughout state government converge at the highest level of the administration in late summer. To handle the vast workload, early September is established as the deadline for receipt of departmental budget documents by DOF. From September through early November, DOF conducts hearings on the BCPs submitted by each department. These hearings are attended by department directors and their budget officers, personnel from the relevant agency at the intermediate level, and analysts and their superiors from DOF. Recommendations of approval or disapproval are agreed on for each BCP. Occasionally, certain BCPs are given no recommendation by DOF staff and are left "open" for the director of DOF or the governor to decide. The outcomes arrived at during DOF hearings, together with decisions on open items, represent the spending levels contained in the governor's budget to be sent to the legislature in January. No matter what their original positions were on particular BCPs, departments are expected to defend the figures in the governor's budget once the spending plan leaves the administration and enters the legislative process.

Several pieces of last-minute business must be concluded before the budget exits the executive branch. In the middle of November, DOF schedules a conference in San Francisco to hear from economists concerning likely economic trends for the FY then

---

BOX 10.1   **New Governor, Old Budget**

As already discussed, the governor, through his Department of Finance, maintains tight control over the preparation of the proposed budget, which doesn't "go public" until it is presented to the legislature on January 10. This timing creates problems when a new governor is elected, however. That person, not inaugurated until the first week of January, was effectively "out of the loop" when the decisions regarding the executive budget were made. With only a few days between inauguration and submission of the budget to the legislature, the new governor hardly has sufficient time to recast it according to personal priorities.

When the takeover is "friendly" between outgoing and incoming governors of the same party, this "inherited" budget need not be a huge problem. The transition team and the governor-elect can expect to be invited to the November budget meetings with the Department of Finance and the governor and to be granted access to the galley proof copies of the proposed budget.

Things can get much dicier when the change in governors also involves a change in party control. In these cases of "hostile takeover," no statute requires that the old administration cooperate with the incoming administration. In the case of the 2003 gubernatorial recall, there was virtually no transition period between the election night and the seating of the new governor (normally, elections are held in November, but the new governor does not take office for another two months). This left new Governor Schwarzenegger a virtual stranger to the proposed "governor's budget" that was the product of the prior administration's planning and priorities.

---

being planned. Discussion of expected sales and employment levels helps DOF project the revenues and expenditures to anticipate for the FY that will begin more than seven months later on July 1. This planning includes substantial uncertainty. For example, prior to the total holiday sales being calculated for the present year, economists are asked to predict what revenues will be generated by holiday spending during the following year.

At this point, the governor's proposed budget is ready to go to print. For the most part, the components of the governor's emerging budget have not been made public, and this pattern of confidentiality continues until that budget is officially presented to the legislature on or before January 10. The state constitution does require that this budget be "balanced," meaning that it must identify projected revenue sources that at least match proposed expenditures. What "balances" on paper, however, may be way out of whack in reality, depending on how much revenue is actually generated by the state's economy over the next 18 months.

Legislative Amendment

On or before January 10, the governor's budget is made public and presented to both houses of the California legislature. Full press coverage attends the governor's submission of the proposed budget. Never again will as much space be devoted to the state's spending plan, despite the fact that the budget is more than five months from final passage. Because the governor's plan is to be treated as a bill, the measure needs an author to introduce it as an official piece of legislative business. Unlike other bills, which may be authored by any of the 120 members of the legislature, the budget bill is introduced by one of only two people—the chair of the Assembly Budget Committee or the chair of the Senate Budget and Fiscal Review Committee, with authorship rotating from one chair to the other on a yearly basis. Also in contrast to normal legislation, the budget is introduced at the same time into both the assembly and the senate.

Before the members of the two houses' budget committees hold hearings on the budget, a six-week period is allowed for the legislative staff to examine the governor's figures. Since its creation in 1941, this staff, titled Legislative Analyst's Office (LAO) has provided the entire membership of the legislature with an independent assessment of all proposals to spend public funds. Each budget analyst at LAO examines the funding proposed for a certain department or for specific programs within large departments. Areas of either inadequate or excessive funding are called to the attention of legislators. To allow members of the senate and assembly committees ample time to hold public hearings on the budget, the analysts and other employees at LAO strive to finish their critiques of the governor's figures by the end of February.

At the legislative committee level, further analysis is provided by staff members with the senate and assembly budget committees. The bulk of these staff people analyze from the majority party's point of view, though the committees also employ a lesser number of minority-party staff. Whereas LAO prides itself on being as objective and nonpartisan as possible, the staffers for these fiscal committees are partisan in character. As the legislature has become more partisan, there is a sense that many lawmakers may depend more on the analysis of their partisan staffs rather than the Legislative Analyst's Office. As well, and despite its critical analytical role, LAO was hard hit by staff cuts that followed passage of Proposition 140 in 1990. Its ability to provide the same breadth and depth of analysis has been stretched to, and perhaps beyond, the breaking point.

After release of LAO's analysis to all members of the legislature in late February, public hearings are conducted for the next three months. With regard to policy bills, it is customary for hearings to be scheduled by full committees. However, given the magnitude of the budget bill, it is broken into parts and then heard in various subcommittees. Assembly Budget and Senate Budget and Fiscal Review have four to six subcommittees each, consisting of three to six members, for the various segments of the budget such as education, health and welfare, and natural resources. A legislator must be a member of a full committee to be seated on any of its subcommittees. After consultation with chamber leadership, the chairpersons of the full budget committees appoint legislators to serve as subcommittee chairs. These fiscal subcommittees are significant for two reasons. First, narrowing the number of departments under a subcommittee's scrutiny allows subcommittee members to specialize and thus become more expert, though term limits have greatly reduced their experience, and hence expertise. Second, subcommittees concentrate budgetary decisions in the hands of relatively few legislators.

Subcommittees generally do not take up items for which the governor's requested figure is the same as that recommended by LAO and the fiscal committee staff. If the figures from these sources differ, the subcommittee is likely to cut or to increase the governor's figure. Easily resolved differences are agreed to in public, and the necessary changes in the budget bill are made. When agreement cannot be reached easily, negotiations move behind closed doors. Relevant analysts from LAO, DOF, the line department, and the subcommittee staff meet privately in an effort to reach a consensus figure that can be presented to the legislators on the subcommittee. If the behind-the-scenes negotiation by this small circle of budget specialists bears no fruit, then a majority of the elected members of the subcommittee will set the figure to be reported out. Analysts from DOF carefully monitor all subcommittee changes to the governor's January figures.

Most legislators want to serve on Assembly Budget or on Senate Budget and Fiscal Review (and subsequently be seated on a fiscal subcommittee) for the prestige and power such a committee assignment confers. Despite the heavy schedule of three subcommittee meetings per week, fiscal committee members like being in a position to influence state expenditures in every legislative district of California. When other legislators need state funds for highways, universities, parks, or levees in their districts, they turn to their colleagues on the fiscal committees for assistance. Though not always appreciated outside the state capitol, the chairperson of a fiscal subcommittee often exercises more power than his or her counterpart chairing the full policy committee in the related area. Changes to statutory law crafted by policy committees have little effect unless they are adequately funded by fiscal subcommittees. Reflecting the desirability of budget committee assignments, about one-third of assembly members and senators serve on their respective chamber's budget committees.

To arrive at the most up-to-date projections possible as the beginning of the new FY approaches, DOF holds a second conference with private-sector economists during the spring. Fresh assessments of probable revenues and caseload costs are prepared by DOF. The so-called May revision to the governor's January budget is sent to the legislature during the first week of May. With updated figures in hand, the subcommittees make a flurry of last-minute decisions. By mid-May, the fiscal subcommittees finish reviewing their segments of the budget bill and send a report of their recommendations to the full committee. Assembly Budget and Senate Budget and Fiscal Review usually accept the reports of their subcommittees within a single day. Though the full committee can make changes in the budget bill, questioning the work of one subcommittee might prompt protracted examination of the other subcommittee reports as well. Current calendars do not allow sufficient time for the full committee to do anything more than a pro forma review of subcommittee reports. The fiscal committees then send the budget bill together with recommended changes to the floor of each house. The annual spending plan for the State of California can sometimes be rushed through the assembly and senate chambers on a two-thirds vote because members understand that this version of the budget is hardly the last word. But brevity of the review accorded the budget bill both in full committee and on the floor reinforces the power of the small number of legislators seated on each fiscal subcommittee.

As stated, the budgets initially passed by each house are just a beginning point. Given the wide variety of budget bill changes recommended by the subcommittees and subsequently adopted on the floor of each house, the senate and assembly versions of the annual spending plan are not identical. So that a bill with a single set of compromise figures may be sent to the governor, the leadership of the two houses appoints a conference committee consisting of three members each from both the assembly and the senate. The majority party holds two of the three positions from each house. The conference committee's decisions must be approved by at least two conferees from each chamber. The chairpersons of Assembly Budget and Senate Budget and Fiscal Review alternate each year as head of the budget conference committee.

The conference committee is presented with a massive agenda (some 1,000 pages) contrasting the figures adopted earlier on the floors of each house. If both the assembly and the senate passed the same level of funding for certain programs, such matters are not considered conference items. Under rules adopted by the legislature, the conference committee may agree to go *below* the lower of the two figures from the senate and the assembly, but the committee may not *exceed* the higher of the two figures. (The possibility that an expenditure might be reduced drastically in conference explains why departments sometimes go to great lengths to encourage the passage of identical figures in both houses.) As they move through the agenda, committee members resolve the less difficult discrepancies between the two houses first and pass over, for the time being, the more serious points of disagreement. Every two hours or so, the members of the conference committee recess to allow staff an opportunity to reconcile the status of the various accounts in the wake of the compromises agreed to by the six legislators.

Each round of compromise decisions, followed by staff reconciliation of the balances, reduces the number of remaining items still in dispute. Members of the budget conference committee meet informally outside the hearing room to engage in hard bargaining on the most difficult issues. The conferees may also receive instructions from legislative leaders and the governor. Once agreement is reached on the remaining items, the committee members troop back into the hearing room to announce the resolution of the last matters on the agenda. The report of the conference committee hopefully arrives back on the floor of each house during the second week of June so that the legislature can approve a budget by a two-thirds vote and send it to the governor by the constitutional deadline of June 15.

If the wishes of the minority party have not received sufficient attention during the conference, achieving a two-thirds vote in each chamber can be difficult. One year Democrat Jesse Unruh, speaker of the assembly from 1961 to 1968, literally locked Republican members of the lower house inside the chamber until they provided the necessary votes to pass the budget bill.

Line-Item Veto

Clearly, the governor enjoys the first word on the budget through its original submission to the legislature back in January, and the last word in the form of the ability to trim back the figures voted out by the legislature. In Chapter 4, we discussed the "bulletproof" nature of gubernatorial vetoes, which applies to budget vetoes as well. Thus, it can be said that if governors want to budget less for any particular item, they will have their way. The only limitation to this power is that, as discussed in Chapter 4, governors may not completely dismantle a program that has been statutorily authorized by decreasing its budget allocation to zero. Just how much a program's budget can be reduced without constituting an illegal breach of statute remains an open question.

Also note that the line-item veto power is unidirectional; it can be used to reduce any given expenditure under what the legislature approved, but it cannot be used to increase spending. If the governor wants to spend more in a given area than does the legislature, however, it may be possible to swap favors. The governor can, for example, withhold a threatened line-item veto in one area in return for a more generous legislative

BOX 10.2

"Big Five" Budgeting

The foregoing account describes the "regular" legislative process for producing a budget. It might also be described as the "micro" process by which marginal adjustments to the budget are made. The 1990s, however, saw few normal budget years. Most involved oceans of red ink that had to be addressed through combinations of hefty tax increases and expenditure cuts. These drastic steps involved a great deal of controversy. Conversely, during 1998, the main discussion was over what to do with a state surplus, but that proved no less controversial. These situations gave rise to a new budgetary entity: the *Big Five*, consisting of the governor, assembly speaker, senate president pro tem, and assembly and senate minority leaders. It falls to this group, usually late in the budget process, to hammer out compromises on these huge fiscal and policy issues, and then it falls to the legislative leaders to sell the compromises to their caucuses back in the assembly and senate.

Thus, informally, because state law contains no statutory or constitutional reference to the existence or role of the Big Five, the budget process can be divided between the micro-functions of the regular legislative process and the macro decisions rendered by the Big Five. Especially during periods of big deficits between expenditures and projected revenues, part of the Big Five's job involves "creative accounting" and other stratagems to produce a budget that at least balances on paper. Pie-in-the-sky projections of federal revenues are one way to bridge the paper gap. "Borrowing" from special funds and scooping up property tax revenues from local governments are also strategies used to make ends meet in the general budget. This process also involves heavy reliance on euphemisms: tax increases are called "revenue enhancements," and service cuts are almost always "temporary."

Legislative reaction to the Big Five is ambivalent. On the positive side, their often unpopular decisions can be laid directly at the Big Five's feet, thus giving individual legislators political cover for unpopular tax increases or program cuts. On the other side, some legislators chafe under the erosion of their control.

allocation in another priority area for the governor. Or, in those years with enough money to go around, the governor can use the line-item veto to put a certain amount of money on the table for future negotiations that would add part of this "set-aside" to the governor's favored programs in a "restoration" or "second budget" passed later in the year. The second-budget concept depends on the availability of extra money, a rare luxury enjoyed only during especially good economic times. For the near future, this concept may be fondly remembered but no longer an option.

REVENUE SOURCES

Whereas expenditures undergo annual review, revenue laws need not be examined each year. If no bills are introduced and enacted to amend the tax codes of the State of California, then the same revenue provisions that were in effect the year before remain in force. Any alterations to California's revenue codes are carried out as separate tax bills, not as part of the annual budget bill. (When tax code changes are enacted, the adjustment in revenues actually collected is reflected in the annual budget.) California employs a wide assortment of taxes to fund the operations of state and local government. More than 75 percent of the revenues at the state level are deposited in the *general fund*, totaling more than 100 billion dollars which may be used to pay for programs in any department of state government. The remainder of the taxes collected by the state are placed in *special funds*, which may be spent only for purposes designated in the law creating the tax.

Until 1970, the sales tax was California's main source of revenue, but since 1970, it has been supplanted by the personal and corporate income tax. Currently, these income taxes account for about 66 percent of general fund money available for the state. The sales tax accounts for approximately 28 percent. A variety of much smaller tax sources, such as insurance and tobacco taxes, supplies the remaining 6 percent of general fund revenues (California Department of Finance, 2007). As noted above, this general fund represents the major portion of the money that is spent by the state each year. For FY 2007–2008, the smaller portion (the special funds) totaled just under $28 billion. This money is allocated to specific areas and programs and cannot be spent for nondesignated budget items. The highway and transportation trust fund, built on gasoline taxes and vehicle registration fees, is the largest of these special funds. Another important special fund was created by Proposition 99, which levied an extra 25-cent tax on a pack of cigarettes and mandated that the money be spent in cigarette/health-related areas. In 1998, voters hit smokers with yet another tobacco levy, this time totaling 50 cents a pack. In all, the total state budget (as of FY 2007–2008) was approximately $145 billion. This amount includes money spent out of the general fund and special funds, revenue, generated by bond issues, and federal money earmarked for specific programs that passes through the state government. This grand total represents an expenditure of about $4,000 for every woman, man, and child living in the state!

Are Californians Over-Taxed?

The answer to this question depends, of course, on how an individual values public-sector programs versus lower taxes, and in many cases that person's perception of the benefits she receives from public expenditures compared to her taxes paid. It also depends on what form of taxes Californians are talking about and what income level they enjoy. Overall, California, which used to be a high-tax state, still ranks about seventeenth, or just at the edge of the top third of states, in terms of its "tax effort" or average percentage of individual income that is paid as state taxes (Morgan Quitno Corp., 2007). But the relative tax burden on Californians also varies according to the type of tax, whether income or sales, and economic situation. Their sales tax burden, again measured against their wealth, is right around the middle of all states. The overall income tax burden is higher, ranking in the top ten among all states. (Californians pay property taxes at a slightly lower percentage of property value than most states. But this tax has traditionally funded local government, not state government programs, and is discussed in Chapter 6.)

However, the state's taxes do not fall evenly across all income levels. Sales taxes hit the poor hardest because a greater portion of their money goes to purchase items that are subject to this tax. On the other hand, the income tax in California is relatively "progressive," meaning the more money you earn, the higher percentages in taxes you pay. The progressiveness of California's income tax ranks among the highest of all states, as does its corporate tax.

A significant amount of disagreement surrounds the issue of how much taxation and spending is "too much" or "not enough." One attempt to measure states' spending "needs" based on population and demographics against those states' revenue sources found that California ranks thirty-seventh among all states in the adequacy of its public revenue sources to meet its needs (Hovey and Hovey, 1999).

WHERE DOES THE MONEY GO?

As previously stated, counting all expenditures, the state currently spends almost $150 billion a year. Many of these expenditures, however, are not funded out of regular state taxes and are not subject to state policy makers' discretion. For example, over 20 percent of the total amount is designated special fund spending, and part of general fund expenditures involves federal dollars that are "passed through" the state government for earmarked purposes. The legislature and governor have only limited discretion in deciding how to spend the remaining general fund revenues, and over 90 percent of general fund expenditures go to just four areas. These "big four" expenditures items are, based on FY 2007–2008 figures:

K–12 education	40.4%
Health and welfare	29.1%
Higher education	11.7%
Corrections	9.6%

Source: California Department of Finance, 2007.

Over the last 30 years, spending for adult and juvenile corrections increased at a rate double that of any other budget category. This jump also represents a twelvefold increase in the actual number of dollars spent on the corrections system. From year to year, total expenditures are "case driven" and thus beyond the legislature's control because the number of prisoners and juvenile detainees is determined by the number of criminal acts and convictions. But in the longer run, spending in this area is at least partially "discretionary" because it is affected by legislative policy regarding the length of sentences for criminal convictions and institutionalization of juvenile offenders. (See Chapter 5 for a fuller discussion of this issue.)

Much of the remainder of the budget is, however, beyond much effective control. The K–12 education and the health and welfare expenditures are caseload driven, meaning that expenditures will largely be determined by how many people require these services. The number of children attending California's public schools is the core factor determining how much must be spent for education, and this figure cannot be controlled by budget makers, absent a state population-control policy. Similarly, the number of individuals eligible for and requiring state-funded health and welfare services is determined by those whose income, or lack thereof, qualifies them for welfare support and state subsidized health care. Tightening eligibility requirements, to the extent allowed by federal law, is the only recourse available to policy makers wanting to reduce health and welfare expenditures.

Economics and demographics determine the numbers requiring these services. This situation, then, leaves corrections and higher education as the only remaining "big-ticket" budget areas subject to Sacramento control. Over the past 25 years, the state's political climate has been supportive of more, not less, spending on corrections. Higher education is left as the one remaining category where large-scale cuts are possible. Moreover, the state's public colleges can be kept open even after state funding is reduced simply by charging students higher fees. And as every student at a California State University or University of California campus has reason to lament, this strategy is the one adopted during bad budget eras. University students attempting to plan future years' tuition costs should pay close attention to state government budget projections!

AN ERA OF PERMANENT BUDGET CRISIS?

The general condition of the state's economy—expansionary, stagnant, or recessionary—is the most obvious influence on the state's fiscal health in any given year. Rises and declines in California's economic barometer parallel, but do not exactly mirror, national economic trends. For example, while the early 1990s witnessed a general economic slowdown nationally, California, which was hit especially hard by military base closures and a reduction in defense spending, suffered a recession that was deeper and longer than that experienced by the rest of the nation. By that decade's end, however, California's economic skies were much brighter. The national economic recovery was punctuated in California with the successful high-tech conversion from the defense industry to dot-com businesses. But the good times did not last long into the new century, and by the end of 2001, the economic skies had again begun to darken. The national economic recession and the implosion of the dot-com businesses in California derailed the state's economy from 2001 through 2003. Then things again began to improve. Currently, however, economic skies are clouded by the downturn in the housing market. This is especially relevant to this state's economy with, until recently, its skyrocketing home values. Homeowners used their burgeoning home equity as a source of ready cash for consumer expenditures. With the closing of this "equity ATM," consumer spending declines, leading to a broader decline in the overall robustness of the economy.

Even natural catastrophes, clearly beyond the control of governors and legislators, can complicate budgetary prospects. Economic loss from the 2007 wildfires in Southern California will reach at least $2 billion (and maybe a good deal more). Extra expenditures necessary for the recovery, and reduced revenue caused by the fires' economic damage, will negatively impact state and local government budgets for years to come.

The state's budgetary condition is very sensitive to these economic tides. When times are good, more people are employed, consumers spend more, and businesses expand their operations. All this means hefty increases in income tax and sales tax collection. But when the economy contracts, so do these revenue sources. Moreover, in bad economic times, more people require public financial assistance, more people are without private medical care, and more people commit crimes. Thus, at the same time that state revenues go down, the demands for state spending actually increase. No matter who controls the legislature or the governor's office, this connection between the economic cycle and the state's fiscal health is the key ingredient in any individual year's budgetary outlook. Thus, with economic storm clouds closing in at the end of 2007, California was anticipating a fiscal year budget deficit of over $14 billion, prompting Governor Schwarzenegger to propose a 10% across the board spending cut. But beyond the boom/bust economic tides and the advent of natural disasters that have always plagued the state's budget process, serious structural problems in California's public-sector revenue flow cloud its fiscal future even further. (See Box 10.3 for a discussion of California's "structural deficit.")

Revenue Constraints

California, the home of Proposition 13, initiated the "tax revolt" felt around the nation. That revolt seems to be almost as robust today as it was back in 1978, when voters used

PHOTO 10.1   October 2007 in San Diego County. Beyond the human and natural costs, the 2007 wildfires created economic losses that will impact state and local revenues for years to come. *(Associated Press)*

Proposition 13 to roll back and freeze their property taxes. (See Chapter 6 for a full description of Proposition 13.) For example, in 1996, voters refused to extend the life of higher income tax brackets for the very rich. In 1998, Governor Wilson forced the legislature to give in on a series of decreases in automobile registration fees. After Gray Davis rescinded those decreases in response to the new round of deficits, Arnold Schwarzenegger, honoring his campaign pledge, made it his first order of business as governor to once again drop the fees. In March of 2004, state voters overwhelmingly rejected a ballot proposition that would have reduced the legislative vote requirement for raising taxes from two-thirds to 55 percent.

Proposition 13 was the first, but hardly the only, ballot proposition that cut taxes and hence reduced public-sector revenues. Certainly, Proposition 13 was the most crucial, resulting in an immediate 57 percent reduction in property tax revenues. Another portion of the proposition's text created the two-thirds requirement for tax hikes (though only a majority is required to lower taxes). Proposition 13 also set in motion a series of follow-up measures, including a virtual end to the state's inheritance and gift taxes and an automatic inflation indexing of income brackets for purposes of computing income taxes. This latter measure means that the floor income for each tax bracket is raised to keep up with inflation; its impact is to keep more taxpayers in the lower tax brackets.

As stated earlier, the sales tax has, relative to the income tax, become a less important source of revenue. More crucial, and ominous, the sales tax also captures less and less economic activity as the state's economic structure changes. Sales tax is levied on purchases of traditional retail goods (with some exclusions such as food and medicine) but not on the provision of services, precisely the sector of the economy that is growing most rapidly. As the state's manufacturing base, relative to other sectors, dwindles, less and less economic activity produces things that, when sold, generate a sales tax; more and more activity consists of untaxed services such as home services, financial services, legal and accounting services, and creative and intellectual services. In addition, many transactions conducted on the Internet, clearly a growing portion of the retail market, are not subject to sales tax. In short, even when the California economy is in a growth mode, sales tax revenues will not grow proportionally.

A portion of what the state spends each year comes from the federal government. This money does not appear on the state's general budget but is "passed through," usually as matching funds, to ongoing state programs. Less of this money is likely to be available in the future. How much less, of course, depends on the course of national politics, but the deficits that once again plague the federal budget do not augur well for federal help to the states. What this means is yet a further reduction in the money that California has available to spend. The choice in Sacramento will be either to reduce the programs by the amount of the federal shortfall or to make up some or all of the difference by reducing expenditures on other programs.

Increased Demands for State Spending

An old saying claims that "demographics are destiny." If it is true, California is perhaps destined for a long period of budget squeeze between uncertain revenue sources and increased demands on those resources. As mentioned earlier, much of the state's spending is determined by caseloads—the number of individuals requiring public serv-

BOX 10.3

The Bad News Bottom Line

Taken together, all these budgetary fiscal and process problems add up to what economists call a *structural deficit* that has been estimated at $8 billion a year. What that means is that in an average year, with neither recession nor boom, available revenues will come in about $8 billion less than desired expenditures. If that's the case, California is in for an era of many more bad than good budget years. The remedy? "Cut spending, raise taxes, or some combination of the two" (Mendel, 2004). But as already stated, most general budget spending is driven by economic and demographic factors, not legislative or gubernatorial decision making. And since California's income tax is already among the nation's highest and most progressive, how much more money can be rung out of that revenue source? Raising corporation taxes might be even more problematical. One estimate places California as forty-fifth of all states in the business friendliness of its tax policies. (Morgan Quitno Corp., 2007).

ices and expenditures—and these caseloads are on the rise. The age distribution of Californians is part of the problem. An abnormally high percentage are young and need schooling, the most expensive and expansive state program. Because the state's birthrates are among the nation's highest, and California ranks in the top three of all states in the percentage of its population aged 5 to 18, more and more children are entering the K–12 system, forcing the state to spend more and more just to keep up. Currently, about 6.3 million children attend the state's public K–12 school system; that's a number greater than the *entire population* of all but 13 of the 50 states! In the late 1990s California enacted an expensive policy to reduce classroom size in the lower grades, and as the numbers swell, the state will have to spend more and more just to stabilize that class size. This pressure comes in addition to other improvements desperately needed in an educational system that lags behind those of most other states.

At the other end of the spectrum, a great many Californians are in their sixties and older. This group will, as a whole, live much longer than did those of their age a generation or two ago, and they are now being joined in retirement by the "baby boomers," those residents born during the middle of the twentieth century. What older people need more of, relative to other age groups, is health care. Thus, California's population in the early twenty-first century will also be heavily skewed in terms of health care consumers. How much of this care will have to be state-provided depends on many factors. One ominous note is the increase of jobs that provide no benefits, including health care. This factor indicates that many more retirees may well be dependent on public health services rather than private health care plans.

Put succinctly, California has entered a demographic era in which relatively fewer gainfully employed taxpayers will be supporting the young and old, who are consumers of public services and tax dollars. The one bright note is that all those schoolchildren will, over the next two decades, be of working age and hopefully paying taxes. This happy prospect depends, of course, on their ability to secure good jobs, which, in the

BOX 10.4 **Howard Jarvis, Con Man or Crusading Populist?**

Until 1978, nobody would have predicted that Howard Jarvis' political career would go anywhere. He had already lost, and lost badly, in election races for U.S. Senate, California Board of Equalization, and Los Angeles mayor. Earlier he had dabbled, without notable success, in careers as a publisher, professional boxer, semipro baseball player, land speculator, Republican publicist, and political fund-raiser, among others. His fund-raising operations were tainted with charges of personal corruption.

After a couple of unsuccessful tries at qualifying antitax measures for the ballot, Jarvis joined forces with Paul Gann in 1978. Gann was also an active member of the anti-tax movement, heading up his own Sacramento-based organization. This time the political tides were running in Jarvis' favor; Proposition 13 qualified easily for the ballot and was passed overwhelmingly. Overnight Jarvis was transformed from a loser on the political margins to a statewide and national hero of the burgeoning tax revolt movement. For the next few years, there probably weren't a half-dozen politicians in the land with more name recognition than Jarvis.

And he played that recognition to the hilt. Always the self-promoter, brusque and crude, Jarvis seemed perfectly cast as the populist leader challenging the established big-money interests, most of whom had opposed Proposition 13, and big government. For the next few years, Jarvis and his "Howard Jarvis Taxpayers Association" engaged in a series of tax-cutting and expenditure-limiting proposition campaigns, some successful, some failures.

In 1986, Jarvis died of the HIV virus, which he had contracted through a tainted blood transfusion. By most measurements, a small, pugnacious man of many failures, questionable financial dealings, an insatiable need for attention, and one singular success, he left in his wake a legacy that towers over that of most California governors, let alone mainline politicians. Of Proposition 13's impact, Peter Schrag wrote:

> It set the stage for the Reagan era, and became both fact and symbol of a radical shift in governmental priorities, public attitudes, and social relationships that is as nearly fundamental in American politics as the changes brought by the New Deal. (Schrag, 1998)

postindustrial "information age," means they will need a good education. The question is whether California's already overburdened public sector can provide them with that good education. (See Chapter 11 for a fuller discussion of this issue.)

Ballot Box Budgeting

Given all California's problems and limitations, making an annual budget will never be an easy task. The job is further complicated by the cumulative effect of past decisions, many of them made by voters, that tie policy makers' hands. The first and most central of these is Proposition 13, which cut the local property tax. The problem here is that while property taxes are unpopular, local government services such as public safety, sewer systems, parks and recreation, libraries, and education, to name just a few, are popular and important. It was inevitable that the state would move in to bail out local governments in the wake of Proposition 13's passage. Initially, because the state had a huge surplus, the bailout was relatively painless; now, with the state badly strapped for money, how much to provide the locals is an agonizing decision. It is also a decision that greatly complicates state efforts to fund traditional state programs.

In 1979, one year after Proposition 13 passed, voters came back to approve Proposition 4, the Gann limitation. The target here was not tax reduction but expenditure reduction. The Gann limitation essentially set a spending limit for state and local governments based on 1978 figures. These figures could not be exceeded except by factoring in population growth and inflation. (This latter standard was later changed to aggregate state wealth.) Money collected in excess of any year's limit was to be returned to taxpayers. Because of problems in the state's public-sector revenue bases, in only one year did the state-collected funds exceed the year's spending limit.

Some real and potential problems accompany the Gann limit. The limit's population factor is based on overall population, but spending requirements are determined by caseload factors such as numbers of schoolchildren, residents on public assistance, and inmates in state prisons. These caseload numbers increased much faster than the general population numbers on which the spending limit is based. Moreover, even if the California economy has an extraordinarily good year and the state's coffers are filled to overflowing, there is no way to bank the excess funds for use in the leaner years that are sure to follow because the law requires that excess funds be rebated. One of the reforms approved by the 2004 primary election voters was the creation of a "rainy day fund" out of annual general budget revenues. How this reform, as well as newly approved balanced budget requirements, fares remains to be seen.

All these budgetary problems and uncertainties motivate program supporters to try to guarantee their "fair share" of the budget. Proposition 98, passed in 1988, specifies that approximately 40 percent of general budget outlays must go to K–14 public education. Proposition 98 stipulates another option: last year's outlay adjusted for inflation and enrollment increases. But the legislature can choose only the *higher* of these two figures. Even though the legislature can suspend Proposition 98 for any given year in the case of a budget emergency, getting Democratic legislators to go along with a suspension has been a difficult undertaking. And the money denied the schools through any year's Proposition 98 suspension must be paid back to the schools in later years and is still a part of the minimum expenditure calculation for future budgets. In 2005 voters rejected Governor Schwarzenegger's attempt to loosen some of Proposition 98's spending mandates.

In a state where only about one in six adults smokes, cigarettes have been a popular tax target of the initiative writers. In 1988 and again ten years later, voters approved special tobacco taxes of 25 cents and 50 cents, respectively, on a pack of cigarettes. The revenues from these "sin taxes" are earmarked for specific health and child care purposes and are not part of the general fund. The result of all these fiscal ballot initiatives, sometimes referred to as ballot box budgeting, is to further reduce the legislature's discretion and flexibility when it attempts to write the annual budget.

Other factors further constrict available choices. Most entitlement programs contain COLA (cost of living adjustment) provisions that automatically increase benefit levels to keep up with inflation. Traditionally, the state relied on the sales of bonds to finance large capital programs, such as school, university, and prison construction. (Bond expenditures do not count against the Gann spending limit.) But in 2004, the state utilized bond issues to pay off its own deficit. Funds to pay the principal and interest of these bonds come out of the general budget. This is an expenditure that cannot be avoided, as failure to pay would ruin the state's bond rating, subject the state to huge lawsuits, and make it impossible to sell additional bonds. Finally, much general fund spending is not negotiable or represents "sunk costs." For example, highway patrol personnel and college professors must receive their salaries; a new state office building started two years ago cannot be abandoned unfinished. In short, creating a budget involves juggling increasing demands for dwindling resources within a process that constrains and limits available options. Finally, when at some time in June, July, or even August a budget plan is finally cobbled together, the whole process can be brought to a halt by a failure to secure a two-thirds majority.

BUDGET REFORM

Perhaps the simplest reform would be to drop the two-thirds requirement and allow budget passage by a simple majority. This reform, recommended by both the Constitutional Revision Commission and the Citizens Budget Commission, would bring California practice into conformity with the overwhelming majority of states and remove one hurdle to timely budget passage. Defenders of the current rule argue that it creates budgets with broader consensus support, but no one who has watched recent budget battles would claim that the atmosphere that surrounded them was consensual. Essentially, the two-thirds rule gives any minority faction with 14 senate or 27 assembly votes an absolute veto power. What ensues is not further debate leading to a consensual broad-based compromise, but ultimate resolution through pressure, attrition, or bribing hold out legislatures with special pots of money for their particular districts. But at least for now, the voters have spoken loud and clear on the two-thirds rule, and it is not likely to go away anytime soon.

The Constitutional Revision Commission also recommended that legislators forfeit their pay for each day the budget is delayed past its constitutional deadline as another lever to pry out timely budget resolutions. This is a popular idea, but is it a good one? It would place a lot of personal financial pressure on lawmakers who rely on their legislative salaries to pay their bills; many do not, however. Neither this approach nor lowering the budget approval vote threshold really get to the heart of budget delays: competing demands, competing philosophies, and limited resources.

The Citizens Budget Commission proposed a whole series of reforms, some general and some quite technical. Among them are:

- A requirement that the budget as passed be balanced. Currently, the constitution requires only that the governor's submitted budget be balanced. Language to this effect was approved by the voters in March 2004. Actually enforcing it is a whole other issue.

- A budget act that references all state spending not just general fund spending, and all sources of revenue, such as federal money and special funds, in order to give a more complete picture of the state's fiscal condition.

- A granting of more local autonomy over local revenues and programs. (California Citizens Budget Commission, 1999)

A good look at this last point indicates that some modification of Proposition 13 would be required in order to free local finance and local programs from their current state of entanglement with the state budget. One option would be to maintain Proposition 13's current 1 percent of assessed evaluation limit but allow those assessed values to rise along with the housing market. Conversely, the current freeze on assessment levels could be maintained, but local governments could be allowed to raise the tax rates. It would be up to local elected officials to decide how much taxes their constituents would be willing to pay. Other approaches suggest ironclad guarantees of local funding through either the property tax or a greater share of the sales tax. Just about everybody agrees that local governments need stronger revenue guarantees and stability, but how would the state make up the money remaining in local hands while attempting to maintain its own programs?

Yet another proposal (suggested by a variety of commissions and advisory panels) would put the state on a two-year, rather than a one-year, budget cycle. This option might allow a better opportunity for long-range planning and more time for deliberation over the budget. It might also temper the impact of year-to-year economic fluctuations on budget prospects. But it also would increase the forecasting period for which budget decisions must be made, thus perhaps requiring even more mid-term budget revisions as the 24-month budget period unfolds.

All these suggestions are pointed at the budget process, and it certainly is a process that could stand improvement. The structural budgetary problem facing the state—namely, the shortfall in fiscal resources required to meet increasing demands—cannot be reformed away, however. State governments possess only limited tools to improve their economic condition and no power to change the demographics of their citizens. Until and unless voters are willing to tax themselves more than they are currently taxed, state and local governments' fiscal prospects will remain clouded at best.

There is, of course, another solution: just spend less. But less on what? The great bulk of state spending is on K–12 education, health and welfare, higher education, and corrections. Should the state reduce its emphasis on any of these programs? One answer is to fully fund the essential elements of these activities but to cut waste. And certainly, in a $150 billion budget, there must be considerable waste. The problem is that there are no sections in the budget labeled "waste," and defining and finding it are not easy tasks. In 2004, a panel assembled by Governor Schwarzenegger proposed a long laundry list of potential cost savings. How much these proposals would save and how many of them are politically viable remain open questions. For example, many of the panel's "streamlining" proposals advocated moving certain independent regulatory entities into the regular executive structure and under the direct control of the governor. In most cases, this would require legislative approval, and legislative reaction to such proposals has been, to date, less than enthusiastic.

California Budget in National and Western State Perspective

State/Local Revenue as Percent of Personal Income
California: 10.6% (Rank: #17)
Highest: New York, 13.7%

Lowest: S. Dakota and Alabama, 8.3%

National Rankings of Other Western States

Wyoming #2

New Mexico #14

Utah #19

Idaho/Nevada/Arizona #29

Washington #32

Oregon/Montana #39

Colorado #46th

Per Capita State Government General Fund Spending

California: #41

Highest: Alaska

Lowest: Nevada

National Rankings of Other Western States

Wyoming #8

New Mexico #11

Montana #13

Washington #17

Utah #18

Oregon #32

Idaho #39

Colorado #44

Arizona #49

SUMMARY

The governor has the first budget word with submission of a budget whose creation is tightly controlled to reflect that governor's priorities. Legislative treatment of the budget is much more open and, as the deadline nears, frantic. With recent multi-billion-dollar deficits, the budget process also requires meetings of top legislative leaders and the governor, the Big Five, in an attempt to juggle the billions necessary to come up with any kind of budget. Ultimately, with the line-item veto, the governor also enjoys the last word. But as Gray Davis found out, governors incur voters' wrath for failed budgets.

Two factors determine the state's budgetary fortunes: the state of the economy and the "fit," or lack thereof, between state spending needs and the resources available to fund that spending. When times are good, such as in the late 1990s, budgeting is a fairly painless exercise. When times turn bad, budget makers are faced with the terrible choices of raising taxes and/or cutting programs. But beyond the economic cycle, California faces a long-term problem of identifying and matching its spending needs with a revenue stream that often can't keep up. Even before the current crisis, concerns with the state's budget condition led to calls for various reforms, but they tended to emphasize the problems in the budget process rather than the fiscal structure of state government, which is less accessible to political reform.

REFERENCES

California Citizens Budget Commission. *A 21st Century Budget Process for California.* Sacramento: 1999.

California Department of Finance. *Enacted Budget Summary.* Sacramento: 2007.

Gray, Thorne. "The Legislature's Skeptic." *California Journal* (June 1986).

Hovey, Kendra A., and Harold A. Hovey. *State Fact Finder.* Washington, DC: Congressional Quarterly Press, 1999.

Krolak, Richard. *California's Budget Dance: Issues and Process.* Sacramento: California Journal Press, 1990.

Mendel, Ed. "It's the Structure, Stupid." *California Journal* (September 2004).

Morgan Quitno Corp. *State Rankings.* Lawrence, KS: Morgan Quitno Press, 2007.

Schrag, Peter. *Paradise Lost.* New York: New Press, 1998.

Walters, Dan. "Governor's Milestone Oozes Irony." *Sacramento Bee* (November 18, 2007).

CHAPTER eleven

BIG STATE, BIG CHALLENGES

T here is no shortage of tough and complicated issues with which California's public institutions, political leadership, and general public must come to grips. But this chapter will focus on two of these: diversity and education. There is a strong connection between these issues and with the budgetary issue discussed in the preceding chapter. But for purposes of organizational clarity, we will deal with them separately.

Diversity, and the issues that surround it, do not fit into an easy definition. Nor is it a subject that can be defined by specific legislative committees, executive departments, or budgetary allocations specifically directed at it. Education, itself a highly complex and multifaceted policy issue, can at least be partially understood by those portions of the governmental and political process that explicitly deal with it (e.g., Superintendent of Public Instruction, State School Board, Department of Education, the education budget, and local school districts). But, as will be demonstrated, the two issues are firmly and deeply intertwined.

DIVERSITY

It is not surprising that issues of diversity are at the heart of many of this state's most contentious issues, since diversity is one of the state's core characteristics. In terms of the ethnic and racial variety and complexity of its population, California is surely, if not the most diverse state in the nation, very nearly at the top of the list; it would even rank high among a diversity ranking of nations throughout the world. Beyond racial/ethnic diversity, the state has traditionally been a magnet for and a home base of those seeking to break out of the bonds of traditional roles and lifestyles.

However, a great irony and even greater tragedy in California's story is its historic inability to deal with diversity, particularly ethnic and racial diversity, with anything approaching a minimum standard of tolerance. The unfortunate truth is that, since the discovery of gold in the middle of the nineteenth century, the treatment of Native Americans, Asians, African Americans, and Hispanics by California Anglos has been characterized by systematic and individual violence at worst, and consistent political, economic, and social discrimination at best.

Of course one could argue that these patterns are not specifically "Californian," but rather a reflection of the darker side of American history that touches all regions. Can anyone name a state with an unbroken record of tolerance and fairness toward those with a different skin color or an unfamiliar language or accent? And haven't we, by the twenty-first century, moved beyond those "bad old days"? The answer to this question is certainly "yes," if we compare contemporary California with the California of the nineteenth and even the early twentieth century and events such as the enslavement and near annihilation of California Indians (Heizer and Almquist, 1977); the systematic economic and political oppression of Asian Americans, culminating in the Japanese Relocation Act of 1942 (tenBroek, 1968); the private but publicly supported segregation of African Americans (Lapp, 1987); and the "zoot suit" beatings of Latinos by mobs of American servicemen in Los Angeles during the World War II era.

It is fair to say that California has moved beyond the savagery of its earlier history. Many Californians now view its racial/ethnic diversity as a plus. This new understanding, more prevalent among the educated and more common in certain regions than others, sees diversity as a real California strong point in terms of our ability to compete in international trade and the global economy, as well as in its contribution to the variety and richness of its social, cultural, and artistic life. But there is still no consensus as to just how power, status, and economic opportunity are to be shared. In particular, we are a long way from consensus on what, if any, is the state's responsibility to make right continuing social, political, and economic inequality that, to some degree, results from past explicit governmental policy or acquiescence in patterns of private discrimination.

The Illegal Immigration Issue: Are Broader Diversity Questions Involved?

As Table 11.1 indicates, California's demographic contours are undergoing, and will continue to undergo, two basic changes into the twenty-first century. The Latino share of the state's population is shooting up; by 2030, Latinos will be the most numerous ethnic grouping in California, and they will constitute an absolute majority by mid-century. On the flip side, Anglos' share of the population is in rapid decline; by 2050, less than one in four Californians will be Anglos.

These numbers are the reason that much of the current debate over diversity is specifically focused on immigration issues, since a large proportion, but hardly all, of new immigrants arrive from Mexico and Central America. Although it is the authors' sense that the immigration issue is driven by many of the same concerns and impulses that fueled unrest among California Anglos throughout the state's history, the legal status of many of these immigrants is a current catalyst for negative political action. Because California (and the rest of the nation's southwest) shares a long, often deserted, and barren border with Mexico, it is possible for those lacking a legal visa to

TABLE 11.1	California's Projected Population by Race/Ethnicity (%)		
	2010	**2030**	**2050**
Latino	38.7	43.0	53.6
Anglo	39.2	29.5	23.3
Asian/Pacific	12.4	13.2	12.5
African American	6.7	6.6	6.4
Native American	1.0	1.7	2.1
Multirace	2.0	2.1	2.1

Source: *California Department of Finance*, Demographic Research Unit: Report 03-P1 *(Sacramento: 2004).*

cross the border illegally. ("Possible" ought not be confused with "easy." Untold hundreds, perhaps thousands, have perished due to heat, dehydration, or betrayal by their "coyotes," individuals who make a good living guiding these illegal crossings.)

Immigration, and hence illegal immigration, is the policy province of the federal government, but the political repercussions emerge at the state/local level. In California (and other states) citizens and politicians opposed to illegal immigration have attempted to discourage it by requiring proof of legal residency from those seeking to receive educational, social, and health care services. The easy passage of 1994's Proposition 187, which mandated these restrictions, was a clear indication of many Californians' unease with the pace of Hispanic immigration, or at least illegal immigration, into the state.

One very intriguing, though unfortunately not completely answerable, question about the large "yes" vote for Proposition 187 was the degree to which it reflected concerns limited to *illegal* immigration as opposed to a more generalized hostility to California's burgeoning Latino population. Certainly, concern about the nation's porous southern border does not automatically equate with an anti-Hispanic bias. Illegal immigration is, after all, illegal. One could argue, then, that law breaking ought not be tolerated, let alone rewarded with benefits and privileges enjoyed by those living here legally.

Still, there is a sense, at least intuitive, that Proposition 187's support was driven to some degree by a more general discomfort with the Latino immigration influx, illegal *and* legal. Ask yourself this question: if California were subject to a large influx of, say, Canadians crossing over the border, some legally, many illegally, would politicians and citizens be similarly alarmed?

Bilingual vs. Immersion Language Instruction: Once Again, Bigger Issues Involved?

As argued immediately above, the issue of illegal immigration ties into the broader question of how California responds to questions of diversity. Similarly, the debate over bilingual education is more than an educational debate over the most effective way to teach English to students whose primary language is not English.

Prior to making these larger connections, however, it is necessary to define what we mean by bilingual versus immersion English language training. *Bilingual education* starts with the assumption that students not proficient in English ought to receive at least part of their instruction in their native language. The idea here is that until students become proficient in the new language, they will fall behind in the subjects that are taught in that language. As their English skills improve, these students are gradually transitioned from native language instruction to English.

Immersion training in English is based on the theory that new language proficiency is most quickly achieved when a person, especially a young person, is immersed in an environment in which only the new language is spoken. To the extent that immersion is diluted by training in the native language, thus requiring students to move back and forth between languages, acquisition of the new language is delayed.

So far, the discussion seems to be about competing educational theories over the most effective form of instruction of non–native English speakers. But in 1998, the debate was thrust into the political arena. At that time, bilingual training was the practice in California public school districts with sizable non–English-speaking student bodies. Complaints had been raised about how the program was being administered in some of those districts, especially over the difficulty some parents encountered in transferring their children out of the bilingual track, and the length of time some students were being kept in the "transitional" bilingual classes. The result was a ballot initiative, Proposition 227, that mandated an almost complete elimination of bilingual instruction and its replacement with English-only instruction.

Both sides of the Proposition 227 debate presented studies that purported to demonstrate that bilingual training was, depending on which side was speaking, superior or inferior to immersion training. But for many voters, the issues were, as was the case with Proposition 187, broader than the specific policy question addressed by the proposition. This underlying current was a philosophical difference over the value of immigrants' speedy assimilation into mainstream American culture versus the value of maintaining ethnic, cultural, and linguistic identification with their pre-immigration roots. Put differently, Proposition 227 evoked broader questions of how and whether immigrants ought to "fit in" their new national home. The melting pot approach, traditionally held by most nonimmigrants, stresses the need to blend in; the ethnic identify approach views the whole immigrant/native mix as a tapestry of a single society that nonetheless consists of identifiable and distinguishable ethnic parts. Understood in this context, the debate over the speed with which schoolchildren learn to speak and perhaps think in English takes on extra meaning.

Like Proposition 187 some four years earlier, Proposition 227 passed handily. In fact, the division between "yes" and "no" votes was very similar to that of Proposition 187. As will be discussed later in this chapter, similarities in the way voters divided over the two initiatives was hardly a coincidence.

Affirmative Action: A Continuation of the Pattern

Native Americans, African Americans, and Asian Americans constitute California's other major racial minorities (Hispanics are, like other European Americans, categorized as "Caucasian"). As Table 11.1 indicates, unlike Latinos, their share of the state's population is growing slowly or not at all. For that reason, their place in current debates over ethnicity and immigration has been less pronounced. Nonetheless, an understanding of the California diversity issue needs to encompass the conditions and prospects of these groups as well. Each of these peoples has its own story, some of which is related in Chapter 2. What they share in common, along with Hispanics, is a history of discrimination and second-class economic and political opportunity.

Vestiges of formal, legal discrimination, have been pretty much wiped away. But the economic and social conditions in which vast numbers of these groups live, with the exception of the sons and daughters of older, established Asian Americans, remain substantially inferior to those enjoyed by most, though certainly not all, Anglo Californians.

This fact, coupled with the understanding that these conditions are at least partially the result of past patterns of discrimination, is the motivating factor behind affirmative action. Affirmative action means that members of ethnic/racial groups (as well as women) who are underrepresented in areas such as university admissions, public employment, and ownership of businesses able to procure government contracts should be give extra consideration, if they are qualified, for these benefits. Beyond the sense of fairness and the realization that our past policies and omissions are part of the current problem, there is also an argument that greater diversity in sectors such as university campuses makes those places stronger and more viable.

The political weakness of affirmative action, however, is that there is a zero-sum game quality to it. There are only so many university admissions slots, public sector jobs, or government contracts to go around. When public policy mandates special consideration for one group, those not in that group are at a disadvantage in the competition for the benefit in question. Affirmative action also runs afoul of many voters' perception that we live in, or are fast approaching, a "color-blind" society. For this school of thought, emphasis on ethnicity and skin color seems a step back from the ideal.

The issue came to a head in 1996 with Proposition 209, which banned affirmative action in the areas of university admissions, public employment, and public contracting. Like the anti-bilingual and illegal immigration initiatives, 209 also passed easily. (The University of California, under the urging of Governor Pete Wilson, had scrapped it's admissions affirmative action program a year earlier.) (Please refer to Box 11.1 for an explanation of why certain diversity-related policies are enacted via initiatives rather than legislative enactment.)

Propositions 187, 209, 227, and, as discussed below, 202, share some common themes and a consistent base of support that is also systematic. But before turning to these patterns, we need to discuss another element in the diversity issue, that of sexual orientation

Sexual Orientation as a Diversity Issue

While, obviously, there is nothing new about homosexuality, the politics of sexual orientation have only lately risen to top-tier status as a political issue. As gays (as well as bisexuals and the transgendered) have increasingly "come out of the closet" and adopted a political self-awareness and action program, there has been a corresponding push back by those who believe, often informed by their religion, that gay rights represent a sinful aberration and a threat to the ideal of family, and hence the very fabric of society. It is not surprising that California, the home of the untraditional and unconventional, has been at ground zero of this new issue.

BOX 11.1 **Initiative Battles: Why Do Minorities Always Lose?**

This chapter discusses ballot propositions that minorities strongly opposed but that won easily. On the other hand, none of the initiatives' policy proposals ever made any headway in the legislature. Why do the legislative and ballot proposition arenas produce such different policy results?

One answer is Democratic Party control of the legislature. The majority of Democrat legislators, mostly urban, are opposed to the content and spirit of propositions such as 187, 209, and 227. While some rural and urban Democrats represent more conservative constituents, the dominant faction can kill those ideas in committee, allowing those other Democrats to avoid politically damaging roll call votes.

Another factor is voter turnout. In particular, Latino voters do not turn out to vote in high percentages. But a low turnout election at the legislative district level will still elect one legislator, just as is the case in a high turnout legislative district. In short, nonvoters still get legislative representation so long as they live in a district that elects "friendly" legislators.

But in a statewide ballot initiative, turnout counts. If the "no" side of a ballot proposition contest doesn't (or can't) muster a heavy turnout and the "yes" side does, the result is initiative-based policies that would have been dead on arrival in the legislature.

In 2000, those opposed to gay rights achieved their biggest victory by passing, with a large majority, a statutory initiative that restricted the legal definition of marriage to opposite-sex couples. On the other hand, just a year later, the state legislature enacted legislation extending certain rights, such as hospital visitation and inheritance status, to "domestic partners." In California, domestic partners are also guaranteed the same public employment retirement and health benefits enjoyed by married spouses. Many of the state's private employers have adopted the same policy regarding their own benefit packages.

But it was, not surprisingly, San Francisco, that pushed the envelope furthest. In 2004, the city's mayor, Gavin Newsom, directed the city and county of San Francisco to issue marriage licenses to same sex-couples. The action created a furor, mostly negative, throughout the nation, but over 4,000 same-sex couples took advantage of the opportunity in the one month prior to a California Supreme Court ruling that the mayor had exceeded his authority and that the licenses were not valid. Significantly, Newsom's popularity within San Francisco soared, and in 2007 he was overwhelmingly reelected. Meantime, the constitutionality of Proposition 202 is being litigated by pro–gay marriage advocates arguing that its limitations violate provisions of the state and federal constitutions.

On certain levels, the politics of sexual orientation are different than those of race and ethnicity. While there is no doubt that homosexuals have been the object of discrimination, they were until recently a mostly hidden minority. Nor have they been so educationally underserved or economically marginalized as have racial/ethnic minorities. But the partisan and electoral constellations around this issue mirror those of the more traditional diversity issues.

The Politics of Diversity

As briefly discussed in Chapter 1, services to illegal immigrants, bilingual education, affirmative action, and gay marriage, all subjects of successful ballot initiatives, were engendered by a common set of concerns among many Californians and a majority of California voters. These voters were reacting to their sense that some basic rules and assumptions, once almost universally accepted, were being undermined by the forces of multiculturalism and moral relativism. Older values, such as a color-blind society, individual identity over ethnic/racial identity, rewards based on individual merit rather than racial/ethnic categories, and the sanctity of marriage, are threatened by policies such as affirmative action, bilingual education, and same-sex marital benefits.

A significant minority of voters opposed the initiatives, and sees the issues they raised in different terms. They would argue, for instance, that the color-blind ideal is something of a sham, given this nation and state's historical discrimination against people of color, and question the concern over affirmative action's preferential treatment, since other groups and individuals have routinely been afforded such treatment. They also question why, in the name of the importance of family to the society, the opportunity for marriage should be denied to a group seeking to embrace it, on the grounds that they are not heterosexual.

Among the state's politicians, there is a decided partisan division over these issues. The great majority of elected Republicans supported all four of the diversity-related ballot propositions. Equally strong majorities of Democrats opposed them. Voters' partisan inclinations mirror this same split. In fact, a voter's propensity to vote for Republican or Democratic candidates may often be determined by how they feel on these issues.

County-by-county analysis of partisan and issue voting demonstrates two very strong correlations: the more Republican a county votes, the more likely it was to support the four ballot propositions; the mirror opposite holds for strong Democratic-voting counties. Second, counties ranking at the top and bottom of voter support for any one of the propositions show up in almost identical positions of support and opposition on the other three.

Diversity and the Future

As we said in Chapter 10, there is a saying that "demographics is destiny." If that's true, coming decades may well see a reversal of the current majority/minority alignment over the issues we have been discussing. The fast changing ethnic makeup of the state is only slowly changing the makeup of the electorate, but that change is constant. As Anglo voters are increasingly displaced by Hispanic voters, the fate of ballot propositions like 187, 209, and 227 may be quite different. As for questions of sexual preference, younger voters are more likely than older voters to be supportive of gay rights or, at the least, not opposed. As older voters leave the electorate, their younger replacements may well render very different verdicts on ballot questions posed by initiatives such as Proposition 202.

EDUCATION

As discussed in this chapter's introduction, the politics of diversity do not fit neatly into any specific niche. In fact, many facets of the diversity issue lay outside the reach of state government. For example, immigration policy is controlled by the federal government; oppressive state policies of the past may be repealed, but their lingering effects cannot be so easily undone; wide disparities of income between ethnic groups are mostly a function of the private economic system and cannot be directly narrowed by state governmental action. One policy area, however, bears directly on the question of equal opportunity, and hence diversity. That policy area is education.

In California's twenty-first century, high-tech economy, education is the absolute key to economic opportunity. In a manufacturing economy, it was possible to start a career on the factory floor and work up to a decent wage through performance and experience, even without a college or graduate degree. But in a high-tech economy, there are many fewer such jobs. Where and how a person enters the work force depends on the educational credentials she brings to that first job. Of course, one element of our modernized economy is a large service component, and entrance into these fields is not dependent on a post–high school education. But these jobs, generally, don't provide the same kind of upward mobility promised by manufacturing sector jobs.

The distribution of educational opportunity, then, is a key determinant of the distribution of economic opportunity. If educational opportunity is widely available across ethnic and racial lines, so will be economic opportunity. If educational opportunity is not available to those ethnic and racial groups that have traditionally been relegated to the lower rungs of the economy, traditional earning power gaps will only widen.

The current and future composition of California's K–12 public school population underscores the connection between education and diversity. As indicated in Table 11.2, public education in California is more and more about the education of non-Anglos.

Public schools across the nation are becoming less white, but this trend is much more pronounced and developed in California. Note also that this report was based on enrollments during the 2002–2003 school year; up-to-date figures would move the totals even further away from Anglos toward Hispanics. What particularly distinguishes this state from the nation, though not from Western states such as New Mexico, Arizona, Texas, and Colorado, is the size of the Hispanic student body. Comparing these figures with those in Table 11.1, we can see that the Hispanic share of public school students outpaces even the burgeoning Hispanic share of the state's general population. Higher birth rates, meaning a higher percentage of school-age residents, explains this discrepancy.

These numbers are well worth pondering, as they hold the key to the connection between education and a more diverse distribution of economic opportunity. Because schools will increasingly be educating non-Anglos, it is these groups who have most at stake in a successful educational system. If the schools succeed, more and more of those

TABLE 11.2	Ethnic/Racial Composition of California's K–12 Public Schools (%)				
	Hispanic	**Anglo**	**Asian American**	**African American**	**Native American**
California	45.5	34.0	11.3	8.3	0.9
U.S.	18.1	59.0	4.4	16.0	1.2

Source: Richard Fry, "The Changing Landscape of American Public Education" (Philadelphia: Pew Hispanic Center, 2006).

entering the workplace with marketable educational credentials will be from ethnic groups whose financial prospects have been traditionally limited.

But there is, of course, an alternative scenario. If California schools do not effectively educate for the twenty-first century economy, California's well-paying jobs will still get filled. But those who fill them will be from other states and other nations whose educational systems produce plenty of graduates able to compete.

California's Schools: A Report Card You Wouldn't Want to Bring Home

There are two ways by which we might gauge the health of California's K–12 public school system. The first is to compare input factors, meaning the resources this state provides its schools as opposed to other states. This is an easier task than the output approach, which focuses on how well or badly educated are the young women and men when they emerge from their public school years. This is a more complex approach, because defining well-educated versus poorly educated is not a straightforward task. But by looking at several measurements, from both the input and output sides of the equation, we can at least begin to estimate just how well California's school system is functioning (see Tables 11.3 and 11.4).

In general, what can we say about all these statistics? It would seem to indicate that California's schools' performance ranges from mediocre to downright horrible. Looking at the input measures, we see that the state is just below the fifty-state medium in terms of spending per student. California classroom sizes are among the nation's very largest.

Measures of student performance paint an even grimmer picture. California ranks well below national averages and toward the bottom of all states in term of high school graduation rates and eighth grade reading and math scores. Yet on one important performance measure, college enrollment, California scores quite well.

Some analysis of these findings may clarify things. California's low input rankings generally indicate that we are not spending as much money on each student as do most other states. So an easy answer is that we must put a lot more money into K–12 education.

But it is also true that the state already spends a great deal in this sector; California's public education budget dwarfs that of all the other states. In fact, if we look at how

---

TABLE 11.3	Selected California Education Input Factors in National Perspective

Spending Per K–12 Student
California: $8,205 (Rank: #29)
National Average: $9,022

Student/Teacher Ratio
California: 22.7 (Rank: #8)
Highest: Arizona, 24.5
Lowest: Nebraska, 17.5

Source: Morgan Quitno Corp., State Rankings (Lawrence, KS: Morgan Quitno Press, 2007).

TABLE 11.4	Selected California Education Output Factors in National Perspective

High School Graduation Rate

California: 80.1% (Rank: #47)

National Average: 84.2%

Best: Wyoming

Worst: Mississippi

Eighth Grade Reading Scores, Proficient or Better

California: 21% (Rank: #46)

National Average: 29%

Best: Massachusetts

Worst: Mississippi

Eighth Grade Math Scores, Proficient or Better

California: 22% (Rank: #39)

National Average: 28%

Best: Massachusetts, 43%

Worst: New Mexico, 14%

College Enrollment per 1,000 Residents Aged 18–24

California: 660 (Rank: #5)

National Average: 591

Highest: Arizona, 860

Lowest: Alaska, 417

Source: Morgan Quitno Corp., State Rankings *(Lawrence, KS: Morgan Quitno Press, 2007).*

much the state spends on education in terms of its *entire population,* that is, per capita spending, California is well over the national average.

This discrepancy can be explained by the state's birth rates, among the very highest in the nation. What that means is that a higher percentage of our residents are school aged. So the state can be spending a lot of money measured against its total population, but not very much as measured by the number of students it must educate.

As mentioned, the percentage of Californians between 18 and 24 attending college is higher than most states. Since the great majority of the state's college students are products of its elementary and secondary school systems, this would seem to indicate that these schools perhaps are not doing such a bad job preparing students for higher education. Or put another way, perhaps the schools are successfully preparing large numbers of certain students but failing to prepare large numbers of others. Table 11.5 indicates that this may indeed be what is happening.

As Table 11.5 indicates, the K–12 system is working fairly well, in terms of turning out college-eligible high school graduates, for white and Asian-American students. But the record for African Americans and Latinos is considerably less positive. Note as well that Table 11.5 deals only with students who have made it through the entire public

TABLE 11.5	Ethnicity and College Eligibility of California High School Graduates*
	University of California System (%)	California State University System (%)
All graduates	14.4	28.8
White	16.2	34.3
African American	6.2	18.6
Latino	6.5	16.0
Asian American	31.4	47.5

*Based on 2003 high school graduation class.

Source: California Post Secondary Education Commission (Sacramento: 2004).

school system. If school dropouts were included, the difference eligibility rates for Latinos and African Americans, versus those of whites and Asian Americans, would be even more pronounced, since dropout rates for the first two groupings are much higher than for the latter two.

The overall picture, then, seems to be that the current public school system is not preparing historically underrepresented groups (except for Asian Americans) for an educational career that can in turn lead to a satisfactory reduction in the employment and income gap that now defines the economic contours of California's ethnically diverse society. In short, education is the hope that opportunity can be more evenly distributed, but at this point, it is only hope, not fact.

What Can Be Done?

There is no disagreement that California's education system must do better. But there is absolutely no consensus as to how that can be accomplished. Instead, there is a myriad of proposals and approaches rising from a variety of perspectives and philosophies. A few of the more prominent approaches are listed below.

- **There's nothing wrong with the system that more money can't cure.** One obvious solution is to spend more money on education. A good argument can be made that the state's school system, serving so many students with special language and other needs, requires considerably more money per student than systems serving a less diverse student body. By this logic, California's per-student spending should be at the very top of the states' rankings, not mired somewhere in the lower middle.

  But as discussed in Chapter 10, California already spends a great deal on its K–12 system. Attempts to raise California higher in the rankings of the states in areas such as spending per student are very expensive. With over 6 million students, the costs of raising expenditures by $1,000 per student would be, at present, over 6 *billion* dollars. That would be the add-on to current levels of school spending that already accounts for over 40 percent of a tightly stretched budget. And maintaining such high per-student spending would require even more spending increases each year as more students are added to the system.

If a lot more money could be added to the state's revenue supply, it might be possible to initiate this policy. What this means, of course, is higher taxes in one form or another. Bearing in mind that Californians are already taxed more than most Americans, the question is how much are the state's taxpayers, and voters, willing to increase their taxes on behalf of more educational spending?

- **There's nothing wrong with the system that competition and consumer choice can't cure.** More conservative observers of California's education problems tend not to view the problem as a funding issue, but rather as the result of a bloated educational bureaucracy and a tenured-in faculty that has become stagnant, rigid, and unresponsive to the educational needs of students. These critics see an infusion of competition into the educational field as the catalyst for better school performance. In their eyes, the traditional public school system is like a monopoly business that has driven out most of the competition. There is no incentive to improve the "product" so long as "consumers" have little alternative but to patronize the existing services.

    The *charter school* movement was the first expression of this outlook. Charter schools can be created by teachers, parents, or anyone else looking for alternatives to the traditional school district campuses. Unlike regular schools, who are guaranteed students because it is difficult or impossible for parents to switch districts without moving, charter schools' enrollments depend on their ability to entice students with a better product.

    Voucher plans are a much stronger form of a push toward school privatization. Charter schools are still public. Voucher systems, on the other hand, envision some form of public money subsidy to parents wishing to send their children to a private school. The argument here is that since private schools charge tuition, often high tuition, many middle- and lower-income parents are denied the opportunity to send their children there, though that would be their preference. Provision of a voucher gives these "consumers" a real choice in their daughters' and sons' education.

    Charter schools are now a reality in California; vouchers remain a distant hope of their supporters. Have charter schools improved education in the state? The jury is still out on this question; studies about comparative performance between charter and traditional schools have produced mixed results. By and large, they have not been the unregulated failures that early opponents of charter systems predicted. Nor have they brought about a revolution in academic performance.

    How a voucher system in California would change things remains pure conjecture. Two ballot initiatives aimed at establishing such a system went down to overwhelming defeat. The combination of those who oppose privatization of the state's school system, those leery about the tax ramifications of subsidizing tuition costs, and voters not willing to support such a fundamental change in the state's educational status quo, so far present a very formidable barrier to adoption of a voucher system.

- Two additional proposals, neither as expensive as the massive money infusion approach nor as radical as a voucher system, may have the best chance of adoption. **Bilingual, multicultural teacher recruitment and training** programs are aimed at increasing the number of teachers, especially Latino and African American, in the school system. The theory here is that students of color do better when some of their instruction, and some of their school role models, share their ethnicity and culture. Incentives such as scholarships for minority students enrolling in education programs and salary bonuses for them if they accept teaching positions in heavily minority schools are the incentives that would drive the policy.

Universal preschool is another proposal currently receiving a lot of attention. There is some evidence that preschool experience pays off in higher academic performance down the line, and middle- and upper-middle-class parents are heavy subscribers to these programs. A universal program, according to its adherents, would make these benefits available to children of parents who cannot afford them. Given the high social costs of student failure, costs of a universal preschool program might be a real bargain for its price.

Of course, there are no guarantees that a more diverse teaching corps or universally available preschool would bring fundamental improvement. While the arguments for more teachers among underrepresented groups seem to make sense, its connection with better student performance remains more conjecture than established fact. And there are practical problems with universal preschool. If the system is to work, there needs to be preschools in the underserved neighborhoods that are geographically and culturally available to local families. How do we ensure that there are adequate facilities and competent, appropriate supervision in areas that, because of their economic condition, have traditionally lacked preschool infrastructure?

One thing seems clear. There are no political, administrative, or fiscal "easy fixes" for California's schools. But the search for answers is required by an even more compelling truth; if California's experience with diversity is going to succeed, and not sink into a rigid two-tier society with opportunity denied to the state's non–white majority, the educational system must succeed.

REFERENCES

California Department of Finance. *Demographic Research Unit: Report 03-P1*. Sacramento: 2004.

California Post Secondary Education Commission. Sacramento: 2004.

Fry, Richard. *The Changing Landscape of American Public Education*. Philadelphia: Pew Hispanic Center, 2006.

Heizer, Robert F., and Allen E. Almquist. *The Other Californians: Prejudice and Discrimination Under Spain, Mexico, and the United States to 1920*. Berkeley: University of California Press, 1977.

Lapp, Rudolph M. *Afro-Americans in California*. San Francisco: Boyd & Frasier, 1987.

Morgan Quitno Corp. *State Rankings*. Lawrence, KS: Morgan Quitno Press, 2007.

tenBroek, Jacobus, Edward Barnhart, and Floyd Matson. *Prejudice, War, and the Constitution*. Berkeley: University of California Press, 1968.

GLOSSARY OF KEY TERMS

Assembly Speaker   Presiding officer of the state assembly. The power of this position to control legislation plus attract campaign donations led observers to conclude that it was the second most powerful job in the state. Term limits may have permanently reduced the speaker's power, however.

Attorney General   Statewide elected official who heads the Department of Justice and serves as the state's top attorney and law enforcement official. This latter role as the state's "top cop" makes this office a coveted stepping-stone to the governor's office.

Ballot Box Budgeting   Through a series of initiatives, California voters established mandates concerning taxing and spending powers. These severely constrict legislative flexibility in writing the annual budget.

Big Five   Consisting of the governor, assembly speaker, senate president pro tem, and senate and assembly minority party leaders, this informal group negotiates major choices in the annual budget.

Big Four   The four leaders of the Southern Pacific Railroad who established that corporation's economic and political domination over the state in the late nineteenth century.

Bilingual Education   Education policy based on the theory that non–English-speaking schoolchildren should receive primary instruction in their native language while mastering English. See also *English Immersion* (bilingual education's policy alternative).

Blanket Primary   Primary election system adopted in 1996 and voided by the U.S. Supreme Court in 2000 that allows all voters, regardless of their party registration, to vote for any candidate for any party's nomination for each of the contested offices. See also *Closed Primary, Hybrid Primary, Nonpartisan Primary,* and *Open Primary.*

Board of Equalization   This four-member elected board (joined by the state's *Controller*) oversees the administration of the property tax and the collection of the sales tax. The board also serves as the state's tax court.

Closed Primary   Under the closed primary system, only voters registered with a party may vote for candidates for that party's nomination. It was the California system from 1909 until 1996, when the voters replaced it with the *Blanket Primary.* See also *Hybrid Primary, Nonpartisan Primary,* and *Open Primary.*

Compulsory Referendum   Certain types of legislation passed by the legislature, including proposed constitutional amendments, bond issues, and changes to laws initially created by ballot propositions, must be submitted to the voters for their approval.

Contribution Limitations   Statutory limits on the amount of money an individual or group may donate to an election campaign. California currently employs a fairly generous set of campaign contribution limits for state offices. See also *Expenditure Limitations.*

Controller   Statewide elected official who is charged with auditing state expenditures to ensure that money for them has been properly appropriated and allocated. The controller's name appears on checks issued by the state.

Cross-Filing   Under laws adopted early in the twentieth century, it was possible to run in the primary elections of more than one party and thus win more than one party's nomination. In 1946, for example, Earl Warren won both the Republican and the Democratic nominations for governor. Cross-filing was repealed in 1959.

Deadwood   Citizens on the voter registration rolls who die or move without notification to election officials may remain on the voting rolls erroneously. Estimates of the number of deadwood registrants in California vary from 1 to 2 million.

Decline to State   Upon registering to vote, individuals may designate a party of choice or decline to state any party preference. Decline-to-state voters are the fastest-growing segment of the state's registered voting population.

English Immersion Immersion education places non–English-speaking students in English-speaking classes almost immediately, based on the theory that in this way they will become proficient in English more quickly than if they are placed in *Bilingual Education*.

Expenditure Limitations Limits on how much money candidates may spend on their election campaigns. Unlike *Contribution Limitations*, such limits, unless voluntarily accepted by the candidate, have been held to be unconstitutional.

Fiscalization of Land-Use Planning Land-use planning is one of the crucial local governmental functions. In making land-use decisions in a revenue-strapped era, however, these governments must heavily weigh the tax revenue consequences of their decisions. The result is often planning that favors proposed development, such as "big-box" retail stores or malls, that generates hefty sales tax revenues.

Gerrymandering When new legislative district lines are drawn (after each ten-year census), it is possible to draw them in such a way that the voting power of certain groups will be enhanced or diminished. Gerrymandering is most often used by the majority party to ensure that most districts will continue to elect that party's candidates.

Grassroots Lobbying Interest groups often use their rank and file membership to contact their elected representatives on behalf of or in opposition to proposed legislation. With term limits and the erosion of established power networks in the capital, grassroots lobbying may be of increased importance.

Hybrid Primary California's current primary system, adopted after the court system voided the state's *Blanket Primary*. It restricts voters registered with a party to voting only in that party's primary election. However, voters who "decline to state" when registering may choose any party's ballot, provided that party agrees to accept participation of decline-to-state voters. See also *Blanket Primary, Closed Primary, Nonpartisan Primary*, and *Open Primary*.

Initiative The most important of the direct democracy provisions established in California early in the twentieth century, it allows for the drafting of proposed legislation by any interested party and the qualification of the proposal through the collection of a specified number of signatures. Once qualified, the idea goes on the next statewide ballot for a "yes" or "no" vote. The initiative has become California's primary method for enacting sweeping and controversial change. See also *Referendum* and *Recall*.

Legislative Analyst's Office (LAO) The center of the legislature's budget expertise. It issues a detailed analysis and critique of the governor's annual proposed budget and provides fiscal projections for proposed legislation and ballot propositions.

Legislative Counsel The legislature's legal division, charged with putting proposed legislation into the form of a legal bill. The legislative counsel also provides the legislature with legal advice regarding constitutional and jurisdictional issues pertaining to legislation and legislative functions.

Lieutenant Governor Statewide elected official who assumes the governorship should that office be vacated. The lieutenant governor also becomes acting governor any time the governor is out of the state. The office possesses few real powers of its own.

Line-Item Veto Upon passage of the legislative state budget, the governor may reduce, though not increase, any specific item in that budget. That reduction can be overturned only by a two-thirds vote in both legislative houses. This veto option gives the governor great budgetary power because it eliminates the dilemma of accepting or rejecting the entire budget bill; the governor can instead pick and choose.

Motor Voter Law A federal statute, the "motor voter" law mandates that public state offices, such as Department of Motor Vehicle offices, provide their customers with voter registration material. The program resulted in many new registrants and an undetermined number of new voters.

Nonpartisan Primary Primary election system in which all voters receive the same ballot and may vote for candidates regardless of the candidates' party or their own party registration. In this sense, it most resembles the *Blanket Primary*, but only the two candidates receiving the most votes for any office appear on the general election ballot. These two candidates are technically not the nominees of their respective parties and, in fact, could be members of the same party. This plan was presented to the voters in November 2004, but it was rejected. See also *Blanket Primary, Closed Primary, Hybrid Primary,* and *Open Primary.*

Nonpartisanship   Political approach and style that emphasize programmatic and broad appeals to voters as opposed to appeals based on party affiliation. This style emphasizes problem solving and pragmatism over ideology. Nonpartisanship is particularly associated with the state's Republican leadership in the 1940s and 1950s, most notably Earl Warren.

Open Primary   Primary election system in which voters can choose which party's primary they wish to vote in, regardless of their own party registration. See also *Blanket Primary, Closed Primary, Hybrid Primary,* and *Nonpartisan Primary.*

Party Raiding   When primary election voters are allowed, as is the case in California, to vote for any party's candidate for nomination, a possibility exists for an organized effort to vote in the weakest candidate on the opposing party's list, thus ensuring the other party's victory in the general election.

President Pro Tem   Presiding officer of the state senate and chair of that chamber's Rules Committee, recognized as the upper house's clear leader. With the advent of term limits and inexperienced *Assembly Speakers,* the pro tem is now the state's leading legislator.

Progressives   In California (progressivism was a national movement), the progressives were swept into power by the voters in 1910 based on their pledge to end the political monopoly of the Southern Pacific Railroad. In power, they enacted a series of reforms, including the *Initiative,* which continues to define California politics. Their leader was Hiram Johnson, who served as governor and subsequently as U.S. senator until 1945.

Recall   One of the direct democracy reforms, it allows for the removal of any elected official through the submission of a specified number of signatures and then a special election to decide whether that official shall be removed. The recall was instituted by the Progressives early in the twentieth century. See also *Initiative* and *Referendum.*

Referendum   Another progressive direct democracy reform, the referendum provides that a law passed by the legislature may, upon the submission of a specified number of signatures, be set aside until a statewide vote is taken on whether it will become operative. See also *Initiative* and *Recall.*

Relocation   In 1942, in the hysteria following the Japanese attack on Pearl Harbor, Japanese Americans on the West Coast were rounded up—despite the lack of any evidence of treason or disloyalty—and moved out of their homes and off their property to relocation centers located throughout the West and South.

Retention Vote   Judges on the California Courts of Appeal and Supreme Court serve 12-year terms. At the end of their terms (and also at the first governor's election following their initial appointment), their names appear on the ballot with a "yes/no" question as to whether they should be retained. This system, in place since the 1930s, has only once resulted in the removal of judges: Rose Bird, Cruz Reynoso, and Joseph Grodin failed their retention votes in 1986.

Secretary of State   Statewide elected official who is responsible for overseeing the conduct of elections throughout the state. The job also includes the roles of "timekeeper"—for example, keeping track of the number of days initiative supporters have to collect their signatures—and of state archivist.

Structural Deficit   A long-term, as opposed to a single-year, state budget deficit that results from an imbalance between the state's average annual revenue flow and the average annual demand for state spending. While short-run economic changes, such as recession or economic boom, affect any given year's budget picture, the structural deficit represents an "average" or expected budgetary shortfall that can be addressed only by permanently increasing the revenue base, generally through higher taxation, or by reducing the expenditure demand through permanent program cutbacks or eliminations.

Superintendent of Public Instruction   Statewide, officially nonpartisan elected official who oversees public K–14 education. The operational powers of the office are not well defined, and the office often competes with several other educational policy power centers, including the state school board, the governor, and the local school boards.

Term Limits   Passed in 1990 as part of Proposition 140, California's term-limits law limits executive officers to two four-year terms, state senators to two four-year terms, and state assembly members to three two-year terms. Although these limits apply over one's lifetime, a "termed-out" officeholder may run for a different office and begin the clock all over again.

Treasurer   Statewide elected official who oversees the selling of state and local bonds, as well as the placement of state funds in interest-bearing accounts and investments.

Voter Fatigue   Because California elections generally consist of many contests for elected office, plus state and local ballot propositions, the ballot can be quite long. After voting on the top offices and the few prominent propositions, many voters leave the remainder of their ballots blank.

INDEX

Page numbers followed by *b*, *f*, or *t* indicate material in boxes, figures, or tables, respectively.